SCENIC DRIVING

SOUTH CAROLINA

THIRD EDITION

SCENIC DRIVING

SOUTH CAROLINA

Including Caesars Head, Coastal Islands,
Charleston, and Congaree National Park

JOHN F. CLARK
&
PATRICIA A. PIERCE

Globe
Pequot

Essex, Connecticut

Globe
Pequot

An imprint of Globe Pequot, the trade division of
The Rowman & Littlefield Publishing Group, Inc.
4501 Forbes Blvd., Ste. 200
Lanham, MD 20706
www.rowman.com

Distributed by NATIONAL BOOK NETWORK

Copyright © 2024 by the Rowman & Littlefield Publishing Group, Inc.
Maps by The Rowman & Littlefield Publishing Group, Inc.

British Library Cataloguing in Publication Information available

Library of Congress Cataloging-in-Publication Data available

ISSN 1552-7298
ISBN 978-1-4930-7056-5 (paper : alk paper)
ISBN 978-1-4930-7269-9 (electronic)

Printed in India

Contents

The Scenic Drives

Overview

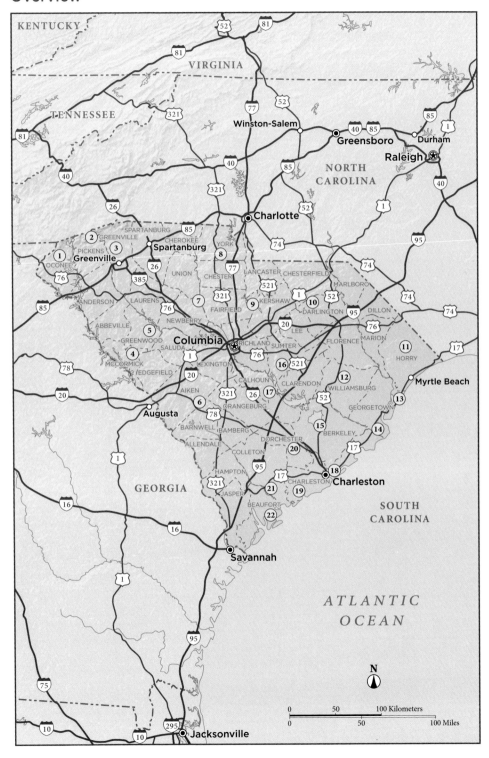

Map Legend

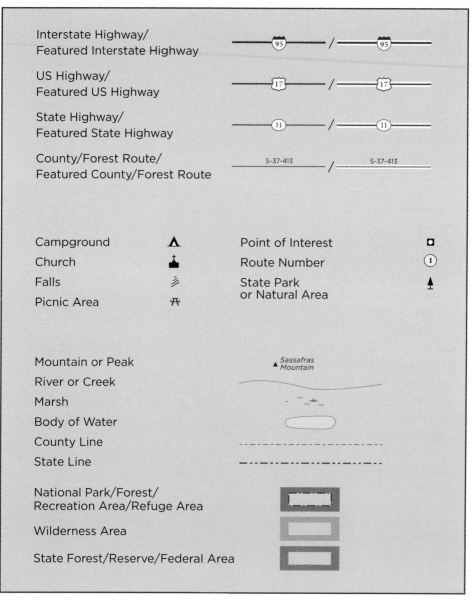

Interstate Highway/
Featured Interstate Highway

US Highway/
Featured US Highway

State Highway/
Featured State Highway

County/Forest Route/
Featured County/Forest Route

Campground

Church

Falls

Picnic Area

Point of Interest

Route Number

State Park
or Natural Area

Mountain or Peak

River or Creek

Marsh

Body of Water

County Line

State Line

National Park/Forest/
Recreation Area/Refuge Area

Wilderness Area

State Forest/Reserve/Federal Area

Sassafras
Mountain

About the Authors

John F. Clark lives in Columbia, South Carolina, where he is a writer and volunteer tour guide. Other books he has authored include *Capitol Steps and Missteps* and *Hiking South Carolina*. He previously worked in state and federal government and taught political science at three universities. A US Army veteran, he holds an AB from Davidson College and a PhD. from Syracuse University, with additional studies at the University of Paris and the University of Addis Ababa. John is a graduate of Leadership South Carolina, is a recipient of the Order of the Palmetto and the Army Commendation Medal, and has served on numerous civic and professional governing boards.

PHOTO BY SUSAN WAY

Patricia A. Pierce lives in Columbia, South Carolina, and is president of Capital Consulting Group of the Carolinas, a government relations and lobbying firm. She previously taught composition at the University of South Carolina, Midlands Technical College, and Tallahassee Community College and English as a second language in Fujinomiya, Shizuoka, Japan. She also served as research director for the South Carolina Senate Agriculture and Natural Resources Committee. Patricia holds degrees from Erskine College, Winthrop University, and the University of South Carolina.

PHOTO COURTESY OF SAM HOLLAND

This book is dedicated to our families—Jay, Jean, Kathy, Marion, Jan, Virginia, Peggy, and Graeme—whose love and support make everything possible, and to the memories of our loving parents no longer with us— Ellen, Franklin, George and Gus—and sister, Leslie.

Acknowledgments

We owe much to many, without whose help this revised edition would not have been possible. Special gratitude is extended to Virginia Pierce, Peggy Jeter, Graeme Rodriguez, Jan Blach, and Kathy Clark.

We are greatly appreciative of the hard work, expertise, pleasant disposition, and patience of our editor at Globe Pequot, Greta Schmitz.

For assistance in many shapes and sizes, we extend our warm thanks to Jay Clark, George Crouch, Andy Smith, Kimi Maeda, Caroline Wolf, and Krystal Buxton.

Finally, we owe special thanks to Marie Goff, who provided us with many excellent photos from her portfolio. Marie is a freelance writer and photographer whose stories and photographs have appeared in *South Carolina Wildlife Magazine*, *The Southern Edge*, *Military Living*, and her travel blog at TravelNotesand Storytelling.com. She holds degrees from Lander University, Webster University, and the US Army War College. Marie is a retired U.S. Army brigadier general and lives in Myrtle Beach, South Carolina, with her husband, Eddie.

Introduction

South Carolina packs delightful variety into a relatively small area. The sliver of mountains at the northwest corner of the state features a dazzling array of gorges and waterfalls, as well as the wild and scenic Chattooga River, famous as the setting for James Dickey's *Deliverance*. Stretching from the mountains to the center of the state are rolling foothills. A belt of sand hills, remnants of ancient sand dunes, separates the foothills from the low, flat coastal plain, which covers the southeastern two-thirds of the state.

The state's population centers are Greenville-Spartanburg, the hub of the state's booming industrial sector; Columbia, the governmental and commercial center; and Charleston, one of the busiest seaports on the East Coast and a thriving tourism mecca. However, in spite of the growth of industrial prosperity and the three midsize metropolitan areas, South Carolina, due largely to its heavily agricultural history, remains primarily a state of small towns and communities and devotion to the rural lifestyle. South Carolinians revere their natural heritage.

The state's tourism industry is huge, hosting more than 30 million visitors annually. Most tourists come for the superb beaches, golf, tennis, entertainment, restaurants, shopping, and fine weather of the coastal areas of Myrtle Beach, Charleston, and Hilton Head. These destinations offer tremendous attractions, but the rest of the state of South Carolina offers mild weather and much more. The Palmetto State presents charming small towns, quaint bed-and-breakfast accommodations, numerous historic sites (the state's recorded history dates back 500 years), beautiful natural resources, attractive farmland settings, and a variety of recreational opportunities.

This book features 22 of South Carolina's most scenic drives, offering more than 2,000 miles of riding pleasure. For the most part, readers are treated to little-known routes through small towns, rural countryside, and public lands. Exceptions are the Charleston and Waccamaw Neck drives, where nature, history, and people blend in unusually splendid harmony.

As you drive through South Carolina's back roads, you will see gracious old homes shaded by oaks and pines and surrounded by flowering shrubs, as well as prosperous farmlands full of cotton, tobacco, soybeans, corn, hay, and vegetables. Horse and cow pastures present idyllic settings, and prolific pecan, apple, and peach orchards decorate some regions.

One thing you will see often, in cities, suburbs, towns, and out in the country, is churches—lots of churches, rich and poor, new and old, and numerous gradations in between. You will also see very modest homes, ramshackle dwellings and farm buildings, and a fair amount of poverty. A majority of the state's less developed areas are in rural counties. Some of these areas are scenic precisely because they are largely untouched by development.

The downtown areas of small communities are often intriguing. Some still manage to thrive, but many are simply ghosts of their glory days in the early and middle parts of the 20th century. Quite a number center around railroad beds, harkening back to a time when trains were the chief intercity carriers of both people and goods.

Public lands make up a fair proportion of the scenery along the routes in this book. State parks, state wildlife management areas and heritage preserves, national and state forests, national wildlife refuges, and components of the National Park System collectively preserve for posterity a great deal of South Carolina's bountiful natural resources.

Regions

Geologists divide the state into several physiographic provinces, all of which extend into the neighboring states of Georgia and North Carolina. The Blue Ridge province, strictly defined, only covers the extreme northwestern mountainous edge of the state. The Piedmont (foothills) province, roughly the northwest third of the state, runs from the Blue Ridge approximately to the center of the state.

The Sand Hills, remnants of an ancient seacoast that provide evidence that the sea level was once much higher, stretch across the state's midriff in a belt from Cheraw through Camden, Columbia, and Lexington, and on to North Augusta. Some scientists consider them to be part of either the Piedmont or Coastal Plain physiographic province, while others identify them as a separate province.

South and east of the Sand Hills, the Coastal Plain province covers the rest of the state. It is characterized by very flat terrain and a plethora of wetlands. A subregion is the Coastal Zone, the narrow strip bordering the Atlantic Ocean.

Other observers identify geographic regions in South Carolina in a variety of ways. Frequently used regional terms include Foothills, Upcountry, upstate, Midlands, Savannah River Valley, Lowcountry, Pee Dee, Grand Strand, and the coast.

South Carolina's tourism promoters present the state in terms of eleven districts: Upcountry; the three-county Pendleton Historic District; Old 96 District; Olde English District; Thoroughbred Country; Capital City and Lake Murray Country; Pee Dee Country; Santee Cooper Country; Myrtle Beach and the Grand Strand; historic Charleston; and Lowcountry and Resort Islands. Information on these districts is contained in Helpful Organizations, located in the back of the book.

Names people use for South Carolina's Coastal Plain can be a bit confusing. Many South Carolinians refer to this entire area as the Lowcountry (also written Low Country, low country and lowcountry), but the boundaries of the Lowcountry are open to question. Some parties refer to the southernmost counties of the state as the Lowcountry, and sometimes the term simply refers to the historic plantation area around Charleston. Others use the term to refer to all of the area formerly dominated by river plantations, from the Waccamaw River wetlands above Georgetown all the way to Beaufort. The Lowcountry and Resort Islands tourism district is composed of Beaufort, Colleton, Jasper, and Hampton Counties, all south of Charleston.

The Grand Strand, the string of ocean resorts on the 60-mile coast centered on Myrtle Beach, is often thought of as a region in its own right. Adjacent to the Grand Strand, but inland, is the Pee Dee section of the state, an agricultural region comprising the watershed of the Great Pee Dee River and its tributaries.

Stretching from northern Charleston County to Georgia are the Sea Islands, once the home of substantial rice and cotton plantations. On these islands, a distinctive African American culture survived and thrived, but this way of life is threatened by resort and other commercial and residential development.

Natural Resources

Rivers dominate South Carolina's terrain. Four major river systems drain the state: the Savannah, Edisto, Santee–Cooper, and Pee Dee.

The Savannah River Basin extends along a narrow strip paralleling the South Carolina–Georgia border for its entire length. Because the Ice Age never stretched into the state, it never gouged any large natural lakes here like those found farther north; all large lakes in the state are man-made, mostly for the creation of hydro-electric power. The Savannah River Basin contains five such lakes in South Carolina: Jocassee, Keowee, Hartwell, Russell, and Thurmond.

The Edisto River is famed as the longest undisturbed black-water river in the world. The Edisto River Basin, which includes the Coosawhatchie, Salkehatchie, Combahee, Ashepoo, and Edisto Rivers, stretches from the Sandhills area between Aiken and Columbia southward to the renowned ACE (Ashepoo–Combahee–Edisto) Basin, a sub-drainage at the southern end of the Edisto system watershed.

The upper reaches of the Santee–Cooper Basin comprise much of the north-central part of the state, from Sassafras Mountain in the west through Greenville and Spartanburg all the way to Rock Hill and Lancaster. Major feeders include the Upper, Middle, and Lower Saluda Rivers; the Broad River; the Catawba/Wateree River; and the Congaree River. The Santee–Cooper Basin narrows to a neck along the Congaree River south and east of Columbia before widening again below Lakes Marion and Moultrie and reaching the sea at Charleston via the Cooper River and below Georgetown via the Santee River. This mighty river system includes Lakes Greenwood, Murray, Wylie, Wateree, Marion, and Moultrie.

The final major drainage area, the Pee Dee River Basin, covers much of the eastern part of the state. This basin, encompassing a rich agricultural region centered on Florence, includes the Black, Lynches, Great Pee Dee, Little Pee Dee, Waccamaw, and Sampit Rivers, emptying into the Atlantic Ocean at Georgetown.

Trees and other plants are as diverse as the geography. The mountains are dominated by oak-hickory forest. Numerous varieties of oak are found in this habitat type noted for its huge diversity of plant species. Wetter areas are dominated by lovely mountain laurel and rhododendron, a special pleasure in the late spring when they bloom riotously.

The rest of the state is mostly covered by oak-pine forest, but exceptions are the rule. A few of our driving routes pass through coastal maritime forests, characterized by a mixture of vegetation resistant to the effects of salt spray and wind. Trees include live oaks, laurel oaks, Carolina palmettos (the state tree), and slash and loblolly pines. Other common vegetation includes hollies, red bays, dwarf palmettos, wax myrtles, and red cedars.

Coastal Plain wetlands are particularly appealing. Swamps feature tea-black water, Spanish moss, and bald cypress and tupelo trees. Another type of enticing wetland is coastal marshland reclaimed from the plantation rice culture of centuries past and managed today as habitat for migratory birds. Such areas are achingly beautiful, especially when wildflowers such as irises, yellow jessamine (the state flower), and spider lilies are blooming.

A Coastal Plain wetland type under serious threat is the Carolina bay. This is an unusual elliptical depression, often, but not always, filled with water. The word "bay" refers not to water, but to the bay trees that are usually the dominant vegetation. Carolina bays are found in their greatest numbers in the Coastal Plain areas of the Carolinas and Georgia. Most have been filled or drained for farming, roads, or development. Efforts to protect the remaining Carolina bays continue, particularly through the work of the Heritage Trust program of the South Carolina Department of Natural Resources.

Humans do not cause all the damage. Nature, too, can be capricious. South Carolina periodically suffers a population explosion of the southern pine beetle. Since 1995, the worst outbreak in state history has affected over half of South Carolina's counties, concentrated in the northwestern and southern parts of the state. Enough timber to build 50,000 houses was destroyed by the beetle.

Hurricane Hugo was another disaster for South Carolina and its ecosystems. On September 21, 1989, this killer storm slammed into the South Carolina coast just above Charleston and dramatically transformed the landscape in its path.

The tidal surge washed completely over many barrier islands, including Bull Island and the Isle of Palms. The fishing village of McClellanville, just north of the spot where the center of the hurricane made landfall, was almost leveled. Furthermore, Hugo tracked rapidly inland, its extremely high winds causing severe damage far from the coast, through Camden all the way past Charlotte, North Carolina. The devastated woodlands of Cape Romain National Wildlife Refuge and Francis Marion National Forest will continue to display the scars of Hugo for decades to come.

South Carolina is home to a great variety of wildlife. The mountains harbor species such as the raven and the endangered peregrine falcon, usually found much farther north in North America. At the southern end of the state are found species common in Florida or other subtropical areas. In between are large populations of white-tailed deer (the state animal) and wild turkey (the state wild game bird). Black bears live secretively in the mountains and, surprisingly, in secluded Carolina bays within a few miles of the highly developed Grand Strand coastal resort area. Other well-represented mammals in the state include beavers, foxes, raccoons, bobcats, feral hogs, and river otters. Opossums, the only marsupials native to North America, are also quite common.

South Carolina is an underappreciated birding region, although sites such as Huntington Beach State Park and Savannah National Wildlife Refuge are becoming better known to international bird enthusiasts. More than 350 species have been identified. Generally, wetlands along the coast are popular year-round host sites for wading birds such as herons and egrets. Ducks winter along the coast, and numerous bird species pass through the entire state during spring and autumn migration periods. Songbirds (look for Carolina wrens, the state bird) and woodpeckers fill the forests during all seasons, while various birds of prey prowl the skies.

South Carolina harbors many endangered or threatened species. The most prominent of these is our national symbol, the bald eagle. This great bird is making a strong comeback in South Carolina. There is even a limited hunting season for alligators, now numerous in swamps and marshlands of the coastal plain but a threatened species for many previous decades. The red-cockaded woodpecker is badly threatened due to habitat loss, but South Carolina has some of the nation's largest remaining populations of this species, important as a bellwether of ecosystem quality.

South Carolina preservationists also work hard to protect nesting areas for loggerhead sea turtles (the state reptile) along the coast, and habitat for gopher tortoises in the sandy areas of the lower Savannah River Valley.

History

Human activity in South Carolina's prehistoric period dates back almost 15,000 years, and there is much remaining evidence of Native American settlement along the coasts and rivers of the state. Ancient shell rings and mounds are particularly noteworthy, and access to such phenomena is available at a few spots along or near the designated scenic routes. Additionally, some of the back roads you will travel and cross were originally Native American trading trails.

Spaniards first explored the South Carolina coast in 1514, and in 1526 they attempted a settlement at Winyah Bay, near the site of present-day Georgetown. Weather, Indian attacks, and disease brought a quick end to this foray. Later, in 1540, Hernando de Soto crossed through the central part of the state in his explorations.

French Huguenots fleeing persecution tried to colonize Parris Island, near Beaufort, in 1562, but this attempt was also short-lived. The Spanish came to Parris Island in 1566 and established Santa Elena, which managed to survive until 1587, when the inhabitants withdrew southward to Saint Augustine. Native Americans had the South Carolina area entirely to themselves again, for almost another century.

However, in 1670, King Charles II established a settlement on the Ashley River, at a spot now protected as Charles Towne Landing State Historic Site, beginning South Carolina's colonial period. The settlers moved across the river to the Charleston peninsula in 1680, to the site of today's downtown Charleston Historic District.

The settled property was part of a large tract of land granted by the king in 1665 to eight lords proprietors, stretching from the southern Virginia border through northern Florida, and extending westward indefinitely. The territory of the Carolina proprietorship was whittled away over time, leaving South Carolina as a wedge between Georgia to the south and west and North Carolina to the north. North Carolina gradually separated from Charleston and the south simply because of geographic separation between Charleston and the area north of the Cape Fear River, and the fact that North Carolina in the early years was mainly settled by southern migration from Virginia, rather than by immigration through ports at Charleston, Georgetown, and Beaufort. The de facto separation became official in 1719.

In the coastal plain, South Carolina prospered during the colonial period, chiefly as a result of the involuntary but heroic efforts of African slaves who cleared swamps and forests to build great indigo, rice, and cotton plantations, generally owned by English and French Huguenot settlers, many of whom arrived by way of Barbados in the Caribbean. South Carolina in general and Charleston in particular were among the wealthiest of colonial locales.

Farther inland, settlement was somewhat less dependent on enslaved people from Africa and more reliant on the work of immigrants from Scotland, Ireland, Wales, Germany, and Switzerland although the use of slavery in that part of the state also took strong root over time, as cotton cultivation spread.

It could be said that the American Revolution in the South began at Fort Charlotte in present-day McCormick County, where, on July 12, 1775, Patriot forces first used force to seize property belonging to the British. South Carolinians played a major role in the events leading up to the American Revolution, and South Carolina became a major battleground. This heritage indelibly marks the state to this day. Needless to say, the Daughters of the American Revolution are an important institution here. Prominent Revolutionary War landmarks are featured throughout the scenic drives in this book.

The period between 1783 and 1860 is the antebellum period of fine mansions, prosperous plantations, blooming magnolias, and, sadly, slavery. When the Old South is caricatured, this is the time that is brought to mind. The Rhett Butler character, of course, was from South Carolina, as were many real-life counterparts. Our scenic drives feature numerous homes, churches, and public buildings constructed in antebellum days.

The Civil War lasted only from 1861 until 1865, but, for some, this four-year period dominates our past. John C. Calhoun and other South Carolinians were among the staunchest defenders of the rights of states to allow slavery, and, in December 1860, South Carolina was the first state to secede from the Union, eventually joining ten other states in forming the Confederate States of America.

The first shots of the Civil War were fired in Charleston Harbor in April 1861, as Confederate troops on Morris and Sullivan's Islands bombarded Fort Sumter, still occupied by Federal forces. Naval and land skirmishes raged along the state's coast throughout the wartime period, and Union General Sherman brought the war tragically home to South Carolinians in the winter of 1865 with his burning and pillaging rampage through the middle of the state, climaxing with the torching of Columbia, the state's capital city.

A number of significant Civil War–era sites are included among our drives, and Confederate memorial monuments are located in virtually every county seat in the state.

Reconstruction, the period of Federal troop occupation from 1865 until 1877, was a period of equality and advancement for African Americans unmatched until the latter portion of the 20th century. African Americans voted in large numbers, and African American jurists, local officials, state legislators, and congressmen took office. Nevertheless, generations of South Carolina children later grew up being taught that this was a period of unmitigated horror ended only by the eventual disenfranchisement of African Americans, who made up the majority of the population of South Carolina until out-migration shifted the balance by the end of the 1930s.

It has taken South Carolina over a century and a half to recover economically from the Civil War disaster. The state went from being very wealthy to extremely poor during the course of the war. The end of the slave labor economy, the shift in importance of industrial strength over agricultural strength, and the physical, human, educational, and political devastation caused by the war itself created a financial hole from which the state has only recently emerged.

In many ways, South Carolina's post-Reconstruction period lasted from 1877 until 1954, when the civil rights movement got under way in full force. Politics and economics became largely local. Small towns emerged as places for farmers to market their produce and buy their necessary wares from local merchants. Small banks arose in the towns, and artisans, lawyers, physicians, and others lived in settlements to provide their services to surrounding communities. Typically, the more important towns were located along railways and at significant crossroads, as access to navigable rivers gradually became less important. In the hilly upper part of the state, industrialists built textile mills beside fast flowing rivers, and towns frequently grew up around the mills.

In the 20 years following withdrawal of Federal troops in 1877, white South Carolinians gradually eroded the political and economic power of African Americans, almost totally disenfranchising them by the turn of the century. Whites gained more prosperity than blacks, but lagged far behind the rest of the country. The Great Depression that hit the rest of the country in the 1930s ravaged the already poor, farm-based South Carolina economy beginning in the 1920s, when boll weevils ravaged cotton fields. Those at the bottom of the economic and political heap, African Americans, began heading north in large numbers, enough so that by the 1940s, whites outnumbered blacks in South Carolina for the first time in more than 200 years.

To some extent, the Old South that you see along our scenic drives is the South Carolina of this post-Reconstruction period. This is the South Carolina of small towns, small farms, small churches, small stores, large concentrations of African Americans and whites living interspersed "out in the country," and unspoiled scenic beauty. It is a land of people living close to the land, of people whose parents, grandparents, and grandparents' grandparents chose to stay in communities where they grew up. It is not a land of huge wealth, but it is a land of considerable satisfaction with the way things are.

South Carolina's civil rights movement era was at its height from 1954, when a Clarendon County lawsuit resulted in the Supreme Court ruling to end school segregation, until 1972, when schools were finally fully integrated and African Americans, empowered by the federal Voting Rights Act, began to make their impact at the polls felt, on behalf of both black and white candidates who were sympathetic to their aspirations. A little church where Clarendon County African American parents met and organized in the early 1950s is featured on the Wateree Basin Scenic Drive.

The time frame since 1972 is the state's New South period. This has been a period of rapid economic growth, educational advancement, industrialization, and tourism development. Although here, as elsewhere, there is much yet to be done, race relations and the economic, social, and political status of African Americans have taken a quantum leap forward.

Hopefully, development of South Carolina will continue to progress without diminution of the natural resources, historic character, and rural charm that make the Palmetto State such a special place.

Public Lands

South Carolina's public lands are controlled by a variety of federal, state, and local entities, which have different rules for public access and use.

State parks are under the management of the South Carolina State Park Service, a division of the South Carolina Department of Parks, Recreation, and Tourism. A few offer access at no charge, but there are small entrance fees for many. Annual passes, which provide unlimited admittance to all 52 state parks and historic sites, are available.

Some parks that preserve important historic features are called State Historic Sites (for example, Oconee Station and Hampton Plantation). Parks with outstanding natural features are deemed State Natural Areas (Keowee-Toxaway and Woods Bay). A majority of facilities belonging to the State Park Service fall into three remaining categories: traditional parks (such as Table Rock), regional parks (Colleton), and outdoor recreation parks (Calhoun Falls).

Wildlife management areas (WMAs) and **heritage preserves** are under the jurisdiction of the South Carolina Department of Natural Resources. WMAs are managed for hunting, and WMA visitors are advised to visit websites indicated in our book in order to learn the hunting seasons, especially the periods for deer hunting in autumn. Hunting seasons vary significantly in different game zones throughout the state.

Heritage preserves are managed to preserve unique habitats, often protecting endangered plant or nongame animal species. Sometimes, they preserve property of historic significance. Hunting for game animals is allowed in some preserve areas. Both WMAs and heritage preserves are sometimes closed to public access in order to protect wildlife during sensitive seasons. There are no fees for admission to these properties.

South Carolina owns five **state forests**, managed for a variety of uses by the South Carolina Forestry Commission. They charge no admission fees and offer miles of pleasant driving, hiking, and mountain biking.

National forests are managed by the US Forest Service, a unit of the US Department of Agriculture, for multipurpose use, including timber harvest and recreation of various types. In South Carolina, there are two national forests, Francis Marion and Sumter. Sumter, located in the upper portion of the state, is composed of three diverse and geographically separate units: Long Cane Ranger District and Enoree/Tyger Ranger District in the piedmont, and Andrew Pickens Ranger District in the mountains. There are no admission fees.

South Carolina has one **national park** and six smaller units of the National Park System called either a **National Historic Park (2), a National Military Park (1), a National Battlefield Park (1), or a National Historic Site (2)**. Our drives take you to all of them. None of these sites charge an admission fee. These are managed by the US National Park Service, a unit of the US Department of the Interior.

National wildlife refuges, operated by the US Fish and Wildlife Service of the Department of the Interior, are primarily managed as wildlife habitat, particularly for migratory birds. Eight national wildlife refuges are in South Carolina. There are no charges for admission to the refuges, but access is sometimes restricted because of wildlife breeding seasons.

Seasons & Weather

The climate in South Carolina is ideal for sightseeing. Winters are mild, and spring and autumn are glorious. Some summer days can be uncomfortably warm, but that is why virtually all vehicles in the state have air-conditioning.

In summer, visitors often say, "It's not the heat, it's the humidity." Actually, it is both the heat and the humidity. However, frequent rains (often in the form of spectacular afternoon thunderstorms) cool things off and make summers pleasing for recreation. Summer temperatures range from average highs and lows of 85 degrees and 62 degrees Fahrenheit in the mountains to 92 degrees and 70 degrees Fahrenheit in the midlands. Because of invigorating sea breezes, the coast, with average highs and lows of 89 and 70 degrees, is slightly cooler than the midlands in the summer.

Apart from midsummer, South Carolina weather is very temperate. The long, delightful spring and autumn seasons make these times excellent for scenic driving.

Average high and low temperatures during the short winter period range from 51 and 28 degrees Fahrenheit in the mountains to 61 and 49 degrees along the seacoast, and many of the best sightseeing opportunities are in winter. In the mountains and other deciduous forest zones, scenic vistas are at their peak in winter, and winter along the mild-weather coast generally means no insect problems, no heat difficulties, low forest undergrowth, and high opportunity to view birds and other forms of wildlife. Winter, along with late fall and early spring, is the best time to travel the coastal plain.

The state's moderate rainfall (about 49 inches annually) is distributed fairly evenly geographically and seasonally. Snowfall occurs, but increasingly rarely.

Highway & Road Designations

Highway and road designations are important and can sometimes be a little confusing. In this guide, our maps and directions indicate six basic types of roadways.

Interstate highways are written as I-26, I-95, and so on. The state is crisscrossed by five interstate highways: 20, 26, 77, 85, and 95. They are shown on our maps with the familiar interstate highway roadside shield symbol.

The older **United States highway** system is indicated on maps by the familiar roadside badge-shaped symbol in use on road signs across the country. These roads are identified as US 17, US 401, and so on. Sometimes, when the particular highway segment runs concurrently with a town or city street, or otherwise has a formal name, the name is shown behind a slash after the numeric designation, or vice versa.

South Carolina highways are state-maintained primary highways marked on roadways by signs displaying the highway number in blue against a white background, with a miniature outline of the state at the top. In the maps in this book, however, these roads are indicated by a number inside a circle. These highways are identified with "SC" followed by the route number. As is the case with other highways, these roads are sometimes co-identified with a name.

Secondary roads are nonfederal roads other than the primary highways in one of the above-indicated classifications. They sometimes have no roadside highway markers other than road signs at intersections. To find the number of a secondary road, look above any stop sign you encounter. A black horizontal sign should be there, emblazoned with a combination of white letters and numbers. For example, if you are traveling to Lower Whitewater Falls, you might find yourself on a road designated S-37-413, or SR-37-413. The 37 refers to the county (in this case, Oconee), and 413 is the road number. In our book, this road is designated as S-37-413, regardless of whether the prefix on the sign is S or SR.

These roads now have written names as well, and these name signs, usually green, are often more prominent than the smaller black numeric signs. Almost all are paved, and the few exceptions are noted in the text.

Keep in mind that secondary road designations often change from county to county. Thus, do not be surprised at occasional sudden changes in secondary road nomenclature. Written names of roads may change without the numeric designations changing, and vice versa.

USDA Forest Service roads in national forests are identified by "FR" followed by the road number. Typically composed of improved gravel or dirt, but often paved, these are shown on our maps with unenclosed numbers and names where they are available.

Town and **city streets** may or may not have numerical designations and are often indicated with names only.

Scenic Drive Descriptions & Related Information

Each drive description contains a standard set of information about the Scenic Drive.

General Description: A brief description of the drive and its highlights.

Special Attractions: Noteworthy places you will see along the way, or which are located nearby.

Location: A short description of where in South Carolina the drive route is located. This description complements the locator map on page vii.

Travel Season: In South Carolina, every route can be enjoyed in every season. However, we provide inklings of seasons that are most appealing.

Services: This item provides information on area towns in which travelers may find conventional hotels and motels, restaurants, grocery stores, automobile care, medical facilities, and other goods and services they may need.

The Drive: The heart of each Scenic Drive presentation is a narrative description of what you can expect to see along the way and background information on areas and places, along with photographs and a detailed route map. We include as many street addresses as possible in order to make your ride GPS friendly.

Nearby Attractions: At the end of each Scenic Drive is a list of nearby attractions not identified on the main or optional Scenic Drive route.

At the end of the book is the appendix section including: **Helpful Organizations**, with contact listings for public and private organizations that can provide additional information, and **Bibliography & Further Reading**, our annotated list of reading materials.

Enjoy

South Carolina is a great place to visit and to live. We hope you have as much fun using this book to explore the nooks and crannies of the Palmetto State's highways and byways as we did in compiling the information contained herein.

Blue Ridge Mountains

Walhalla to Whitewater Falls

General Description: A spectacular 45-mile drive through forests, around and over mountains, and across rivers and gorges, offering majestic vistas and cool, idyllic resting spots. There are several opportunities to stretch your legs and visit waterfalls or follow mountain streams.

Special Attractions: Historic Walhalla, Stumphouse Park and Tunnel, Issaqueena Falls, Oconee State Park, Cherry Hill Recreation Area, Burrells Ford Recreation Area, Chattooga National Wild and Scenic River and Chattooga and Foothills Trails, King Creek Falls, Spoonauger Falls, Winding Stairs and Big Bend Trails, Walhalla State Fish Hatchery, Ellicott Rock Wilderness Area, Oscar Wigington Scenic Byway, Bad Creek Reservoir, Lake Jocassee, Lower and Upper Whitewater Falls.

Location: Northwest corner of the state.

Travel Season: All year. The upstate is especially beautiful in the spring when it is covered in wildflowers and mountain laurels are in bloom and in the fall when the trees are aflame in yellow, orange, and red foliage. Winter is good for distant vistas, and summers are shady and pleasantly mild. The area offers good birding opportunities for spring and fall migrants and forest birds.

Services: Walhalla and Westminster have limited accommodations and services. A full range of hotels, restaurants, and other services is available in Seneca, Clemson, and Greenville.

The Drive

You begin in charming, historic **Walhalla** and then step back in time as you climb past apple orchards into the forests of the southernmost Blue Ridge Mountains, at the bottom of the Appalachian Mountain chain. At Stumphouse Park, you see Issaqueena Falls, a breathtaking 100-foot waterfall, visit the incomplete Stumphouse Tunnel, and a variety of walking, hiking, biking trails. Head north to lovely Oconee State Park and Walhalla State Fish Hatchery. You can visit Burrells Ford, hub of some of the state's most attractive hiking opportunities and site of two nearby spectacular waterfalls before winding along scenic Wigington Scenic Byway, and heading northward and upward to Bad Creek Reservoir, the Whitewater River and Lower Whitewater Falls, Jocassee Gorges, and Lake Jocassee. End your journey crossing into North Carolina to view the spectacular Upper Whitewater Falls.

Blue Ridge Mountains: Walhalla to Whitewater Falls

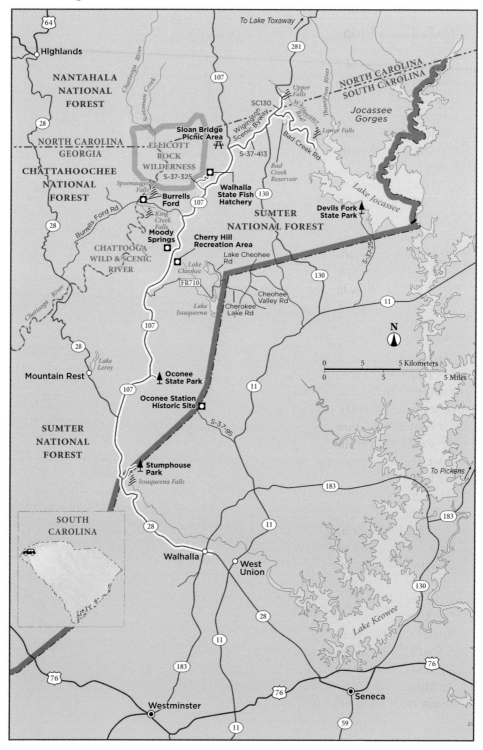

Walhalla to Stumphouse Park

Begin at the corner of SC 28/East Main Street and John Street in downtown **Walhalla**, an attractive town settled in 1850 by the German Colonization Society from Charleston. Nestled at the foot of the Blue Ridge Mountains, its name derives from a Norse mythology term meaning "Garden of the Gods," a place for fallen warriors to spend eternity as reward for their valor. Walhalla features a traditional mid-20th-century main street lined with monuments, 19th-century churches, and stately old homes.

Head northwest through the downtown shopping area with an abundance of colorful brick buildings filled with unique shopping and dining opportunities. Travel 0.4 mile on East Main Street/SC 28 West/Highlands Highway.

Just after College Street, turn left (south), onto Browns Square Drive to visit the **Oconee Heritage Center** (123 Browns Square Dr.). Housed in an old tobacco warehouse (1892), the facility provides exhibitions and educational programs relating to the history of Oconee County, including the history of Native Americans, railroads, agriculture, and manufacturing.

Exit the center by crossing South Tugaloo Street and heading west onto Short Street. On your left is the **Museum of the Cherokee**, featuring the history of the Cherokee Indians in Oconee County and upstate.

To your right is the **Oconee County Courthouse** (205 W. Main St.) and **Patriot's Hall Oconee Veterans Museum** (13 Short St.), housed in the "Old Rock Building" (1933). Exhibits highlight the contributions that Oconee County war veterans and others have made in serving their country.

Continue to the intersection with South Church Street. Directly ahead is **Saint John's Evangelical Lutheran Cemetery and its church** (301 W. Main St.), begun in 1859 and dedicated in 1861. The town clock is located in the steeple of this attractive, white wooden church with vaulted ceilings. An obelisk dedicated to the original German settler leaders rises in the median across from the church.

Turn right (north) on South Church Street and then left (west) onto West Main Street. As you head north out of town, you pass pretty old homes and a confederate monument in the median before winding north past roadside stands selling apples and apple cider in the fall. Climb into the hills and enjoy distant vistas to the east and west.

After about 4.5 miles, you enter the **Andrew Pickens Ranger District** of Sumter National Forest. (General Andrew Pickens was a Revolutionary War hero in South Carolina's upcountry; General Thomas Sumter led Patriot troops in the Midlands.) Also stretching from the town of Walhalla to Stumphouse Mountain is the **Stumphouse Youth Wildlife Management Area**, which includes **Stumphouse Mountain Heritage Preserve** (Issaqueena Falls, the railroad tunnel, the

Stumphouse Mountain Tunnel KATHY CLARK

Turnip Top tract and the nearby forested mountains covering more than 1.2 million acres).

The entrance to **Stumphouse Park** is less than a mile farther, on your right (east), immediately after the Yellow Branch Picnic Area on your left (west) on Yellow Branch Road. Turn right into the 440-acre park on S-37-226/Stumphouse Tunnel Road. Ease your way down about a half mile around hairpin curves into a gully, and along a roadway framed with dark, overhanging mountain laurel and dogwoods.

Turn right (southeast) into the **Issaqueena Falls** parking area. Explore the beautiful 100-foot cascade by hiking a short distance down a pathway to the foot of the falls. Legend says that Issaqueena, a Cherokee woman married to an Englishman and subsequently captured by her countrymen, escaped and, in her flight, leapt over a precipice near the top of the falls. She eluded capture by hiding under an overhang now visible from the trail. The 6.5-mile **Blue Ridge Railroad Historical Trail** starts just above Issaqueena Falls, on the other side of a footbridge across Cane Creek. A few picnic tables are located on this side of the park. Exit the parking area. Straight ahead 0.1 mile is a picnic area and gazebo on a small pond.

Turn right onto the paved road and travel 0.1 mile to see the **Stumphouse Mountain Tunnel**, where the ill-fated Blue Ridge Railroad ended in this area. It was a grand dream of South Carolina statesman John C. Calhoun, who was a member of the original surveying team. The idea was to link the port of Charleston with the farms and burgeoning cities of the Midwest. The Civil War intervened, and the railroad was never completed. Its greatest monument, Stumphouse Mountain Tunnel (which wasn't completed either), can be explored if you are not afraid of the dark.

This area has great natural variety. Trees include oak (mainly chestnut and chinquapin), maple, pignut hickory, tulip poplar, sassafras, pine, black walnut, locust, piedmont rhododendron, mountain laurel, dogwood, and sourwood. Trailing wild muscadine, arbutus, elderberries, asters, wild hydrangea, Indian pink, honeysuckle, nettles, and snakeroot are under the trees. Birds you may see include red-eyed and blue-headed vireos, tufted titmice, warblers (black-throated green, hooded, Blackburnian, black-and-white, and worm-eating varieties), ovenbirds, American redstarts, and Acadian flycatchers.

Stumphouse Park to Walhalla State Fish Hatchery

Exit Stumphouse Park and turn right (north) on SC 28 West/Highlands Highway/SC 107 North. After 2.6 miles take a slight right (north) to remain on SC 107 to head toward Oconee State Park.

Travel 2.4 more miles on SC 107 North and then turn right (east) onto State Park Road to visit **Oconee State Park** (624 State Park Rd., Mountain Rest).

Created in the 1930s, this park and its rustic facilities bear the stamp of the Civilian Conservation Corps (CCC), President Franklin Roosevelt's Depression-era army of public works builders. A CCC statue is located outside of the park office honoring the memory of the more than three million members who served in the CCC between 1933 and 1942. At 1,165 acres, the park encloses two mountain lakes and lovely rolling terrain where black bears occasionally visit. The park offers challenging hiking, and also features lake swimming, canoeing, kayaking, fishing, geocaching, and biking.

Hiking is delightful, as Oconee State Park offers five trail opportunities, each with its own special attractions. Oconee and Old Waterwheel Trails are about 2.5 miles each and entirely contained within the park, while Tamassee Knob Trail and Hidden Falls Trail are each 2 miles one-way and extend beyond the park's boundaries. Finally, Oconee State Park is the western terminus for the Foothills Trail, which extends more than 100 miles to Table Rock and Caesars Head.

Exit the park from State Park Road by turning right on SC 107 and drive north 6.4 miles toward Cherry Hill Recreation Area.

Cherry Hill Recreation Area (Cherry Hill Recreation Road/FR 735) is the northwestern trailhead for **Winding Stairs Trail**, a pleasant, easy 3.5-mile jaunt. On your left is the trailhead for **Big Bend Trail**, which takes hikers 3.2 miles to crashing Big Bend Falls on the Chattooga River, as well as connections with the Chattooga and Foothills Trails.

Continue north 0.2 mile and look for the Moody Springs pullover on your left. Artesian well water flows from a pipe jutting from the side of the mountain. Moody was an early settler in the area, and Moody Springs became a favorite stopping point in the 1800s for travelers heading northward to High Hampton in North Carolina.

If you'd like to access the Foothills and Chattooga Trails and the Burrells Ford Campground Area, after 1.3 miles, turn left (west) on Burrells Ford Road/FR 708. The road is paved for 0.6 mile and then dirt and gravel for about 2.3 miles where you'll reach the Burrells Ford Campground and access points to the trails.

The large parking area is an access point for the **Foothills Trail***, which crosses Burrells Ford Road just east of the parking area, as well as connections to the Chattooga Trail. The Foothills Trail stretches for more than 100 miles south and east from here, and is the premier backpacking experience in South Carolina. A primitive campground is a few hundred yards south, and modest restroom facilities are available at the parking area.*

A great short-term experience is to hike southward along the Foothills Trail about a mile, taking a left on a short spur to visit roaring **King Creek Falls***, which makes a spectacular 70-foot tumble down a steep granite face into a lush gorge smothered in mountain laurel and rhododendron.*

Turn left out of the parking lot and go another 0.3 mile where you will see trailheads for the Chattooga Hiking Trail and the **Ellicott Rock Wilderness Area***. A short distance is a small bridge that crosses the Chattooga River. Park along the roadside and view the river from the bridge. The water is usually peaceful on this stretch.*

The **Chattooga Trail** *runs north and south from this point, and this is the best place to access it. A wild, rushing river, crashing waterfalls, coves lush with mountain laurel, and brilliant wildflowers make the Chattooga Trail a favorite of hikers who share their delights with occasional fly casters. The trail follows the edge of the Chattooga River, often along the banks of the river and sometimes high up on bluffs. The mountains and cliffs of the Georgia side of the river form a scenic backdrop. Hikers ascend and descend frequently as they cross numerous small streams and wind around and through a seemingly endless series of coves and ravines and along mountain ridges.*

If you head northward on the Chattooga Trail, you will have opportunities to connect with other beautiful pathways, including the Foothills Trail, East Fork Trail, and Fork Mountain Trail. However, you need only walk about 0.2 mile north to reach a sign indicating that **Spoonauger Falls** *is on a spur 200 yards to the right (east). Take this spur. The trail follows switchbacks up a cascading series of small falls along Spoonauger Creek until it reaches the base of Spoonauger Falls, a spectacular crashing cascade also known, for self-evident reasons, as Rock Cliff Falls.*

Return to SC 107 after turning around at the Chattooga River Bridge and driving east on Burrells Ford Road. Turn left (northeast) onto SC 107. A scenic outlook is just 0.2 mile past Burrells Ford Road on your right. Stop here for breathtaking views.

Walhalla State Fish Hatchery (198 Fish Hatchery Rd/SC 107 North, Mountain Rest) is 1.5 miles past Burrells Ford Road. Turn left (west) onto S-37-325/Fish Hatchery Road and travel 1.8 miles farther down a shady, curving mountain road to a parking lot.

Formerly a federal facility built by the Works Progress Administration and Civilian Conservation Corps in the 1930s, it is now operated by the South Carolina Department of Natural Resources and open to the public. More than 250,000 rainbow, brown, and brook trout are raised here and released annually into streams in the upper part of the state. In addition to the large outdoor tanks where the growing fish can be seen, visitors can view an interpretive display.

The picnic area offers many spots to relax in the shade of giant hemlocks and white pines, and to play in the shallows of the East Fork of the Chattooga River. The area is a great spot for bird-watching. Broad-winged hawks, pileated woodpeckers, great crested flycatchers, eastern wood pewees, wood thrushes, red-eyed vireos, warblers, blue jays, bluebirds, cardinals, and Carolina chickadees are among the numerous feathered friends seen here.

The fish hatchery is also the northeastern trailhead for the East Fork Trail, which leads 2.5 miles to the banks of the Chattooga River through a lush, fertile gorge filled with unusually large white pines, along with hemlocks, mountain laurels, winterberries, and sweet pepperbushes. The trail is often smothered in rhododendrons and also features maples, oaks, hickories, tulip poplars, yellow birches, Fraser magnolias, hollies, and dogwoods. The East Fork is a large, swift, rocky stream that dances over rocks and around boulders along the south side of the pathway throughout the length of the trail.

Except for short distances at the two ends of the trail, the entire length of the East Fork Trail lies within the southernmost region of Ellicott Rock Wilderness Area, a pristine 9,012-acre preserve on national forest lands closed to logging, vehicles, and activities that disturb the natural state of the area.

Walhalla State Fish Hatchery to Whitewater Falls

Turn left out of the Fish Hatchery to continue north on SC 107 for 2.3 miles. When you reach a stop sign on SC 107, you might consider stopping for a picnic. *If so, consider turning left (north) to remain on SC 107 and drive 0.2 mile to stop at Sloan Bridge Picnic Area. This is the site of the northeastern trailhead for the Fork*

Wigington Scenic Byway view of Lake Jocassee Kathy Clark

Mountain Trail, as well as another access point for the Foothills Trail, which heads both east and south from here.

To continue to Whitewater Falls, turn right onto S-37-413, **Wigington Scenic Byway**. This 2.3-mile stretch offers scenic outlooks and picnic areas, views of mountains and forestlands, and great distant vistas of lakes and lowlands. A scenic outlook is almost a mile after your turn onto the scenic byway. Pull over here to take in the breathtaking views of distant mountains and Lake Jocassee.

Proceed 1.5 farther until Wigington Scenic Byway ends at the intersection with SC 130. Turn left (north) on SC 130/Whitewater Falls Road and travel just 0.7 mile, and then turn right (east) on Bad Creek Road into Duke Energy's Bad Creek Reservoir, with signs pointing toward the Foothills Trail and Whitewater River. Travel 3.5 miles (northwest) to the Visitors Overlook Parking Area.

Observe on your right **Bad Creek Reservoir**, a 1,200-foot-high rock-lined bowl of water. At night, when electricity demand is low and nuclear power is in maximum supply, water is pumped from Lake Jocassee below to Bad Creek Reservoir above. At peak demand times during daytime hours, the reservoir water is released by Duke Energy through hydroelectric turbines to produce electricity when it is most needed. There is no public access to the reservoir itself.

After 2 miles, you come to a left turn (north), where signs point to Muster Ground Road and an access point for the Foothills Trail, the **Jocassee Gorges Wildlife Management Area**, and **Lower Whitewater Falls**. You can park at the far end of the lot and walk 0.6 mile over a ridge to the **Whitewater River** and several hiking options. Two bridges offer a good view of the Whitewater, an unusually clear and pristine stream with native populations of rainbow and brown trout, unusual for South Carolina streams, which normally rely on stocking with hatchery-reared fish.

Upper Whitewater Falls, the highest waterfall east of the Rockies KATHY CLARK

Exit the parking area. Turn left and continue east on Bad Creek Road for another 1.5 miles, enjoying enticing views of mountains and valleys. Pull into **Visitors Outlook** and stroll under shade trees in the viewing area surrounding the parking lot. To your east and north is a deep, blue-green arm of **Lake Jocassee**, and a peninsula jutting from the Jocassee Gorges area. On clear days, a distant view of Lower Whitewater Falls is possible. To the south is the larger body of Lake Jocassee.

Backtrack and return to SC 130. Turn right (north), and travel a half mile to end your drive at Upper Whitewater Falls. Cross the North Carolina state line and immediately turn right (east) into the parking lot for **Upper Whitewater Falls** in the **Nantahala National Forest**. This is the highest waterfall east of the Rockies. Park and walk a half mile to a spectacular overlook of the 411-foot Upper Falls. The walkway is paved. Steps (154) allow you to go downward for vistas that are even more dramatic. If you continue farther downward, you will reach the Foothills Trail, leading southward and across a suspension bridge to the Bad Creek area, and westward toward the Chattooga River.

Nearby Attractions

Brasstown Creek and Buzzard Roost Heritage Preserves, Chattooga Belle Farm, Chau Ram Park, Clemson University, Historic Pendleton, Lake Issaqueena, Oconee History Museum, Seneca Historic District, South Carolina Botanical Garden, South Cove County Park, Walhalla Performing Arts Center, Westminster, Whitewater Lake, Yellow Branch Falls.

2

Mountain Bridge Natural Area

Keowee-Toxaway to Jones Gap

General Description: This 85-mile drive takes travelers through the Mountain Bridge Natural Area and up and down the Blue Ridge Escarpment. A long precipice at the southern edge of the Blue Ridge Mountains, the escarpment was aptly named "The Blue Wall" by the indigenous Cherokees. Along the way are spectacular views, mountain lakes, and the highest mountain peak in South Carolina.

Special Attractions: Keowee-Toxaway State Natural Area, Lake Keowee, Cherokee Interpretive Center, Eastatoe Creek, Reedy Cove Falls, Sassafras Mountain, Jocassee Gorges, Eastatoe Creek Heritage Preserve, Table Rock State Park, Lakes Oolenoy and Pinnacle, Cherokee Foothills Visitor Center, Bald Rock Heritage Preserve, Caesars Head State Park, Raven Cliff Falls, Rainbow Falls, Symmes Chapel/Pretty Place, South and Middle Saluda Rivers, Wildcat Branch Falls, Jones Gap State Park.

Location: Northwest corner of the state.

Travel Season: All year. The upstate is especially beautiful in the spring when it is covered in wildflowers and in the fall when the trees are aflame in yellow, orange, and red foliage.

Services: Full accommodations and other services are available in Pickens, Easley, Greenville, and Travelers Rest.

The Drive

This ride takes you through the forested peaks and valleys of one of the most varied ecosystems in the eastern United States. You will be amazed and delighted with the variety of flora, fauna, and diverse wildlife, as well as the striking views at Caesars Head Lookout and Pretty Place, and the 360-degree panorama atop Sassafras Mountain. This area is home to two of the four National Wild and Scenic Rivers in the southeastern United States, Chattooga and Horsepasture, as well as more than 50 white-water waterfalls, some of which are the most spectacular in this part of the country, including Whitewater Falls, Laurel Creek Falls, Reedy Cove Falls, Toxaway Falls, Raven Cliff Falls, and Rainbow Falls.

Begin at Keowee-Toxaway State Natural Area and then ride through the enchanting Eastatoe Valley before heading up curving roadways to reach the top of Sassafras Mountain, the highest peak in South Carolina. Head back down the mountain and travel over rolling hills to see spectacular views of bald Table Rock, Pinnacle, and Caesars Head Mountains. Next wind your way up the Blue Ridge

Mountain Bridge Natural Area: Keowee-Toxaway to Jones Gap

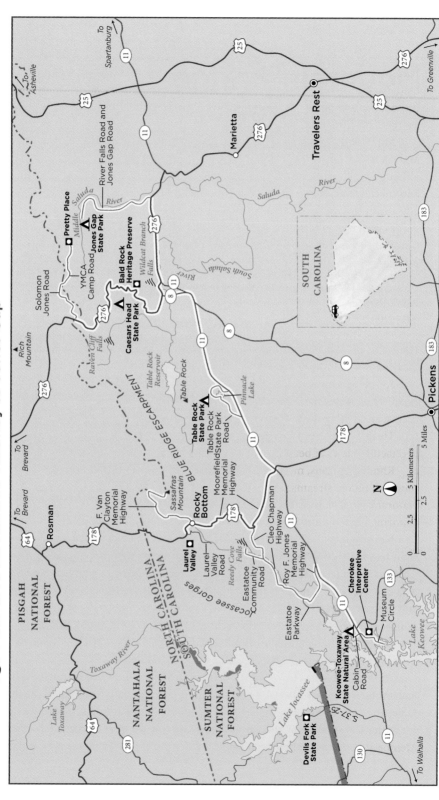

Escarpment to visit Caesars Head State Park, which combines with Jones Gap State Park to form the bulk of the 10,000-acre Mountain Bridge Natural Area, and meander along the North Carolina state line to visit the idyllic Symmes Chapel at Pretty Place. You end in the cool, rustic river valley of Jones Gap.

Much of this upstate area has been carefully preserved through state, federal, and private initiatives, so future generations can continue to enjoy its pristine state although there continue to be new developments here. In addition to state parks and several smaller heritage preserves and wildlife management areas, the state is also the proud owner of 32,000 acres of the Jocassee Gorges, an area of mountains, gorges, rivers, and lakes connecting Sumter National Forest on the Georgia–South Carolina border on its west side with the Mountain Bridge Natural Area on its east flank.

Keowee-Toxaway State Natural Resource Area to Sassafras Mountain

Begin this drive in **Keowee-Toxaway State Natural Area** (108 Residence Dr., Sunset), which straddles Cherokee Foothills Scenic Highway/SC 11 on the east bank of **Lake Keowee**. Enter the north section of the park on S-39-74/Cabin Road. This side of the 1,000-acre park provides the park's campgrounds, lake access, and hiking trails. Campers can fish in Lake Keowee and picnic in the shelters. Head down Cabin Road a half mile to the shore of Lake Keowee and enjoy spectacular views of beautiful rock outcroppings and the Blue Ridge Mountains.

Rhododendrons, mountain laurel, and other lush mountain vegetation can be found along the streams and trails in the park, which offers the moderate 1.1-mile Natural Bridge Nature Trail and the strenuous 4.2-mile Raven Rock Hiking Trail featuring great overlooks of Lake Keowee.

Next, return to SC 11, turn left (northeast) and drive 0.1 mile before turning right (south) onto S-39-347/Museum Circle to visit the **Cherokee Interpretive Center**. This facility tells the story of the Cherokee Indians who once roamed this area and the Cherokee Nation capital, Keowee, once beside the Toxaway River and now under lake waters. In the Cherokee language, *keowee* means "place of the mulberry groves," and *toxaway* means "land of no tomahawks."

Exit the south section of the park and turn right to head northeast on SC 11 to enjoy a pleasant jaunt along the Cherokee Foothills Scenic Highway. Bootleg, Dug, Pine, Wadokoe, Horse Gap, and Little Rock Mountains are on your left. On your right are Buzzard Roost, Cedar Creek, Rocky Bald, Gilstrap, Big Rock, Pink, Odle, and Mosley Mountains.

After 3.7 miles on SC 11, turn a sharp left (north) onto S-39-143/Roy F. Jones Memorial Highway and go 2.2 miles.

Reedy Cove Falls, in the Eastatoe Creek valley KATHY CLARK

Just after you cross Eastatoe Creek, 1.3 miles along the way, is a turnoff to the right where you can park and walk down a path to get a good look at the creek.

Bear right on Granny Gear Road and travel only 0.2 mile. At the next intersection, turn right (northeast) on S-39-100/Cleo Chapman Highway to travel 2.8 miles along the west bank of **Eastatoe Creek**. Old tin-roofed mountain houses, forests, cabins, Eastatoe Baptist Church, horses grazing in green fields, and rolling hills decorate this idyllic valley.

When Cleo Chapman Highway heads right, to the east, veer left to continue (north) on S-39-92/Eastatoe Community Road, a dead-end road. Travel almost a mile and turn right (east) onto Water Falls Road, to visit **Reedy Cove Falls**.

Mountain bungalows and some newer homes are tucked in here and there. Follow Water Falls Road/Holcombe Hollow Road less than a half mile to reach a gravel parking lot. From here, a quarter-mile path northward along Eastatoe Creek leads to the spectacular twin cascades of Reedy Cove Falls, well known as the cover shot on *Hiking South Carolina*. The falls are accessible from dawn to dusk.

Exit Water Falls Road the way you entered, turn left (south) on S-39-92/Eastatoe Community Road, and return 0.9 mile to the intersection with S-39-100/

Cleo Chapman Highway. Turn left (east), cross Eastatoe Creek again, and enjoy the wildflowers, grazing horses, farms, and mountain views that cover quiet Eastatoe Valley.

After 2 miles, you reach an intersection with US 178/Moorefield Memorial Highway. Turn left (north) and travel 4 winding miles north to reach the Rocky Bottom community, past campgrounds, mountain bungalows, and beautiful Reedy Cove Lake. Where US 178 veers left, turn right onto S-39-199/F. Van Clayton Memorial Highway, which goes to the top of Sassafras Mountain.

The drive to the top is 4.6 miles on a paved road through a forest of oaks, white pines, maples, tulip poplars, locusts, black birches, witch hazels, mountain laurels, rhododendrons, and Fraser magnolias. About 1.3 miles along the way is a small parking area on the left with access to the boulder-strewn area of Chimneytop Gap, less than a mile away along the Foothills Trail.

From the parking area just below the mountain summit, step out of your car and stroll along a paved walk to observation deck at the peak of **Sassafras**

Northward View from Sassafras Mountain, highest point in South Carolina Kathy Clark

Mountain. There are 26 steps up to the deck, or you can reach the deck via a disability access gravel path and ramp approximately 0.2 mile in length from the parking area. At 3,554 feet above sea level, this is the highest point in South Carolina. Enjoy spectacular views of the mountains and valleys below, filled with oaks, hickories, and other hardwoods. On a clear day you can see four states at once. And you can stand one foot in North and the other in South Carolina on the observation deck.

This is a great birding area. You may spot or hear a plethora of warblers, such as black-throated blue, worm-eating, Blackburnian, Swainson's, and chestnut-sided varieties. Other often-glimpsed birds in this area are ruffed grouse, ravens, dark-eyed juncos, Carolina chickadees, pileated woodpeckers, and solitary vireos.

The mountaintop provides access to three sections of the Foothills Trail. The Gum Gap Segment takes hikers to the Raven Cliff Falls area and US 278, 12 miles eastward. A trail segment heading southeast, leads to the Nature Center at Table Rock State Park, 9.4 miles away, and a pathway heading southwest leads 4.7 miles downward to Laurel Valley. Restrooms and educational signage are available.

Sassafras Mountain to Caesars Head

Head back down S-39-199/F. Van Clayton Memorial Highway to the bottom of the mountain, and turn left (northeast) onto US 178 for a sharply curving 7.2 miles downhill ride that passes through the Garvey and Jim Timmerman Wildlife Management Areas before reaching a major intersection with Cherokee Foothills Scenic Highway/SC 11.

*For an interesting detour, turn right (northwest) at the intersection with US 178 in Rocky Bottom and drive 0.9 mile to the left (west) turn for Laurel Valley Road. Turn here and cross the bridge over **Eastatoe Creek**, turn left onto S-39-237/Laurel Valley Road into Laurel Valley, on the eastern edge of the **Jocassee Gorges**, and travel 0.3 mile to end of this shady road that parallels the trout-filled stream gurgling swiftly by an assortment of mountain cottages.*

To the right (west) of Laurel Valley Road is Horse Pasture Road and access to the Foothills Trail. A red wooden sign marks the spot, and cars can park here if there is space at the trailhead.

*Horse Pasture Road also continues as a dirt road to a parking lot and trail-heads for the Eastatoe Creek Trail (1.8 miles) in **Eastatoe Creek Heritage Preserve**, and the Jocassee Gorges Segment of the Foothills Trail (31 miles). At times, the road past this point is barricaded. When it is not barricaded, a rough, rocky road provides access for high-suspension four-wheel-drive vehicles to travel 7 more miles to the camping and picnic area beside the top of the 80-foot straight drop of **Laurel Creek Falls**. The South Carolina Department of Natural Resources*

controls this area of the Jocassee Gorges and can be contacted for further informa-
tion about access.

After the downhill ride on US 178, turn left (east) on SC 11 and continue
4 miles to **Table Rock State Park**. Look straight ahead for a fantastic view of
Table Rock Mountain. The park headquarters (158 E. Ellison Lane, Pickens) and
Cherokee Foothills Visitor Center are to the right of SC 11. The headquarters
is a log cabin on the bank of Lake Oolenoy, named for the Cherokee Chief who
sold the property to the state. The headquarters building offers restrooms, snacks,
and a porch with rocking chairs where you can enjoy a fantastic view of Table
Rock's bald face. Cherokees believed their ancestral chieftain god used the "Sah-
ka-na-ga," the Great Blue Hills of God, as he chose. He dined by sitting on 2,600-
foot Pinnacle Mountain and used the 1.3-billion-year-old granite of Table Rock
Mountain as his table.

To visit the park and its restaurant and camping area, cross SC 11 and enter a
dark, forested area on S-39-25/Table Rock State Park Road, a slender 3-mile loop.
The forest is thick, deep, and filled with rhododendrons.

Listed on the National Register of Historic Places, the park was established
in 1935 in an effort to protect the beauty of the area. The Depression-era Civilian
Conservation Corps (CCC) developed the park using rustic designs and locally
available building materials. Evidence of this original construction can be seen in
the lodge, restaurant, bathhouse, two picnic shelters, the lake spillway, and dozens
of other log and stone structures.

Table Rock Mountain, reaching 3,200 feet, overlooks one of the state's oldest and most popular recreation areas. Camping, boating, fishing, swimming,
nature trails and programs, summit hikes, a restaurant, and rental cabins are
among the offerings. The park covers 3,000 acres of mostly oak and mixed
pine and hardwood forests, home to such birds as peregrine falcons, ravens,
and worm-eating warblers. A naturalist at the nature center schedules daily
programs during the summer for visitors, and the 36-acre Pinnacle Lake offers
supervised swimming, rental canoes, and pedal boats. The park has playgrounds,
picnic tables, and shelters. Fishing for bass and catfish is allowed in nonmotor-
ized boats.

The park has a substantial trail system that is designated a National Recreation Trail. The short Carrick Creek Nature Trail begins behind the nature center and connects with two longer hiking segments. On the west side of the Trail
loop is the Sassafras Mountain Segment of the Foothills Trail, leading to Pinnacle
Mountain, 4 miles away, past Sassafras Mountain, 9 miles away, and on to Oconee
State Park, 85 miles from Table Rock. On the east side of the nature trail, the hike
to the top of Table Rock Mountain is a rugged 3.4 miles.

Exit the park by continuing on Table Rock State Park Road past the camping area and turning left (east) on West Gate Road. Go 0.4 mile and take a left (east) back onto Cherokee Foothills Scenic Highway/SC 11.

On this tree-lined highway segment, Table Rock, Caesars Head, and other mountains sit to your left.

After 5.1 miles, veer left (north) on SC 8/Caesars Head Highway. Go 1.2 miles and merge left onto US 276/Geer Highway, winding northward and uphill into northwest Greenville County.

Continue (north) on US 276, a narrow, curving road through thick forest. Making an extremely steep climb up the Blue Ridge Escarpment, you experience several hairpin turns while enjoying a mountain stream, bald rock faces, and small waterfalls. Sometimes it looks as if the road drops completely off the mountain. Several pull-offs are here and there, where you can stop to explore the dark and dense woods or just savor the view.

After 1.8 miles, look for a pull-off along US 276, on your right beside a granite vista, to enter the **Bald Rock Heritage Preserve**. The 165-acre preserve adjoining Caesar's Head State Park is part of the Mountain Bridge Wilderness Area. The broad granite rock provides a panoramic view of the eastern side of Table Rock Mountain and the surrounding foothills of Pickens and Greenville Counties.

The tract contains granite outcrops, seeps, and waterslides. Two headwater streams found here have aided in the growth of some rare plant species, including one nationally threatened, the Piedmont ragwort, and one state threatened, the grass of Parnassus. Take in the view and the beauty of the rock formations before heading north on US 276.

Once you see the old Mountain House Restaurant on your left after 4.5 miles, you're almost at the **Caesars Head State Park** entrance (8155 Geer Hwy., Cleveland) 0.1 mile ahead.

This park is a popular spot because its elevation of 3,208 feet allows for unusually good visibility. Barring fog and haze, you can see 50 miles on a clear day at Caesars Head Lookout. Table Rock and Pinnacle Mountains are in easy view, and in the distance the Blue Ridge mountain range and the skyline of Greenville can be discerned.

An on-site park naturalist conducts visitors' programs and workshops throughout the year, as well as bird walks, nature hikes, and overnight backpacking trips.

A network of trails takes hikers across several mountains. Raven Cliff Falls near Caesars Head State Park is reached via a 2-mile trail to an overlook, or a 3.3-mile hike to a suspension bridge above the falls. It is one of the highest waterfalls in the eastern United States, with a splendid 420-foot cascade. Bill

Viewing point atop Caesars Head outcrop, looking southward KATHY CLARK

Kimball–Coldspring Branch Loop (4.6 miles) and the Naturaland Trust Trail (9.5 miles), both quite strenuous, also connect near here, as do the western end of the Jones Gap Trail (5.5 miles) and the eastern end of the Gum Gap Segment of the Foothills Trail (12 miles).

Caesars Head to Jones Gap

Leave Caesars Head and turn left out of the parking lot onto US 276. A mile north of Caesars Head is the parking area, on your right, for the moderately difficult trail to **Raven Cliff Falls**. The trail is on your left. The awe-inspiring views of the Blue Ridge Escarpment and the falls make it well worth the effort to get there. Another 0.4 mile farther north on US 276 on your right, is a parking area for the Silver Steps Falls trail, a 1.4-mile (each way) walk in the woods to a waterfall on the Middle Saluda River.

Continue north on US 276 for 1.2 miles and turn right (east) on YMCA Camp Road/Solomon Jones Road toward Camp Greenville YMCA (100 YMCA Camp Rd.), immediately south of the North Carolina state line. After 0.2 mile, the road becomes S-23-15/Solomon Jones Road. Mountain houses, brick bungalows, cornfields, and flower gardens filled with hollyhocks, zinnias, and wild daisies adorn this winding drive that crisscrosses the North and South Carolina border. Solomon Jones Road becomes YMCA Camp Road again after 2.4 miles.

After traveling 4.3 miles, you reach the Camp Greenville entrance. Bear right and continue almost a mile farther to visit Pretty Place and Symmes Chapel.

Two large marker stones, a few hundred feet past the entrance, indicate the entrance to the short but strenuous 1-mile trail to the bottom of **Rainbow Falls**, *a beautiful setting where Cox Camp Creek plunges 100 feet and crashes onto rocks just in front of you. On sunny days, rainbow prisms glisten in the mist.*

A stone wall and iron gates adorn the entrance to **Pretty Place**. Pass through the gates and see **Fred W. Symmes Chapel** perched on the edge of the mountain overlooking the Middle Saluda Valley. Park and walk into the stone structure, where you will see a spectacular panoramic view of the valley and nearby mountains. When not reserved for weddings or other private use, the chapel is open to the public. It is quiet and peaceful, a great place for a breezy picnic or just a reflective break.

Return on Solomon Jones Road/YMCA Camp Road to US 276, and then head south and east and downward on the curving highway past the Caesars Head Park headquarters until you reach the intersection of US 276 and Cherokee Foothills Scenic Highway/SC 11, 15.5 miles away.

Bear left (east). Along this stretch, you'll see a few exclusive residential developments, as well as cute bungalows, log cabins, and horses grazing in green pastures tucked on both sides of the road, along with the **South Saluda River** on your right. Wildcat Wayside (5500 Greer Highway, Cleveland), a parking area for a short walk to **Wildcat Branch Falls**, is 0.6 mile along the way.

At the intersection of S-23-97/River Falls Road and SC 11/US 276, 3.4 miles farther east, turn left (north). Take a slow, winding ride north and then west along S-23-97/River Falls Road and S-23-97/Jones Gap Road for 5.8 miles until you reach a dead-end at Jones Gap State Park. The road hugs mountains and fields of corn, beans, tomatoes, and kudzu. Pines, oaks, magnolias, and cedars form a canopy over the road in places, giving the passage a cathedral-like mystery—dark, cool, and serene. Old barns, grazing horses, and mountain bungalows are tucked behind trees or atop steep hills lavished with wildflower gardens. Along the way you'll catch glimpses of the Middle Saluda River and Tankersley Lake.

The visitor center and park office for **Jones Gap State Park** (303 Jones Gap Rd., Marietta) are a short walk across a bridge and through the woods off the shady parking area on the **Middle Saluda River**, the first river in South Carolina to be designated a State Scenic River. The Middle Saluda and its Cold Spring Branch tributary are part of the local beauty. The visitor center houses an interpretive environmental learning center with nature exhibits. Please note that the parking area is often full on weekends and holidays, so plan accordingly if you plan to stay for a while rather than just do a drive-by.

Jones Gap State Park MARIE GOFF

Between 1840 and 1848, Solomon Jones, for whom the area is named, built a 5.5-mile road across Caesars Head to Cedar Mountain, North Carolina. Originally, Jones Gap Road was a toll road, but it was abandoned in 1910. Now it is Jones Gap Trail, a pleasant walkway that allows hikers to meander along and across the Middle Saluda River and to the Caesars Head area.

Three much more difficult trails also interconnect here: Rim of the Gap (5.2 miles), Pinnacle Pass (13 miles), and Falls Creek–Hospital Rock (6.1 miles).

Nearby Attractions

Clemson University, downtown Greenville, Hagood Creek Petroglyph Site, Hagood Mill Historic Site, Paris Mountain State Park, Pickens County Museum of Art and History, Travelers Rest.

3

Cherokee Foothills Scenic Highway

Oconee Station State Historic Site to Cowpens National Battlefield Park

General Description: This 100-mile drive, passing by state parks, fruit orchards, roadside markets, and small villages on the Cherokee Scenic Highway (SC 11), follows an ancient Cherokee pathway in the looming shadow of the southern edge of the Blue Ridge Mountains known to the Cherokees as the "The Great Blue Hills of God." It begins at Oconee Station State Historic Site, an old Indian trading site and militia outpost, and ends at Cowpens National Battlefield Park, site of a pivotal battle in the American Revolution.

Special Attractions: Oconee Station State Historic Site, Station Cove Falls, Devils Fork State Park, Lake Jocassee, Keowee River, Keowee-Toxaway State Natural Area, Table Rock

Mountain, Poinsett Bridge Heritage Preserve, Chestnut Ridge Heritage Preserve, Campbell's Covered Bridge, Cowpens National Battlefield Park.

Location: Northwest corner of the state.

Travel Season: All year. Spring and summer are especially beautiful, with blooming flowers and orchards. Autumn guarantees a spectacular, colorful show. Peaches are celebrated in the summer and apples in the fall with local festivals.

Services: Conventional accommodations and services are plentiful in Clemson, Easley, Greenville, Spartanburg, and Gaffney. Limited services are available in Walhalla, Pickens, Landrum, and Chesnee.

The Drive

Along the Cherokee Foothills Scenic Drive, you enjoy magnificent views of foliage, lakes, and apple and peach orchards as you drive the ancient foothills of the Blue Ridge Mountains, one of the oldest mountain ranges on earth. The roadway follows an ancient Cherokee pathway, often right at the foot of the mountains. Beginning in Oconee Station State Historic Site, you travel to Devils Fork State Park on the banks of Lake Jocassee and continue past Keowee-Toxaway State Natural Area, on the shore of Lake Keowee, Table Rock and Jones Gap State Parks, through fruit orchard country all the way to Campbell's Covered Bridge and Cowpens National Battlefield.

The Cherokee Foothills Drive begins at Oconee Station State Historic Site, in Oconee County. Oconee, meaning "water eyes of the hills," is situated in the extreme northwestern corner of the state, almost surrounded by the waters of the

Cherokee Foothills Scenic Highway: Oconee Station State Historic Site to Cowpens National Battlefield Park

Chattooga River and Lakes Jocassee, Keowee, and Hartwell. The area was home to several Native American tribes, including the Creek and the Cherokee, but they gave up their lands in treaties signed in 1777 and 1785. After the American Revolution, settlers from other parts of the state began moving in.

Oconee Station State Historic Site to Devils Fork State Park

Begin your drive in **Oconee Station State Historic Site** (500 Oconee Station Rd., Walhalla), a militia outpost and Indian trading place dating from the late 18th and early 19th centuries. The parking area is a few tenths of a mile from the park entrance.

The 210-acre park has two historic structures, **Oconee Station** and the **William Richards House**. From the parking area hike uphill several yards to see Oconee Station, the oldest extant structure in Oconee County, built in 1792 as part of a series of blockhouses along the South Carolina frontier during a tense period between settlers and the Creek Indians. Oconee Station is considered the last western militia outpost to be decommissioned in the upstate. Troops remained until 1799, when the site was turned into a trading post, operated by Irish immigrant William Richards until his death in 1809. The William Richards House, constructed in 1805 and believed to be the first brick house in northwestern South Carolina, is adjacent.

The park also features a fishing pond and a nature trail leading into the Sumter National Forest and ending at **Station Cove Falls**, a 60-foot waterfall. Here, the nature trail connects to a 3.2-mile segment of the Palmetto Trail that takes hikers to Oconee State Park. This segment forms the northwestern terminus of the mountains-to-the-sea Palmetto Trail, which begins on the coast in the Awendaw area north of Charleston. If the park entrance is closed, you can drive 0.2 mile farther to a trailhead on our left that takes you to the falls.

Exit Oconee Station by turning left (southeast) back onto S-37-95/Oconee Station Road and driving 2 miles to SC 11. Turn left (northeast) and drive through rolling hills for 8.3 miles to a left (north) turn on Jocassee Lake Road/S-37-25 that takes you to **Devils Fork State Park** (161 Holcombe Circle, Salem). Drive 3.7 serene, winding miles all the way into the park, passing gardens, wildflowers, and mountain homes, to the boat landing for a great view of Lake Jocassee. A brown sign marks the turn.

The park's central feature is **Lake Jocassee**, named after an Indian princess whose name means "the place of the lost one." Devils Fork is also the only public access to the 7,500-acre lake. One thousand feet above sea level, deep and icy cold, and surrounded by forested mountains, its waters teem with brown trout, rainbow trout, white bass, smallmouth bass, largemouth bass, bluegill, and black crappie.

Lake Jocassee, at Devils Fork State Park KATHY CLARK

A 3.5-mile walking trail and 1.5-mile nature trail offer opportunities to view bloodroots, trout lilies, violets, jack-in-the-pulpits, and rare Oconee bells as you walk through forest inhabited by wild turkeys, white-tailed deer, raccoons, and gray foxes. In the trees are a variety of songbirds, including red-eyed vireos, scarlet tanagers, and many species of wood warblers. Peregrine falcons soar above.

In addition to a gift and tackle shop, and a variety of campsites, the 622-acre park offers 20 mountain villas that overlook the lake, complete with screened porches and fireplaces.

Devils Fork State Park to Campbell's Covered Bridge

Exit Devils Fork and backtrack 3.7 miles on S-37-25/Jocassee Lake Road to turn left onto the Cherokee Foothills Scenic Highway/SC 11. Travel northeast, crossing **Keowee River** after 3 miles and passing through **Keowee-Toxaway State Natural Area** (see Scenic Drive 2) 2 miles farther. Stop and enjoy the park's interpretive center and walking paths.

When you cross Keowee River, you enter Pickens County, established in 1826 in an area that was Cherokee territory until the American Revolutionary War, when the Cherokee sided with the British and suffered defeat.

View of Table Rock Mountain, from Cherokee Foothills Scenic Highway KATHY CLARK

Continue 8.4 miles past forests and mountains to the intersection with US 178. A detour to the left (north) here takes you to Sassafras Mountain and Eastatoe Creek Heritage Preserve (see Scenic Drive 2).

Be sure to look directly ahead here for a terrific view of majestic **Table Rock Mountain**. Table Rock State Park (158 E. Ellison Lane, Pickens) and the Cherokee Foothills Visitor Center (see Scenic Drive 2) are 4.3 miles past the intersection.

Almost 5.3 miles farther is the left (northwest) turn for SC 8 that leads to Caesars Head State Park (see Scenic Drive 2). Next, 1.5 miles down the road, SC 11 joins US 276/Geer Highway at the Greenville County line. Founded in 1786, Greenville County has the largest population in South Carolina, but this portion is sparsely populated. US 276 and SC 11 run concurrently to the right (southeast).

Bear right (east) on US 276/SC 11. Christmas tree farms, grazing horses, and huge old trees line the highway. Mountain cottages and bungalows are dispersed throughout the hills and valleys. Wildcat Wayside (5500 Greer Highway, Cleveland), a parking area for a short walk to Wildcat Branch Falls, is on your left 0.4 mile ahead. About 3.4 miles farther is S-23-97/River Falls Road on your left, leading north to **Jones Gap State Park** (see Scenic Drive 2) 5.5 miles down the road.

Continue on US 276/SC 11 crossing over the Middle Saluda River. At 1.5 miles past River Falls Road, turn left (northeast) toward Gowensville to continue on SC 11. US 276 heads south to Travelers Rest and Greenville.

Mountains and forests predominate this stretch of the drive. After 2.6 miles, the entrance to Pleasant Ridge County Park (4232 SC 11, Marietta, SC) is on your left. Continue 2 miles past horse pastures framed by mountains to the intersection with US 25 which connects Greenville with Hendersonville, NC.

About 3.7 miles on SC 11 past US 25 is the left-hand turn (northeast) on S-23-91/Old South Carolina 11 leading, 2.4 miles away, to **Poinsett Bridge Heritage Preserve**, a 12-acre preserve containing Poinsett Bridge, a 183-year-old stone bridge (580 Callahan Mt. Rd., Landrum). This is believed to be the oldest surviving bridge in South Carolina and possibly designed by famed South Carolina architect Robert Mills.

About 6 additional miles along SC 11 past the Poinsett Bridge turnoff is the entrance to **Chestnut Ridge Heritage Preserve** (2101 Oak Grove Road, Landrum).

This stretch of the Cherokee Foothills Scenic Highway is dotted with fresh produce markets offering, in season, such enticements as fresh apples, blackberries, raspberries, peaches, pears, plums, grapes, muscadines, figs, boiled green peanuts, honey, sweet corn, and a variety of fresh vegetables. Mountains puncture the horizon to the north as horses, goats, and cattle graze in vibrant green fields.

To visit Campbell's Covered Bridge, turn right, 3.4 miles past the Chestnut Ridge turnoff onto Tugaloo Road/S-23-978 and travel southwest 1.2 miles to S-23-175/North Campbell Road. Turn left (south) and drive through a picturesque agricultural valley with seasoned farm homes and scattered barns. Continue 1.4 miles to the intersection with SC 414.

Turn left (east) on SC 414 and drive 0.4 mile to the first road on your right, S-23-114/Pleasant Hill Road. Turn right (west) and go 0.2 mile to a gravel parking lot on your right to visit **Campbell's Covered Bridge**.

Refurbished and managed by the City of Greenville, the bright red wooden structure spanning Beaverdam Creek is the only remaining covered bridge in South Carolina. Constructed in 1909, it has been restored several times.

Campbell's Covered Bridge to Cowpens National Battlefield

Exit the parking lot by turning left (northeast) on Pleasant Hill Road/S-23-114. Travel 0.2 mile and then turn right (east) and travel 1.1 miles on Pleasant Hill Road/S-23-114 to SC 14. Turn left (northeast) on SC 14 and drive 2.3 miles to the Gowensville crossroads with SC 11.

Turn right (east) on SC 11 toward Campobello.

For an interesting detour, go straight (north) for 5 miles to the charming village of **Landrum**, *filled with antiques, book stores, gift shops, and fine dining. Pretty* **Lake Lanier** *is just west of town.*

Continuing eastward on SC 11, cross into northern Spartanburg County, the name of which is derived from the Spartan Rifles, a local militia that played a major role in the Battle of Cowpens during the American Revolution. In spring, this highway is ablaze in pinks and yellows. In autumn, red and orange foliage leads you past rolling hills to the peach country of Spartanburg County, "the fresh peach capital of the South," and for good reason. At one time Spartanburg County produced more commercially grown fresh peaches than the entire state of Georgia.

In the village of Campobello, 4 miles from the junction with SC 14, you reach a traffic light at the intersection of SC 11 and US 176; US 176 goes right. Remain on SC 11 by veering left. Peach tree orchards line the highway. With the mountains at your back, you traverse rolling hills past cultivated row crops, towering pecan trees, spicy fruit orchards, green pine forests, and horse and cow pastures.

Cross I-26, 3.3 miles from Campobello, and continue 9.5 more miles on SC 11 through New Prospect and Fingerville, past attractive houses, well-manicured yards, grazing cows, peach orchards, country homes, and old barns. Insistent signs beckon travelers to the numerous peach orchards and fruit stands on both sides of the road.

Enter downtown **Chesnee** 15.6 miles past I-26. Here, SC 11 becomes West Cherokee Street, lined with two-story homes adorned by huge porches decorated with swings and rocking chairs. Verdant yards and lively flower gardens enhance the attractiveness of this small town. The quaint downtown features art and furniture.

Continue east on SC 11/West Cherokee Road/US 221 Alternate. Enter Cherokee County after 0.2 mile and drive 2.5 miles to Cowpens National Battlefield Park.

Turn right (south) into **Cowpens National Battlefield Park** (4001 Chesnee Hwy., Gaffney) on Park Gate Road. A frontier pasture, Cowpens was the scene of one of the decisive battles of American history. On January 17, 1781, the British sustained one of the worst disasters of their Southern Campaign. American General David Morgan, surprised to learn of British Colonel Tarleton's approach, led his army to victory, achieving a vital link in the chain of British disasters in the South that led to a final defeat of the British at Yorktown, Virginia.

Originally called Cow Pens, the locale was a natural grazing area for cattle. Cow Pens was well known to the militia who Morgan hoped to assimilate with his Continentals to help win this battle. The previous October, some of the same men

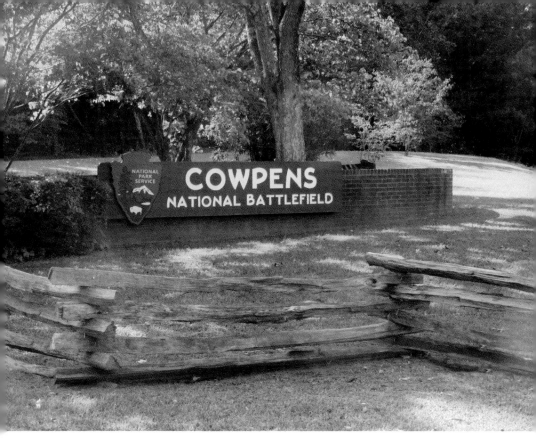

Cowpens National Battlefield entrance John Clark

had camped here on their way to the Battle of Kings Mountain, so when Morgan sent out the word to meet him at Cow Pens, his men knew where to come.

Cowpens National Battlefield Park is operated by the US Department of the Interior's National Park Service. The excellent visitor center and its museum are on your left shortly after you drive through the park entrance.

The center presents a battle reenactment movie, *Day Break at Cowpens*, a narrated slide presentation, and a self-guided fiber optic map presentation. Follow the Auto Loop Road around a 3.8-mile circuit to complete your scenic drive. The park also offers a 1.3-mile walking tour of the battlefield and a 2-mile nature trail that begins in the picnic area.

Nearby Attractions

Cherokee County Museum, Falls Park on the Reedy, downtown Greenville, Greenville County Museum of Art, Peace Center, The Peachoid water tower, Pickens County Museum, Travelers Rest, Walhalla.

4

Upper Savannah River Valley

Lakes Hartwell, Russell, and Thurmond

General Description: Beginning on Lake Hartwell, this 100-mile drive past farmlands and rural towns to large lakes takes visitors along the Savannah River National Scenic Highway through the Upper Savannah River Valley along the state's western border with Georgia, South Carolina's Freshwater Coast.

Special Attractions: Sadlers Creek State Recreation Area, Lake Hartwell, Calhoun Falls State Recreation Area, Richard B. Russell Lake, Mount Carmel, Willington, Long Cane District of Sumter National Forest, Hickory Knob State Resort Park, Baker Creek State Park, historic McCormick, Plum Branch, Parksville, Price's Mill, Modoc, Hamilton Branch State Park, Savannah River, J. Strom Thurmond Dam and Lake.

Location: Western border of South Carolina, north of North Augusta and west of Anderson and Greenwood.

Travel Season: All year. Spring displays wildflowers and blossoming trees, and fall is full of autumn color, especially throughout the Sumter National Forest.

Services: Full services are available in Anderson and North Augusta, and most services are available in Abbeville, McCormick, and Edgefield.

The Drive

This ride winds past Lakes Hartwell, Russell, and Thurmond, through some of the most popular recreational areas in the state. In the 18th century, this area was South Carolina's western frontier, teeming with soldiers, frontiersmen, and Native Americans. The Cherokee owned Anderson County, the starting point of this ride, until the Patriots defeated them in 1776. Many of the towns you visit were developed in the 1800s around railroad stops that thrived during the heyday of cotton but became deserted when the boll weevil devastated the industry.

Built and operated by the US Army Corps of Engineers to generate hydroelectricity, the three lakes total 153,000 acres of water, surrounded by 128,000 acres of public land in South Carolina and Georgia. Visitors along the Savannah River National Scenic Highway pass through sleepy villages and pastoral settings, in addition to the woodlands and water of the Long Cane District of Sumter National Forest and five state parks.

Upper Savannah River Valley: Lakes Hartwell, Russell, and Thurmond

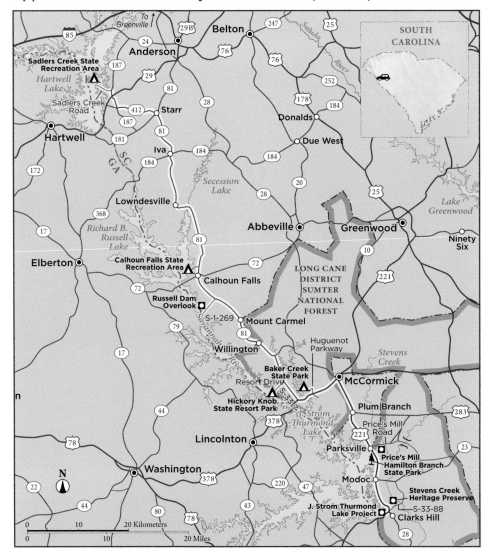

Lake Hartwell to Calhoun Falls

Begin just off SC 187 at **Sadlers Creek State Park Recreation Area** (940 Sadler Creek Rd., Anderson), which covers more than 395 acres on a peninsula extending into Lake Hartwell. The 56,000-acre lake with 1,000 miles of shoreline borders both South Carolina and Georgia and offers vast areas for sailing, waterskiing, fishing, boating, swimming, jet skiing, camping and hiking on the lake's shore. Drive all the way to the park office and picnic area that sit on the banks of Lake

Hartwell. Picnic tables are found near the lake's edge, and a half-mile walking trail begins beside the parking area. Head out of the park, and after 0.2 mile turn left to visit a fishing pier that offers expansive views of the lake.

Exit the park on S-4-745/Sadlers Creek Road and travel 1.2 miles through rolling hills and cornfields to SC 187. Turn right on SC 187 and head south. After 0.7 mile, cross US 29 and continue 1.5 miles to the intersection with SC 417/Rainey Road. Turn left (east) on SC 412/Rainey Road toward **Starr**. Enjoy 5.3 miles of undulating terrain and winding roads through picturesque farming country dotted with hay fields, pecan orchards, and old barns and farmhouses. If you're lucky, you'll catch glimpses of farmers tilling fields or harvesting hay in this bucolic setting and even deer leaping across the road. Small towns dot the road every few miles, remnants of water stops for the Savannah Valley rail system in bygone eras.

In Starr, named in honor of a popular railway engineer when the railroad was completed in 1884, you will see the town that once thrived around the cotton industry. As you enter Starr, slow down and look to your left to see the abandoned block of buildings and the pretty redbrick **Starr United Methodist Church** at 624 Professor Brown Lane.

Turn right (south) on SC 81 toward **Iva**, 5.5 miles away. As you roll into town, old homes and an abandoned textile mill line the highway. Originally a shipping station incorporated in 1904, Iva was once called "Cook's Station," for Dr. Augustus "Gus" Cook, a prominent local physician and businessman. The post office was named for his daughter, Iva Cook Bryson. The name Cook was dropped in favor of Iva for both the town and the post office when it was discovered there was another Cook's Station in the state.

In town turn left on East Broad Street and then right on East Front Street to visit Iva's downtown. The newly renovated square on East Front Street has an old-fashioned barbershop, a few shops, and several downtown eateries. The **Iva Museum and Visitor Center** is located on the corner of Central Street at 106 E. Broad Street. and a gazebo decorated to reflect the current season adorns the downtown block.

Continue on East Front Street to East Jackson Street and turn right. Drive one block on East Jackson Street and turn left on West Front Street/SC 81 to head south towards Lowndesville. Less than a mile from Iva, veer left to continue south on SC 81/SC 184/West Front Street. SC 184 goes right at the edge of town, and you remain on SC 81/Lowndesville Road as you cross into Abbeville County after 3.3 miles.

Sadlers Creek State Park on Lake Hartwell Patricia Pierce

Continue 3 miles to Lowndesville, "The Town of Seven Hills," a sleepy little town established in 1823. In town, SC 81 is also Main Street. Slow down as you enter town, and on your right, notice **Smyrna United Methodist Church** (439 Main St.), established in 1808; the present building dates from 1917. On your left is **Lowndesville Community Center and Town Hall** (1935), housed in the old high school building at 416 Main Street.

Where Main Street goes left (east), turn right (west) onto Marshall Avenue/S-1-368 to get a good look on your right at the beautiful **Providence Presbyterian Church** (1842) perched on a hill at 363 Main Street. A cemetery sits behind the church. Across from the church is a ballfield and small pavilion and picnic area where you can stop and rest, have a picnic, or just stretch your legs.

From Marshall Avenue turn around in the church parking lot and head back towards Main Street. Turn slightly right to return to Main Street/SC 81 (east). On your right is a country store where you can get boiled peanuts, red worms, and cold drinks. Pass old homes to head east toward Calhoun Falls 10 miles ahead.

A half mile past town, veer right (east) to remain on Main Street/SC 81/Savannah River Scenic Byway. After crossing the W. D. Nixon Bridge over a branch of Lake Russell after another half mile, take another right (southeast) where the road forks to continue on SC 81 toward the town of Calhoun Falls, another old railroad community.

Just north of town, 7.8 miles from the last SC 81 fork, is the entrance to **Calhoun Falls State Recreation Area** (46 Maintenance Shop Rd., Calhoun Falls). A brown park sign notes the right-hand turn (west) onto Calhoun Falls State Park Road into the 318-acre park on the shores of **Richard B. Russell Lake**, a little over a mile away. It is one of South Carolina's (and Georgia's) most popular fishing lakes. The 26,650-acre lake is home to largemouth bass, bluegill, crappie, and catfish. Drive all the way to the park office and boat ramp, where you'll have a terrific view of Lake Russell with its pine-lined shore.

Calhoun Falls to Hickory Knob State Resort Park

Exit the park by returning to Calhoun Shores Parkway/SC 81, turning right (south) and entering the old mill town of Calhoun Falls. Travel a mile into town, passing John C. Calhoun Elementary School (750 Calhoun Shores Parkway) on your left, to the junction with SC 72.

Turn left (east) here on North Cox Avenue, toward Abbeville, to see Calhoun Falls' quaint one-block downtown; you'll make a half-mile loop.

Calhoun Falls State Park on Lake Russell Patricia Pierce

Downtown Calhoun Falls PATRICIA PIERCE

Drive 0.2 mile and turn right (south) on South Cox Avenue, named for Judge W. F. Cox, who was one of the original investors when the town was founded in 1891. Cute antiques stores, Pettigrew Hardware, and the Red Dot Grocery (102 Cox St.), going strong since World War II, line the downtown street. Cross over East Savannah Street, and drive one more block to turn right on Seneca Street/S-1-31. Then after one more block, turn left onto West Savannah Street. Travel another block and turn left (south) on Calhoun Shores Parkway/SC 81.

Three and a half miles past Calhoun Falls, look for the Russell Dam Overlook Road/S-1-269 on your right. Turn right (west) and travel 3 miles to the end of the road to enjoy great views of the **Richard B. Russell Lake and Dam Project**.

Backtrack to SC 81 and turn right (southeast). You will enter McCormick County, largely engulfed by the Long Cane District of Sumter National Forest. McCormick is the state's smallest county in land area and the second smallest in population.

After 4.6 miles from your turn onto SC 81, enter **Mount Carmel**, a National Historic District. Slow down and take in this almost abandoned town. Old wooden homes topped with tin roofs look as if they have stories to tell as they sit silent, covered in overgrown ivy and wisteria.

There is no mountain here. Mount Carmel's name, decided upon by French Huguenot refugee families, is derived from a town in France. Mount Carmel originally served the surrounding farmers as a small trading center, and it boomed in the 1880s. A post office was established in 1854, a pottery and brick factory were established in 1885, the same year the town was officially chartered, and the Savannah Valley Railroad ran through the town in 1886. Mount Carmel thrived until a boll weevil infestation wiped out the cotton farms in the 1920s, followed by the Great Depression in the 1930s.

Fort Charlotte, built 7 miles southwest of the town between 1765 and 1767 to protect the French, British, and German settlements near Long Cane, was the site of the first overt act of the American Revolution in South Carolina. The site is now under Lake Thurmond.

McAllister and Sons (100 Main St., Mount Carmel), on the corner of Main and Depot Streets, is the oldest business in the county. Listed on the National Register of Historic Places, it is nearly the only visible commerce here. Established in 1888 as a drug store, but later serving as a bank, hardware store, and furniture store, this old shop still thrives under the fifth generation of McAllisters.

Leaving Mount Carmel on SC 81, travel 4 miles southeast to **Willington**.

The town of Willington was settled by French Huguenots in the 1760s. It gained prominence when Willington Academy was founded in 1804 by Reverend Moses Waddel. The academy attracted many of the best students from 1804 to 1819, some of whom became notable men in the South, including John C. Calhoun, a US senator and US vice president, and James L. Petigru, a lawyer who was among the few prominent South Carolinians who openly opposed secession from the Union. Dr. Waddel later became president of the University of Georgia.

As you drive into town, look to your left to see a former school building, the white, wooden **Mims Community Center** (2958 Hwy. 81, North McCormick), built in 1907. Next, 0.2 mile farther, on your left, are the tiny Daniel P. Juengst Railroad and Post Office Building (2368 SC 81, McCormick) and the Green Olive School House, both built around the turn of the 20th century. The Juengst Building has interesting exhibits, and the one-room School House serves as an African American Cultural Center.

This small village was thriving in the early 1900s in the heyday of cotton, but fires and the boll weevil devastated the community. Today, a nonprofit group called **Willington on the Way**, located in a group of historic structures in the heart of town at 1801 Morrah Bridge Road, is revitalizing the community.

Stop to explore the **Willington Bookshop** (1803 Morrah Bridge Rd., McCormick) and the **Willington History Center** (2352 Main St.) to enjoy displays of vintage quilts, Cowan family String Band musical instruments and photographs, historical dioramas, antique farm equipment, and a history of educational impacts of Dr. Waddel.

From Willington, continue 2.6 miles southwest on SC 81 to the intersection with S-33-7. Turn right (southwest) and travel 5 miles to visit Hickory Knob State Resort Park.

After 2.4 miles, you will pass Huguenot Parkway on your left, where **New Bordeaux**, the last of seven South Carolina French Huguenot colonies, was founded in 1764. The British Crown granted Protestants who were fleeing religious persecution in France 28,000 acres in the Hillsborough Township. Almost 200 hundred French Huguenots landed in Charleston and began settling at New Bordeaux. Others followed a few years later. The colony produced silk and wine on a modest scale.

Hickory Knob State Resort Park (1591 Resort Dr., McCormick) is a 1,091-acre, well-manicured park on the shores of Lake Thurmond. Turn right onto Resort Drive/S-33-421, lined with a verdant, rolling 18-hole championship golf course along the lake on the left and thick woods to the right. Ride to park headquarters and take in a good view of Lake Thurmond, the second largest lake in the southeast, encompassing 70,000 acres. The park offers hiking, walking, and biking trails, a boat ramp, archery and skeet shooting ranges, a swimming pool, and tennis courts. A motel, cabins, campsites with electricity and water, restaurant, lodge, and meeting facility are also available.

About 1.5 miles from your turn into the park is the **Guillebeau House**, built in the mid-1770s and just off the main road to your right, tucked in the woods. The cabin, home of Revolutionary War veteran Andre Guillebeau, was moved to Hickory Knob from New Bordeaux and is the only remaining documented structure of the French Huguenot settlement in South Carolina's upcountry. Circle around the park offices 0.3 mile farther, and head back out of the park.

Hickory Knob State Resort Park to McCormick

Exit the park and turn right (south) on S-33-7 to visit **Baker Creek State Park** (863 Baker Creek Rd.). Travel 1.6 miles to US 378. Turn left (northeast) and travel 2.1 miles to cross the bridge over Little River, and then turn left onto S-33-467/Huguenot Parkway. Drive less than a mile, and turn left onto Baker Creek Road/S-33-329 to visit the park, tucked in the heart of Long Cane District of the Sumter National Forest.

The heavily wooded road through rolling terrain of the 1,305-acre park takes you all the way to the Lake Pavilion, where you can enjoy a panoramic waterfront view of the Little River Branch of Lake Thurmond. Two 50-site campgrounds are located on the lake, and this is a good place to enjoy fishing, boating, and nature trails.

Exit the park by backtracking 3 miles to the intersection of Huguenot Parkway/S-33-467 and US 378. Turn left (east) on US 378 to head toward McCormick, 3 miles ahead.

Continue past commercial and residential areas scattered along US 378 toward downtown **McCormick**, a town where shops are built over old gold mine tunnels that date as far back as the mid-1800s. The town of McCormick was named for Cyrus McCormick, the inventor of the reaper and owner of the land where a large portion of the town was eventually built. After investing in the gold mine and then the railroad, McCormick purchased property, ordered the town to be surveyed, and ensured that two rail lines came through his land.

Another influential family in McCormick's history was the Dorn family. William "Gold Mine" Dorn discovered gold here in the mid-1850s, and the first town was called "Dorn's Gold Mines." He also built the flour and grist mill on Main Street, and others in the Dorn family owned the lumberyard that provided wood chips and sawdust that powered it. Even the first postmaster was a Dorn when the post office opened in 1857.

As you enter downtown McCormick on West Gold Street/US 378, cross over SC 28, and continue uphill to cross the railroad tracks. Ahead on the right-hand corner of South Main Street is the **McCormick Visitor Center and Chamber of Commerce** (100 S. Main Street), in a 1920s building that was once the town's service station. Turn right onto Main Street and pass a downtown block filed with antiques stores and other interesting shops and eateries on your left and railroad tracks to the right. The ***Journal Messenger***, a weekly newspaper established in 1902, is at 120 S. Main Street, one of the few local papers in the state still going strong.

Directly ahead is the **Old Train Depot** (1910). Turn right onto Augusta Street, cross the railroad tracks, and then turn right again on Main Street. On your left is the old McCormick Hotel (1884) at 127 South Main Street.

Next is the **Keturah Hotel** (1910) at 115 South Main Street, named after the builder's wife. Once a boardinghouse and an inn, the hotel is now listed on the National Register of Historic Places and serves as the home of the McCormick Arts Council.

Continue on Main Street to cross West Gold and Virginia Streets toward the **Dorn Mill Complex** (200 N. Main St.), once the center of the town's economy in the late 19th century. The steam-operated mill, built beside the railroad track in 1898, originally processed cottonseed oil. In the 1920s, however, the facility was converted into a flour and grist mill. It was the only steam-powered mill of its type in South Carolina. The structure contains the original steam engines and milling equipment.

From the Mill, backtrack a half block on North Main Street, turn left on Virginia Street, cross the railroad tracks, and immediately turn right on South Main Street. Go one block, and just before the visitor center, turn left on East Gold Street. Travel 2 blocks, and on your left is the home of former state senator **Joseph Jennings Dorn**, built around 1917 at 206 East Gold Street. A prominent businessman, Dorn was involved with farming, manufacturing, banking, and the lumber business. The Dorn home was one of the first built with brick in McCormick.

Turn right (south) on South Oak Street, across from the Dorn house, go one block, and turn right (west) on Augusta Street to head back downtown. After 2 blocks, pass the old train depot on your left and cross the train tracks again. One block directly ahead is the **McCormick County Courthouse** (1923) at 133 South Mine Street.

If you'd like to try your hand at panning for gold, turn right on US 28/North Mine Street and head 0.2 mile to the **Heritage Gold Mine** *(211 N. Mine St.) on your left. Cyrus McCormick, for whom the town is named, once owned the mine, which continued in operation off and on until the 1930s. Today the Gold Mine Park offers self-guided and docent mine tours, as well as panning for gold, minerals and gemstones two Saturdays each month.*

Turn left (south) onto South Mine Street/US 221/SC 28 toward Plum Branch and Augusta, Georgia.

McCormick to J. Strom Thurmond Dam & Lake

Plum Branch, named for a nearby stream framed with plum bushes, is 4.5 miles southeast of McCormick on SC 28/US 221. Bracknell's (108 Depot St.), a local store that opened in 1902, was once the largest merchandise house between Augusta and Greenville. The store closed in the 1980s and was later a farmhouse restaurant. The railroad runs parallel to the highway on your left.

In Plum Branch turn left (east) on Old Edgefield Street and then right (south) on North Depot Street to see the 2-block downtown that faces the railroad. Only the essentials remain here now: The fire department, **Town Hall** (106 N. Depot St.) with a tiny library in front, and the **post office** (102 Depot St.) fill the downtown.

Cross Edgefield Street, and on your left is **Woodlore Grove**, a woodworking shop, housed in a grey two-story wooden structure adorned with metalworks. Turn right (west) on S-33-29/City Cemetery Street, cross the rail tracks, and turn left on Main Street/SC 28/US 221 to continue southward toward Parksville, 5

Wood and metal works in downtown Plum Branch PATRICIA PIERCE

Plumb Branch Town Hall and Library PATRICIA PIERCE

miles ahead. Forests and rolling hills filled with horses and grazing cattle line the road.

Parksville, the only town located on the shore of Lake Thurmond, is quite small. Quaint wooden houses with tin roofs and small porches line the highway on your way into town.

In Parksville, if you'd like to see **Price's Mill**, *turn left (northeast) onto Price's Mill Road/S-33-138. A brown sign marks the turn. Cross the railroad tracks and travel 1.5 miles to Price's Mill, a tall 2-story wooden mill on the banks of Stevens Creek listed on the National Register of Historic Places. One of only two water-powered gristmills that operated in South Carolina, the mill is now on private property and is closed. The structure was built in the late 1890s to replace the original mill (1768), which was washed away in a flood. The mill remained in production until the 1970s.*

Turn around and backtrack 1.5 miles on Price's Mill Road/S-3-33-138, cross the railroad tracks, and continue to US 221/SC 28. Turn left (south) onto US 221/ SC 28 toward Hamilton Branch State Park.

To continue your drive from Parksville, remain on US 221/US 28 and travel south 2.5 miles to **Hamilton Branch State Park** (111 Campground Rd., Plum Branch). Turn right on State Park Road to visit the park that covers a peninsula extending into the 70,000-acre Lake Thurmond. This is a great place for outdoor enthusiasts to experience scenic views and access to the lake. It is perfect for fishing, boating, picnicking, and lakefront camping. A short bike trail also connects to the 12-mile Stevens Creek Bike Trail.

Backtrack to exit the park and turn right (south) on US 221/SC 28. Travel 1.5 miles farther to reach the tiny town of Modoc, named for the Indigenous Americans tribe of Northern California that fought in the Modoc War (1872-1873). Some of the tribe members who were captured in the conflict were sent across the continent to live on the eastern side of the Savannah River.

Continue another 4.5 miles past Modoc to the intersection where SC 28 goes straight ahead (south) and US 221 turns right (west) to become US 221/Clarks Hill Highway. Turn right and drive a mile on Clarks Hill Highway to end your drive and visit the **Savannah River** and the **J. Strom Thurmond Dam and Lake**, one of the largest inland bodies of water in the South, surrounding more than a hundred islands that host a diversity of plants and animals. The dam, completed in 1954 as a US Army Corps of Engineers hydroelectric project, impounds a lake that stretches 40 miles northward up the Savannah River and 26 miles up the Little River. On the south side of the dam, the Savannah River heads toward Augusta, Savannah, and the Atlantic Ocean.

When the dam and lake were completed in the 1950s, they were known as Clark's Hill Dam and Lake, after the nearby South Carolina community. In the 1980s, Congress changed the name to J. Strom Thurmond Dam and Lake. Georgians still call the body of water Clark's Hill.

The **J. Strom Thurmond Dam and Lake Visitor Center** (510 Clarks Hill Hwy., Clarks Hill) offers a superb view of the dam and lake. Offering interpretive materials and programs, this is a good spot for nature walks and bird-watching. Wild turkeys, Bonaparte's gulls, loons, and double-crested cormorants make their homes here, along with a wide variety of other waterfowl and songbirds.

Nearby Attractions

Anderson County Arts Center, Anderson Downtown Historic District, Ashtabula Historic House, Clemson University, Clemson Area African American Museum, Blue Hole Recreation Area, Due West and Erskine College, Fort Hill, Hanover House, Lick Fork Lake Recreation Area, Modoc Campground, Parson's Mountain Recreation Area, Pendleton Historic District, South Carolina Botanical Garden, Stevens Creek Heritage Preserve, Woodburn Historic House.

5

The 18th-Century Frontier and Historic Towns and Settlements

Abbeville to Edgefield

General Description: This 75-mile drive begins in Abbeville's picturesque Town Square and takes you through Hodges, Cokesbury, Ninety Six with its Revolutionary War–era Ninety Six National Historic Site, and ends in the eclectic town square of Edgefield.

Special Attractions: Historic Abbeville, Parson's Mountain Recreation Area, Long Cane District of Sumter National Forest, Hodges, Cokesbury, Ninety Six, Ninety Six National Historic Site, historic Edgefield, and Lick Fork Lake Recreation Area.

Location: Western part of the state, between Aiken and Greenville.

Travel Season: All year. In spring, this area of the state celebrates flowers and peaches with weekend festivals.

Services: Conventional accommodations and services are plentiful in Greenwood, while many services are available in Abbeville, Edgefield, Ninety Six, and Johnston.

The Drive

This ride begins in charming, historic Abbeville and takes you over rolling hills and past green pastures to the colonial-era Ninety Six National Historic Site, before passing through more farmland and forests to the fascinating pottery center of Edgefield, a community alive with the past and known as South Carolina's Cradle of Governors.

Historic Abbeville

Begin in **Abbeville's Town Square**, bricked in 1919 and lined with vibrantly colored storefronts restored to their turn-of-the-century style. You'll feel as if you are stepping back in time in this "Pretty Near Perfect" town. Ancient oaks and flowers decorate the center of the square. Abbeville exudes southern charm.

French Huguenot and Scots-Irish farmers settled the area in the early 1800s on land that once belonged to the family of Andrew Pickens, a Revolutionary War leader. Since its establishment, important political figures have helped shape this quaint town. Patrick Calhoun, father of John C. Calhoun, helped found the county. John C. Calhoun, born in Abbeville, practiced law on the square from

The 18th-Century Frontier and Historic Towns and Settlements: Abbeville to Edgefield

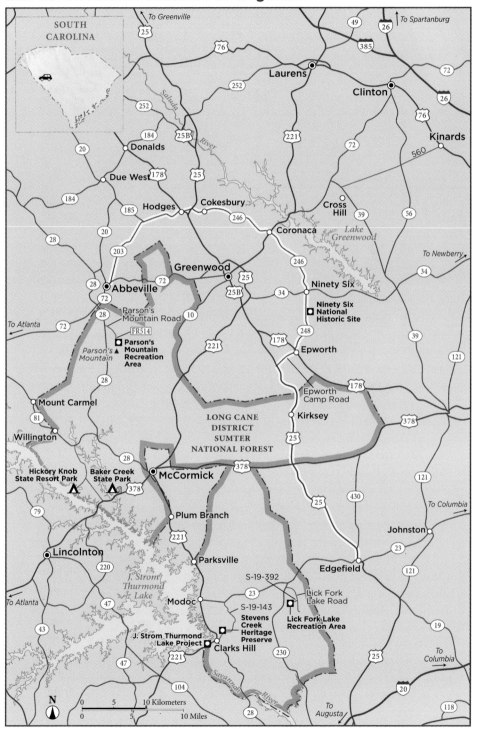

Dowtown Abbeville Marie Goff

1807 until 1817, and here he launched his career in public service that led to his becoming vice president, secretary of war, secretary of state, and US senator. Post–Civil War President Andrew Johnson had a tailor shop just off the square, and Robert Mills, the architect who designed the Washington Monument, lived in Abbeville for a time. Abbeville's historic district is listed on the National Register of Historic Places.

On the southeastern corner of the Town Square is the refurbished Victorian lodge, **Belmont Inn** (104 E. Pickens St.), formerly known as the Eureka Hotel. Built in 1903, the inn was a popular stopping point for travelers who came to the area by rail on their way from Atlanta and New York. This lovely hotel, bedecked with an enormous front porch and antique-filled rooms, invites visitors to enjoy fine dining in its restaurant or an ale from the pub downstairs.

The **Abbeville Opera House** (100 Court Sq.) on the corner of East Pickens and South Main Streets that also serves as City Hall is the state's "Official State Theater of South Carolina." Built in 1908 and fully restored to its turn-of-the-20th-century condition, the Opera House at one time served as a movie theater until a community theater group in the late 1960s turned it back into a playhouse. Now live theater can be enjoyed throughout the year, making it an entertainment hub for the Abbeville community.

To the left of the Opera House is the **Abbeville County Courthouse** (1908). In front, you'll find a monument to Thomas Dry Howie, an Abbeville native known as the "Major of St. Lo" for his heroism in a World War II battle in France.

The eastern side of the square is lined with retail stores, real estate offices, and a pool hall, the **Rough House** (116 Court Sq.), which remains very much as it was when it opened in 1932. Decorated with old seats from the Abbeville Opera House, nostalgia-producing vintage posters, and old-fashioned pocket pool tables, this is a great place to stop in for a cold beer or soft drink and a hot dog.

The center of downtown Abbeville is decorated with huge oaks, park benches, and lovely flowers. In the center of the Town Square is a 1996 Confederate monument that replaced the 1906 monument erected by the Daughters of the Confederacy of Abbeville County, destroyed in 1991 by fire from a nearby Christmas tree. On the south end, a 1912 watering trough installed by the Humane Society Alliance, designed with an upper pool for horses and a lower pool for cats and dogs, is now a fountain. At the north end is "Big Bob," a black alarm bell that once hung on city hall.

The western side of the square is filled with restaurants, more antiques shops, law offices, and **Abbeville's Visitor Center** (107 Court Sq.), located in the old **Nations Bank Building** (1860). The building served as a bank until 1996. Now you can step into the vault, which serves as a gift shop, and pick up brochures, the updated walking tour guide produced by the Abbeville County Historical Society, and books relating to the history of Abbeville and its historic structures and homes found in town. Inside the visitor center, you'll also find five paintings done by Wilbur Kurtz in 1922, depicting life in Abbeville from 1756 to Reconstruction.

Drive to the northeast end of the square and head north through the traffic light onto North Main Street/SC 20.

At the corner of North Main and East Pinckney Streets is the beautifully restored **Sacred Heart Catholic Church** (1888). Across East Pinckney Street on your right is **the Main Street United Methodist Church**. The church was organized in 1826 and the present building was constructed in 1884–87. To your left on West Pinckney Street is the **Abbeville Presbyterian Church**, built in 1888–1890.

Cross Pinckney Street. On your left at 305 North Main Street, hidden by holly and dogwood trees, is the recently restored **McGowan-Barksdale-Bundy House**, built in 1888, that serves as the Abbeville County Historical Society's headquarters. The Society has developed a walking tour guide available here, highlighting sixty historic sites in Abbeville. Behind the House are several servants' cabins and the 5759 CSX caboose, part of the Ann and Franklin Pursley Railroad Museum found in the lower level of the home.

The First Baptist Church organized in 1871 is on the corner of N. Main and Ellis Street. The current church building was constructed in 1911.

Cross Ellis Street and directly ahead, in the fork in the road, is the **Burt-Stark Mansion** (400 N. Main St.), built around 1840. This National Historic Landmark is significant not only for its architecture and the preservation of the home, its contents, and lifestyle of the early 19th century, but also for an historic Confederate meeting that took place here on May 2, 1865. Jefferson Davis held the last Confederate Council of War meeting at the Burt-Stark Mansion agreeing to give up the fight and dissolve the Confederate government. To visit the home, turn left onto Greenville Street/SC 20. A gravel parking lot will be on your left where there is also the **Jefferson Davis Park**, a lovely green space.

On your right is the **Parker-Green House** (1859), the oldest house on Greenville Street, at 200 Greenville Street. The stately columned home at 204 Greenville Street is the **Gary-Little-Dupre House** (1905).

Continue northeast on SC 20/Greenville Street for 1.3 miles. The **Upper Long Cane Presbyterian Church** (194 SC 20) on your right was established in 1763 and the present building was constructed after World War II. A few tenths of a mile farther on your left is **Long Cane Cemetery**. The first burial here is believed to have been in 1760, and the first marked graves date back to the 1770s.

Turn around in the cemetery and turn right onto SC 20/Greenville Street to return to Abbeville's Town Square and North Main Street.

If you'd like to see more beautiful homes highlighted in the town's walking tour, turn right at the light onto North Main Street. On your right at 500 North Main Street is the **Calhoun-Smith House**, *believed to be built by a relative of John C. Calhoun in the early 1800s. Also on your right at 506 North Main Street is the* **Morse-Wier-Garstka House** *(1883).*

On your left is the **Lee-Hite House** *(1885) at 505 North Main Street, built in the Second Empire style, and the Brown* **Neuffer Ford House** *(1900) at 507 North Main Street, adorned with double columns across its front porch. On your left is the* **Robertson-Hutchinson House** *(1881) at 509 North Main Street. The home is difficult to see hidden because it is behind huge trees, but take note of the redwood tree in the front yard. It is the largest and oldest redwood in South Carolina.*

Once back on the Town Square, at the traffic light, turn right (southwest) onto Trinity Street. On your right, is a restored livery stable (1820) that is used for community functions such as farmers' markets.

Directly ahead is the **Trinity Episcopal Church** (200 Church St.), the oldest church building in Abbeville. The first congregation assembled in 1842, and a small but devoted congregation continues to thrive here. The church, built between 1859 and 1860, houses a Tracker organ installed by John Baker of Charleston and features a chancel window imported from England in 1863. Stained-glass windows break the sunlight and keep the chapel dimly lit and cozy. Visitors are welcome to explore the church and its grounds. Trinity's cemetery at the rear of the church has graves dating to the 1850s, including those of Confederate soldiers and a Union soldier.

Turn left (south) on Church Street and go one block. To your right facing Vienna Street is the **Associate Reformed Presbyterian Church**, organized in 1889 and built in 1892–93. Continue south to get a good look at the **Quay-Wardlaw House** on your right at 502 Church Street, built in the 1790s and believed to be Abbeville's oldest standing house.

Turn left, (northeast) on West Pickens Street to return to the Town Square. Pass on your right the **Press and Banner** (107 W. Pickens St.), Abbeville's community newspaper since 1844.

On the corner of South Main Street at 101 W. Pickens St. is the **White Brothers Building** (1888), which frequently serves as an antiques store.

If you would like to visit a natural area, **Parson's Mountain Recreation Area** *(Parson's Mountain Road, Abbeville), in the midst of the Long Cane District of the Sumter National Forest, is attractive. Turn right off of West Pickens Street onto South Main Street/SC 20 and travel 0.4 mile passing weathered old homes, diners, coffee shops and the* **Abbeville County Library** *(201 S. Main St.), on your left, housed in the former US Post Office building (1912) designed by James Knox Taylor.*

At the intersection with SC 72, turn right (southwest) onto SC 28/SC 72 Connector. Travel almost 2 miles through a commercial area. At the light, turn left onto SC 28 and travel 2.1 miles. Turn left onto S-01-251/Parson's Mountain Road and drive 1.5 miles to Parson's Lake Road. Turn right to enter the recreation area and campground. The lake is a mile ahead.

The Long Cane District of the Sumter National Forest covers about 120,000 acres in Abbeville, Edgefield, Greenwood, McCormick, and Saluda Counties, and has an array of recreational opportunities to offer.

A 4-mile loop hiking trail begins at 28-acre Parson's Mountain Lake and climbs up Parson's Mountain, past an abandoned gold mine to an observation tower. The 22-mile Long Cane Trail loop also passes through the recreation area.

The surrounding oak-hickory and mixed pine forest is a terrific place to spot a number of interesting birds, such as wild turkeys, Bachman's sparrows, Kentucky warblers, and a variety of woodpeckers. The crest of the mountain offers especially picturesque views in the fall. Although the granite outcropping peak is only 800 feet high, the relatively flat surrounding land allows you to see for miles in all directions.

Continue east on Pickens Street past the Belmont Inn to the intersection with Poplar Street. Turn right and then immediately left onto Henry M. Turner Street. On your left at 309 Poplar Street is Abbeville's old county jail (1854), designed by Robert Mills and now serving as the **Abbeville Museum**. On your right at 100

Henry M. Turner Street is the Charles Dendy House (1791) which is believed to be the oldest standing public building in Abbeville County.

Next on your left at 203 Henry M. Turner Street is the redbrick **St. James AME Church**, built in 1899. The bricks are said to have been made by members of the congregation.

At the end of the block, turn left (north) on Secession Avenue. **Secession Hill** on your right is the site of the first organized secession meeting, on November 22, 1860, where resolutions were adopted in support of South Carolina's seceding from the Union. One month later, South Carolina was the first state to secede.

Continue over Branch Street, past Abbeville's 19th-century dilapidated **train depot**, onto Chestnut Street and go one more block to the intersection with Washington Street/SC 203. Turn right (east) onto SC 203 to head toward Hodges.

If you want to return to the Town Square, turn left. Washington Street takes you back to the northeast corner of the Square.

Abbeville to Ninety Six National Historic Site

Continue 7.5 miles on SC 203 toward Hodges. After about a mile, Washington Street becomes Old Douglas Mill Road. After 6.3 miles, Old Douglas Mill Road becomes SC 185.

*If you wish to visit the picturesque town of Due West, home of **Erskine College**, established in 1839, and its uniquely labeled "Flying Fleet" athletic teams, turn left at the SC 185 junction and travel 10.5 miles west. SC 185 takes you right into town and Due West's Main Street. Turn left on Main Street to see more of the college and this quaint town.*

At the intersection with SC 185, bear right (east). You'll cross Long Cane Creek 2.3 miles past the SC 185 junction and enter Greenwood County after another mile, on your way to the crossroads community of **Hodges**, 4.7 miles from the SC 203/SC 185 intersection.

In Hodges continue a half mile on SC 185/Main Street. On your left at the crossroads with Moorefield Street/SC 246 is the **Hodges One Stop** (4528 Main St.). For decades this market has been the meeting place for breakfast and lunch, filling up with gas, and shopping for hardware and groceries. You can even visit the butcher shop and buy homemade sausage, country ham, or honey. Stop in for a bite to eat or just to look around for local treats.

Continue southeast on SC 185/Main Street for another 0.2 mile to pass the **Town Hall** (4511 Main St.) on your right and see pretty **Hodges Presbyterian Church** (4413 Main St.), established in 1899 and built around 1901.

Old Cokesbury College campus in Greenwood County, now a wedding and events venue
PATRICIA PIERCE

Go 0.1 mile farther and turn left (east) on Freeman Road. Proceed one block, cross Moorefield Street, and merge right (south) onto Emerson Street/SC 246.

Drive southeast a mile, cross over US 25, and enter the village of **Cokesbury**. This was once a thriving community and an educational center for the entire state formerly known as Mount Ariel for its educational academy opened to students in 1825. In 1834 the community changed the name from Mount Ariel to Cokesbury after the first two Methodist bishops, Thomas Coke and Francis Asbury.

A half mile into the town, turn right on Asbury Road. A brown sign marks the turn to see the refurbished **Cokesbury College** (210 College Rd.), built in 1854 for the purpose of educating young women. The college operated until 1876 as a Masonic Female Collegiate Institute, one of the earliest in the southeast teaching Greek, Latin, modern languages, music, drawing and painting.

From 1876 to 1911 the college served as the Cokesbury Conference Center. Today the Cokesbury College Historical and Recreational Commission oversees the operation and preservation of the college building where weddings, meetings and other community functions are held. A beautiful garden adorns the entrance to the campus.

Exit Cokesbury College by turning right on Allen University Road and then right again onto SC 246 to continue southeast. After 0.6 mile cross over SC 254/ Cokesbury Road.

Continue on SC 246 for 7.5 miles to **Coronaca**, passing grazing cows, hay fields, and pretty farm ponds.

In Coronaca cross over SC 72/US 221 and travel 7 more miles to Ninety Six. After a little more than a mile, pass Fuji Film's North American Manufacturing Headquarters and Distribution Center (211 Puckett Ferry Rd., Greenwood) on your left. Remain on SC 246 all the way to Ninety Six, driving over more green hills and through forests that inspired Greenwood County's name.

The town of **Ninety Six** dates back to colonial times when the settlement began at the 96th milepost that marked the distance northward to Keowee, the Cherokee village in the Blue Ridge Mountains. The Cherokee Trail through here was used by traders and Native Americans, and a store was located here, supplying traders with rum, sugar, and gunpowder. The store was in operation as far back as 1737, and by 1753 it rivaled some in Charleston.

Many historic events took place in Ninety Six, including a blockade during the war with the Cherokees in 1760 and one of the first battles of the Revolutionary War in the South, November 19–21, 1775. The skirmish ended in a truce. Later, the British fortified the settlement, building a star-shaped fort and holding the post against the Patriot army for almost a month, from May to June 1781. However, the British abandoned the fort later that year.

In 1785 the community attempted to establish a college, Cambridge, and the settlement's name was temporarily changed to Cambridge. The college failed and the area declined. In 1852 a railroad was constructed through the village and citizens renamed the area Ninety Six.

A half mile into Ninety Six is the intersection of SC 246/Cambridge Street and Highway 34/North Main Street. Ahead to your right is the refurbished train depot built by Norfolk Southern in 1892.

The **Ninety Six Visitor Center** and Chamber of Commerce (SC 34/North Main Street), is to your left on North Main Street/SC 34 beside the old stone fountain. *If you'd like to pick up information about local attractions, turn left onto North Main Street to access the Visitor Center.*

Continue on South Cambridge Street/SC 246/William Bruce Ezell Memorial Highway (named for former President of Erskine College in Due West, SC). As you leave town, passing beautiful old homes in the heart of Ninety Six, Cambridge Street becomes SC 248.

Travel 2 miles southward on SC 248/South Cambridge Street to visit the **Ninety Six National Historic Site** (1103 SC 248, Ninety Six) and its Star Fort, on your left (east). This 1,000-acre property is the frontier outpost chosen for its convenient campground along the Cherokee trail that traversed the state. The Ninety Six park preserves the site of the most famous action that took place in the town during the American Revolution, the Siege of 1781. You can relive this battle by following a 1-mile paved interpretive walking tour through dark woods and green fields featuring the historic roads, reconstructed stockade, sites of the 1781 siege and battle and site of the Ninety Six village. A cannon used in the battle sits at the trailhead.

A 1.5-mile Gouedy Trail passes the grave of Robert Gouedy's son, James. Robert Gouedy built the first trading post in the area, in the early 1750s.

Adjacent to the parking lot is the visitor center that offers maps, a bookstore, and a museum including a 10-minute film about the historic site. Free ranger-led tours are available, as well as picnicking, fishing, bird-watching, and wildlife viewing.

Picnic tables beyond Logan Cabin near the parking lot and clean bathroom facilities make this a good place to stretch your legs and take a break.

Ninety Six National Historic Site colonial frontier post MARIE GOFF

Ninety Six National Historic Site to Edgefield

Exit the Ninety Six National Historic Site by turning left (south) onto SC 248. After a half mile, cross Ninety Six Creek.

After 1.7 miles farther, pass beautiful **Kinard United Methodist Church** (2217 SC 248 South), built in the late 1800s, on your left, and its cemetery, on your right. Travel 2 more miles past green pastures and farms until SC 248 ends at US 178.

Turn left, (southeast) on US 178. An old red farm building sits at the crossroads. Drive slowly and go 0.2 mile to turn right (southwest) onto S 24-44/East Epworth Camp Road. Grazing horses, the Epworth Camp Meeting Grounds, old houses, and green forests decorate the winding road.

East Epworth Camp Road intersects with US 25 after 2.5 miles. Turn left (south) onto US 25 and travel 23 miles toward Edgefield through a beautiful stretch that takes you past rural homes, pecan groves, peach orchards, and horse pastures. You can easily envision carriages bumping along this route through hills adorned with white cotton fields in the autumns of the early 19th century.

After 3 miles, enter the crossroads of Kirksey.

Travel 5.5 miles farther and enter Edgefield County, passing more old homes, barns and other farm structures, and rolling fields of hay.

Cross Turkey Creek after 5 miles and then pass pretty Berea Baptist Church (1675 Highway 25 North, Edgefield) on your right after almost 2 more miles. Edgefield is 6 miles ahead.

English, German, Irish, Dutch, and French traders and farmers settled in the **Edgefield** area in the middle of the 18th century. The founders built a politically active community, supported by cotton and other agricultural crops on the fertile lands of the area. These lands also seemed to nurture public leaders. The entire community took part in an ugly civil war between Patriots and Tories during the American Revolution. Later, Jim Bonham, a hero of the Alamo, was born here, as were ten South Carolina governors, five lieutenant governors, and several US senators and representatives, including Strom Thurmond, who began his political career here by successfully running for county superintendent of education. He later became governor and then served in the US Senate from 1954 to 2003, when he retired at age 100.

The entire town of Edgefield is listed on the National Register of Historic Places; thus, it has numerous 18th and 19th-century churches, homes, farms, and plantations that help tell the story of the Old Ninety Six district. Roadside vegetable and fruit stands, blooming peach orchards in the spring, and fields white with cotton in the fall decorate the outskirts of the picturesque community.

As you enter town on US 25 Business/Buncombe Street, turn left onto Simkins Street just before you reach Courthouse Square and just before you reach the gray stone **St. Mary's Catholic Church** (305 Buncombe St.) on your right. Irish stonecutters were brought to America to construct the church in 1858.

Simkins street parallels Court House Square. On your left is a small white wooden structure that served as the law offices of many prominent Edgefield lawyers who later became elected officials in South Carolina. An historical marker sits in front of the house.

The old Edgefield Pottery studio at 230 Simkins Street is on your right. The potter's studio displays 19th-century pottery named Edgefield Pottery by Dr. Abner Landrum, who developed the unique method and design. He shaped vessels from local clay and applied an alkaline glaze to give it a distinctive green or brown tone. Local potters produced practical and decorative stone pieces.

The most famous Edgefield potter was an enslaved man named Dave who worked for Dr. Landrum. Dave's pottery is easily recognizable by the original verses he inscribed on his pieces. His work and the work of others are a distinctive folk-art form exhibited in many major museum collections. In front of the Visitors Center on Court House Square is a video kiosk that you can tap to view examples of Dave's pottery and a history of his work.

Continue one block past Lynch Street and turn left (north) on Church Street. The **First Baptist Church** and **Willowbrook Cemetery** (1823) are on your right at 212 Church Street. The gravesites of Strom Thurmond and other notable Edgefield natives, including 150 Confederate soldiers, are here.

Backtrack to Simkins Street and turn left (east). Ahead on the left side of the street is the brick **Trinity Episcopal Church** (1836) at 317 Simkins Street.

Drive two blocks past old homes to the end of Simkins Street. Turn right onto Hart Street/S-19-132, and drive one block to Main Street.

*If you'd like to visit an antebellum home built in 1835, turn left on Main Street/SC 23. Travel less than a half mile to the **Oakley Park Museum** (300 Columbia Rd./S-19-300), sometimes referred to as the "Oakley Park Red Shirt Shrine," located at the junction of SC 23 and US 25. Oakley Park is the former estate of Confederate General Martin Witherspoon Gary who, with General M. C. Butler, guided the "Red Shirt" terrorist movement to elect Wade Hampton as South Carolina governor in 1876 and effectively end the state's Reconstruction period. The house is operated by the United Daughters of the Confederacy as a museum.*

This drive ends in the heart of Edgefield and its Courthouse Square, so turn right (west) onto Main Street/SC 23. On your right at 405 Main Street is the **Edgefield Historic Society and Discovery Center Museum and Theater** housed in a 1940s renovated farmhouse. The facility focuses on the history of

Abbeville, Edgefield, Greenwood, and McCormick Counties, including highlights of the cotton trade, the Revolutionary War, antebellum politics, mill villages, and more. Local and regional artists' works are exhibited throughout the year, and information about tours and educational programs in this region of the National Heritage Corridor is plentiful.

On your left is Edgefield's Town Hall. Cross over Bacon Street and continue west to **Courthouse Square**, in the center of town. Directly ahead is the **Edgefield County Courthouse** (124 Courthouse Sq.), designed by famed South Carolina architect Robert Mills and built in 1839.

Turn left onto Courthouse Square and park along the square. In the center of the square is a Confederate monument, a life-size bronze statue of Senator J. Strom Thurmond, and a granite marker listing the 10 governors and 5 lieutenant governors of South Carolina who were natives of Edgefield County. Park benches and beautiful flowers adorn the square, a great place to stop and linger to visit any of the restaurants, confectionaries or pubs located on and near the square.

On the northern side of the square is the **D. A. Tompkins Memorial Library and Genealogy Research Center** (104 Courthouse Sq.) the official Welcome Center of Edgefield County. The library is a repository of hundreds of volumes, microfilm, and loose files on the families and histories of the Old Edgefield District including estate records, plats, deeds and court records. Brochures are available in front of the Welcome Center as well as an educational video kiosk about the history of Edgefield and Dave the potter.

On the corner of US 25 and SC 23/Jeter Street (northwest of the square) is a small green space and the Edgefield History Wall. The wall provides the history of the town and county of Edgefield from local Native American tribes to the twenty-first century.

If you'd like to see more of Edgefield and a portion of the Long Cane District of the Sumter National Forest, drive west from Courthouse Square on SC 23/Jeter Street. On your right, just past the Edgefield History Wall, is the Village Blacksmith at 206 Jeter Street. In the early part of the 20th century, this was a blacksmith shop operated by an African American craftsman, McKinley Oliphant. Today, a working artistic blacksmith can be found here. Visitors are welcome.

Continue 8 miles west on SC 23 and then veer left (south) onto SC 230/Martintown Road. Drive a half mile to reach S-19-263/Lick Fork Lake Road on your left (east). The area is identified with a brown wildlife viewing area sign. Turn left onto Lick Fork Lake Road and travel 2 miles before turning right (west) onto S-19-392 to enter **Lick Fork Lake Recreation Area***.*

The facility boasts a 12-acre lake nestled in the southeastern portion of the Long Cane Ranger District of the Sumter National Forest, offering fishing for catfish, bream, and bass, as well as boating and swimming. Mountain biking and hiking in the heavily wooded park are also available.

Two interlocking loop trails, the 1.7-mile Lick Fork Lake Trail and the Horn Creek Trail, a bike/hike trail of 5.4 miles, are major attractions.

To see more peach country, return to Main Street/SC 23 in Edgefield and head 8 miles east toward Johnston. Pass through the quaint towns of Ward, Ridge Spring, Monetta, and Hibernia and continue on to Batesburg-Leesville. This is an especially lovely drive during the spring and summer when the peach trees are a lush green or in full bloom. If you take this route, just a few tenths of a mile out of town you'll pass the birthplace of Strom Thurmond at 305 Long Meadow Lane on your left. A historical marker stands in front of the white 2-story home.

Nearby Attractions

Benjamin Mays Historic Site, Edgefield County Peach Museum, Erskine College and its Bowie Arts Center and Discovery Garden, Furman University Monument, Greenwood, Groundhog Kiln, Horn Creek Baptist Church, Lake Greenwood State Recreation Area, Ten Governors' Rail Trail at Slade Lake, National Wild Turkey Federation, and Winchester Museum.

6

Thoroughbred Country

Aiken to Barnwell

General Description: Explore elegant Aiken before travelling 80 miles through horse pasture countryside, past the dark waters of the South Edisto River, through old railroad towns and finishing in charming, historic Barnwell.

Special Attractions: Historic Aiken, Hopeland Gardens, Hitchcock Woods, Aiken County Historical Museum, The Willcox Inn, Aiken Horse District, Aiken Training Track, Aiken Visitors Center and Train Museum, Center for African American History, Art, and Culture, Aiken Farmers Market, Gaston Livery Stable, Aiken State Natural Area, South Edisto River, Wagener, Salley, Springfield, Williston, Blackville, Healing Springs, Barnwell State Park,

historic Barnwell, Lake Edgar Brown, and Barnwell County Museum.

Location: Western part of the state, in the middle portion of the Savannah River Valley.

Travel Season: All year. In Aiken, Hopeland Gardens' flora and fauna are prettiest in spring and fall. Aiken hosts a number of festivals throughout the year as well as polo matches almost year-round and flat, steeplechase, and harness races in the spring and fall.

Services: Hotels, motels, restaurants, and other accommodations and services are plentiful in Aiken and along I–20. Barnwell and Blackville have some services.

The Drive

Begin this drive in elegant, sophisticated Aiken, amid the lush beauty of Hopeland Gardens and Hitchcock Woods. Pass through the town originally made wealthy by early 20th-century winter resort residents and traverse lovely residential areas and an attractive downtown that hosts equestrian, art, food and festival events throughout the year. Next head into the countryside, where horse, cattle, goat, and cotton farms abound. Then visit Aiken State Natural Area beside the dark, foreboding South Edisto River before beginning a tour of several quiet railroad towns whose heydays were in the early part of the 20th century. The drive ends in beautiful Barnwell, full of history, grace, and Spanish moss.

Aiken

Aiken, like many towns in South Carolina, prospered with the development of the railroad in the mid-1800s. Named for William Aiken, founder of a railroad company in Charleston, the town grew popular as a favorite respite for affluent South Carolina planters and Northeastern vacationers. These visitors brought with

Thoroughbred Country: Aiken to Barnwell

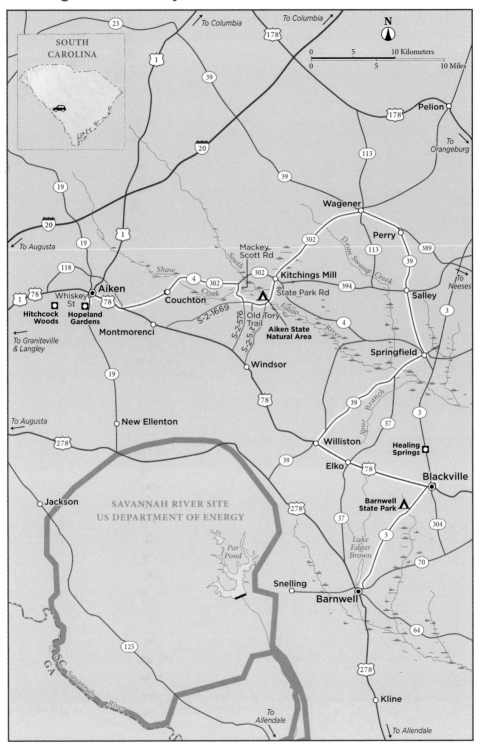

Hopeland Gardens in Aiken PATRICIA PIERCE

them their love of polo, horse racing, and breeding. Today Aiken continues to be one of the most popular horse-breeding areas in the United States, and the horse industry remains a staple of the Aiken economy, as well as the area's most notable pastime.

In the 1950s, with the construction by the old US Atomic Energy Commission of the huge nuclear weapons complex straddling Aiken and Barnwell Counties, scientists, engineers, and other topflight technicians and executives made Aiken County their permanent home. Now named the Savannah River Site, this 300-square-mile facility employed 38,000 workers at its peak, and employment today ranges from 12,000 to 20,000, depending on assigned missions from the US Department of Energy.

Aiken County is also the site of **Redcliffe Plantation**, one-time home of former US congressman, US senator, and South Carolina governor James Henry Hammond. A staunch defender of both slavery and male supremacy, Hammond is most famous for his "Cotton is king" speech on the floor of the US Senate in 1858.

Begin in **Hopeland Gardens** (135 Dupree Place SW), site of the Thoroughbred Racing Hall of Fame. The Gardens provide a lovely setting for an easy stroll over bricked pathways past lush flora and fauna. A fountain and seating area are the perfect place for a shaded picnic. The 14-acre park was once the estate of Oliver and Hope Iselin, who donated the property to the city. Winding pathways take visitors through the shade of sprawling, moss-hung live oaks and past creeks and ponds to enjoy an immense variety of flowers and other vegetation. Camellias, azaleas, and dogwoods are prominent. A special feature is the Touch and Scent Trail with Braille signage for the visually impaired. Connected to the gardens is Rye Patch, an elegant residence now owned by the city, with a memorial rose garden and the Carriage House Museum on its grounds. During the summer Hopeland Gardens hosts summer concerts to enjoy the garden in the evenings.

On the Hopeland grounds just to the left of the first long brick pathway into the garden is the **Thoroughbred Racing Hall of Fame**, housed in a former carriage house of the Iselin estate. The Aiken area is the breeding ground for a number of Kentucky Derby, Preakness, Hambletonian, and other flat racing and harness champions. The museum is a tribute to Aiken's heritage of thoroughbred breeding and training, and honors horses bred or trained in the Aiken area since 1942.

From Hopeland Gardens, exit right (east) from the parking lot onto DuPree Place SW. Travel one block to turn left onto Whiskey Road SW/SC 19 and head north past lovely homes and gardens. After 2 blocks turn left (west) on Easy Street SW. Drive 2 blocks to the end of Easy Street and turn right (north) on Newberry Street SW.

The **Aiken County Historical Museum** at 433 Newberry Street is on your left located in a 1930s winter resort home called Banksia. The museum offers more than 30 rooms of exhibits, plus other items of interest outdoors, including a log cabin built around 1808 and a one-room schoolhouse built around 1890. The grounds also feature a nature trail and an arboretum.

If you'd like to visit another natural area and take a stroll through a forest, drive one more block and turn left (west) at the stop sign on South Boundary Avenue SW to experience **Hitchcock Woods** *(444 S. Boundary Ave. SW), one of the largest privately owned urban forests in the nation. Cross over Lauren Street SW and travel 0.4 mile and park on South Boundary Street. The road becomes dirt as you enter the parking area for the Woods. Maps and a kiosk are provided at the entrance to the 2,100 acres of longleaf pine forest. Visitors, including equestrians, hikers, walkers, and joggers, enjoy the 65 miles of sandy trails that pass through a variety of ecosystems. (The main entrance to Hitchcock Woods is on Dibble Road off SC 118.)*

From Hitchcock Woods, head east on South Boundary Avenue SW.

To continue your drive from the museum, drive one block north to the end of Newberry Street and merge right (east) onto South Boundary Avenue SW to enjoy an oak-canopied passage. Drive one mile on South Boundary Avenue past beautiful old Aiken homes. (South Boundary Ave. becomes SE after Chesterfield St.) As you near the end of South Boundary Avenue SE, slow down to turn right (south) onto Powderhouse Road SE to visit Aiken's Equestrian District.

You'll travel 0.7 mile on Powderhouse Road SE. On your right is the historic Aiken Training Track that extends all the way to Audubon Drive SE. You'll get a closer look when you get deeper into the Horse District.

Turn right (west) on Audubon Drive SE. On your left is Bruce's Field (1337 Audubon Dr. SE), an expansive area filled with steeple chase competition areas, tracks, and barns in the distance. Spectator parking is available on your left so pull into the grassy parking area to see riders on horses practicing jumps, participating in a competition, or just exercising their horses in the fields.

Be sure to slow down to 15 miles per hour in this area because you may need to share the road with riders and their horses moving between barns, tracks, and private property.

Continue a half mile on Audubon Drive SE and turn right (north) at the end of the road onto Two Notch Road SE. The road becomes hard packed dirt after 0.2 mile, and it might be challenging to drive after a heavy rain. On your right is the historic Aiken Training Track chartered in May, 1941 and opened in November that same year. The track was designed by Frank Phelps modeled after the Keeneland Race Track in Lexington, Kentucky. Since the 1940s some of the wealthiest and most famous people in the world housed and trained their horses here and 40 of the alumni horses have been crowned national champions.

At 0.4 mile from Audubon, turn left and travel 0.3 mile west on Mead Avenue. On your right is the Winthrop Polo Field.

Turn right (north) on Sumter Street SE and travel one block to get a better view of the polo field. Then turn right (east) on Grace Avenue SE and travel 0.4 mile past more barns on your right and beautiful homes on your left adorned by open fields and grazing horses.

To exit the Equestrian District, turn left (north) on Orangeburg Street SE. It's a paved road but a sign may not be visible. Travel one block back to South Boundary SE. Turn left (west), drive 3 blocks back through the canopy of oaks and turn right (north) on Marion Street SE.

Drive one block and turn left (west) on Colleton Avenue SE to enjoy a slow drive past beautiful, old homes on your left and right. Travel 0.7 mile on Colleton Avenue. As you cross over York Street look to your left for the Aiken County Library housed in a former school building.

Cross over Chesterfield Avenue SW to enjoy a sweeping view of the elegant front facade of the lovely **Willcox Inn** (100 Colleton Ave. SW). Built in 1898 as a winter resort hotel for northern clientele escaping brutal weather, it remains to this day a splendid restaurant and inn, with four-poster beds and decorative fireplaces. At minimum, step into the gracious lobby with its huge stone fireplace, usually stoked with a roaring fire in winter, where Franklin Roosevelt and Winston Churchill conspired and sipped toddies during World War II. Peek at the old-club-style Pheasant Room, which serves continental cuisine and traditional Southern specialties.

Travel the length of the hotel grounds, and then turn right (north) on Newberry Street SW. Cross the bridge and proceed one more block to Park Avenue SW.

Turn right (east) on Park Avenue SW. Travel 4 blocks and veer left (north) onto Union Street SE to enter the parking lot of the **Aiken Visitors Center and Train Museum** housed in Aiken's old train depot constructed in 1899. Stop here for visitor guides, to tour the train museum, or to enjoy a trolly tour of the historic churches and homes in downtown Aiken.

Exit the Visitors Center parking lot by turning right (west) on Park Avenue SE to enjoy Aiken's bustling downtown center. Drive 0.3 mile and turn right (north) on Newberry Street SW.

Parking is plentiful on Newberry Street in front of the Performing Arts Center and Community Theater. A statue of William Aiken, Sr. (1779-1831) for whom the City was named in 1895 decorates the lovely median on Newberry Street. Aiken was president of the South Carolina Canal and Railroad Company.

Willcox Inn in Aiken PATRICIA PIERCE

In 1833, it was the world's longest railroad at the time from Charleston to what is now the City of Aiken.

Newberry and Laurens Streets are connected by "The Alley," a wide brick walkway so you can meander the unique antiques and artworks shopping and dining district easily. Check out the **Aiken Center for the Arts** at 122 Laurens Street SW that features exhibits by local and regional artists.

Aiken to Wagener

From Newberry Street SW, turn right on Richland Avenue/US 1 North/US 78 East/SC 19 South, a pretty street with a grass and tree-filled median, and head southeast.

Two blocks ahead on your left on the corner of York Street NE and Richland Avenue SW, is the **Center for African American History Art and Culture** (120 York St. NE) housed in the Immanuel Institute built in 1889 and renovated in 2021. The Institute was established by Reverend W.R. Coles, an African American Presbyterian missionary, to provide a school for freed previously enslaved people. Today the Institute serves as an educational center that hosts lectures, art shows, exhibits, special events, and concert series to celebrate Aiken's diversity.

Continue 0.7 mile farther on Richland Avenue/US 78. On your right is the historic **Aiken County Farmers' Market** (115 Williamsburg St. SE). Founded in 1951, it is the oldest county farmers market in continuous service in the same location in South Carolina. Forty-five of the original tables constructed to display fruits and vegetables for sale at the market are still being used today. The market is listed on the Aiken Historic Register.

As you head east out of town on Richland Avenue after 0.4 mile past the market, on your right is the **Gaston Livery Stable** (1315 Richland Ave. E.). The stable, built in 1893 by D. W. Gaston Sr. and his son D. W. Gaston Jr., served as a full-service livery stable from 1909 until 1932. The structure features an original Victorian style operational carriage lift to move carriages and equipment from ground level to the second floor and is the only known operational lift of its kind in the United States. The Gaston Livery Stable was designated as an historical landmark in Aiken and is listed on the National Register of Historic Places.

Travel 1.4 miles farther and veer left onto SC 4/SC 302/SC 21/Wagener Road. Your next destination is Aiken State Natural Area about 12 miles ahead.

Travel east through a folksy area of neat lawns, modest homes, pastured cattle, woodland patches, and pecan trees. After 3.6 miles, you reach the settlement of Couchton, a spread-out, rural community of rambling homes and small convenience stores. Cross the swampy wetlands of Shaw Creek a mile on the other side of Couchton, and stay right (east) on SC 4/SC 302/Wagener Road as SC 21 veers northeast to the left.

Now you enter rolling horse country. Pastures, stables, and horse training facilities dot the attractive countryside, punctuated with farmhouses, pecan trees, and hay fields. Continue northeast toward Aiken State Natural Area.

Cross the bridge over Shaw Creek, and after 6 miles from Couchton, turn right (south) on S-2-576/Mackey Scott Road, and continue for 1.6 miles on the narrow country lane that takes you once again over Shaw Creek and through mixed hardwood/pine forest. Turn left (east) past the bridge, onto S-2-1669/Old Tory Trail and travel about 1.7 miles through more forest to **Aiken State Natural Area** (1145 State Park Rd., Windsor). To enter the park, turn left onto Picnic Circle.

Centered beside the **South Edisto River** and four spring-fed lakes, the park is a combination of river swamp, bottomland hardwood forest, and dry sand hill forest. The sand hills of this area are remnants of an ancient era when the ocean reached this far inland. Built in the 1930s as a Civilian Conservation Corps project, the 1,067-acre park teems with wildlife. It is a birder's delight. Woodpeckers are everywhere, and many varieties of warblers populate the woodlands. Butterflies are plentiful, and near the water you may see wood ducks, hooded mergansers, pied-billed grebes, and wading birds. The water and moist forestlands provide excellent habitat for amphibians and reptiles.

The park offers fishing and a 3-mile nature trail, as well as a segment of the Edisto River Canoe Trail. Bear left in the park and follow a 2.3-mile loop road along a shady, heavily forested road. After about a mile, turn into the parking area for the canoe trail and enjoy views of cypresses and tulip poplars protruding from the dark waters. Continue along the tree-canopied lane past the fishing lake, a picnic area, recreation fields, and a camping area before exiting Aiken State Natural Area back onto S-2-1669/Old Tory Trail.

Exit the park by turning left (east) on Old Troy Trail. Drive 0.1 mile and turn left (northeast) onto S-2-53/State Park Road to head towards Wagener. You cross the black waters of the South Edisto River after a half mile and continue 1.7 more miles to the Kitchings Mill crossroad settlement. Cross over Salley Road/SC 4, where State Park Road becomes SC 302/Wagener Road to continue northeast toward Wagener, 8.5 miles away.

Pass by farms and wetlands before entering more undulating countryside, featuring horse pastures, hay and cotton fields, farmhouses, ponds, and a variety of trees, including pines, oaks, sycamores, magnolias, dogwoods, and pecans. Horse training grounds are scattered here and there.

Enter downtown **Wagener** by turning left (northeast) onto SC 302/SC 113/Main Street and traveling 2 blocks to the intersection with SC 39/Railroad Avenue, the beginning of Festival Trail Road. A quiet town, Wagener's downtown faces a green median, once a railroad bed that brought commerce to the community when cotton was king. The old tracks are long gone, but in their place is an attractive 4-block-long park, the centerpiece for the annual Wagons to Wagener festival in May.

Wagener was first known as "Pinder Town" and then later Guntersville or "Gunter's Crossroad," after the many Gunter families who settled here in the 1880s. The town's commerce was mostly agricultural until the Southern Railroad brought trains through the town. Wagener farms grew mostly asparagus and cotton.

Turn right (southeast) on Railroad Avenue/SC 39 and drive 2 blocks past old storefronts on your right. The **Wagon House** with a Conestoga wagon, a pavilion, and shade trees in the park over the old railroad bed are on your left.

Wagener to Barnwell

Continue 3 blocks past Wagener City Park on your left where you can stop for a picnic, along Railroad Avenue/SC 39 (southeast), which becomes Festival Trail Road/SC 39 as you head toward tiny Perry, 3 miles away.

In Perry bear right (southeast) to stay on SC 39/Festival Trail Road, which is Railroad Avenue in town. Salley is 4 miles ahead.

Salley, another modest community with a green space through the middle of town occupying the old rail bed that the downtown once faced, owes its fame to the annual fall **Chitlin Strut**. Since 1969 the community has held the festival after the Thanksgiving holiday to celebrate and consume several tons of boiled and fried hog intestines and to hold hog-calling contests. Salley claims to be the "Chitlin Capital of the World." The community was nearly leveled during Sherman's burn and pillage march through South Carolina near the end of the Civil War. To see one of the first buildings constructed after the fire, turn right on Pine Street, the third street on your right after you enter town.

The **Hemrick House** (ca. 1870) at 124 Pine Street NW is an example of an early Victorian home decorated with geometric green and navy stained-glass windows. Hemrick House is the first home on your right on Pine Street. A cast-iron gate encloses the front yard. Backtrack to SC 39 to resume your trip toward Springfield.

Turn right (south) on SC 39/West Railroad Avenue/Festival Trail Road. Drive 5 miles beside an old rail bed to cross into Orangeburg County and reach another railroad town, **Springfield**. Festival Trail Road continues here since Springfield is the site of the fall **Governor's Frog Jump Festival**. The winner gets to fly to Calaveras County, California, accompanied by his or her frog as the state's official entrant in the National Jump-Off. Springfield's pretty railway median is decorated with an old caboose, and the little community is dotted with nice shade trees, comfortable old homes, and some downtown stores.

If you'd like to visit the Orangeburg County Military Museum, turn left onto Springfield Road/SC 4. Cross the railroad tracks and turn right onto Railroad Avenue/SC 3 Business. Drive 3 blocks and turn left on Brodie Street. On your left located in the old Springfield High School is the **Orangeburg County Military Museum** *at 210 Brodie Street.*

Backtrack to Railroad Avenue, turn right, and go 3 blocks back to Springfield Road/SC 4/SC 39. Turn left (southwest) onto Springfield Road/SC 39.

From Springfield Road/SC 39, continue 11 miles to Williston. This is a pretty stretch, as you first dip into the verdant South Edisto River wetlands and cross a bridge over the serenely flowing black-water stream, emerging in Barnwell County. You pass several miles of mixed hardwood and pine forests, farmhouses, cotton fields, vegetable plots, and pastures.

Williston is next on your tour of old railroad villages, yet another small town fronting another abandoned train track converted into a nicely appointed greenway park. This downtown area, however, is healthier than many, with several

Ashley-Willis House in Williston, occupied by federal troops during and after the Civil War PATRICIA PIERCE

active shops and some former store space converted into attractive downtown apartments.

In the late 19th and early 20th century, Williston's agricultural operations produced mostly asparagus. In fact, the town was considered the "Asparagus Capital of America" before the Great Depression, until California's long growing season allowed it to overtake Williston and the surrounding area.

In Williston, turn right (northwest) onto Main Street/S-6-33. Drive just 0.6 mile and turn left (southwest) to cross the old rail bed, and turn left again (southeast) onto West Main Street/S-6-108. Look to your right for the stately, Greek Revival **Ashley-Willis House**. A historical marker to the right of the road will help you Identify the house. Built in the 1830s, the home was used as quarters by Sherman's troops, and thus avoided being burned to the ground. It continued in use by Union soldiers during the first four years of Reconstruction, until 1869.

Head back toward downtown (southeast) on West Main Street. Proceed southeast through the shopping district, following the rail bed on your left, and merge onto US 78 to reach the tiny crossroads town of **Elko**, 2 miles away.

Continue southeast through Elko on US 78 toward Blackville, 6 miles away, traveling beside a rail bed and past farms, pleasant homes decorated with magnolias and pecan trees, and crop fields and pastures.

As you enter **Blackville** on US 78/Dexter Street, you pass **Floyd Manor**, at 3614 Dexter Street, on your left. This stately home was once the manor house of an 8,000-acre plantation. The columns that frame the front of the house were shipped from England in 1886.

At the next corner, turn left (north) on Walker Street to visit downtown Blackville. At the corner of Walker and Main Streets, look to your right to see the shell of the old **Shamrock Hotel** (1912). To your left is the Blackville Heritage Museum (655 Main St). Across Main Street is the **Farrell-O'Gorman House** (650 Main St.), named for the Irish merchant who lived here and fought with the Confederate army. Patrick Farrell built the home in 1875, and he and his sons built some of the brick buildings that can be seen in Blackville today.

Turn right (east) on Main Street to pass by old storefronts facing the railroad tracks. In the median is a historic marker noting that in the early 1800s, Blackville was a major stop on the Charleston-Hamburg Railway, the first commercial rail line in America and once the longest commercial line in the world.

Cross over Solomon Blatt Avenue. Blackville is the hometown of Solomon Blatt Sr., a longtime Speaker of the South Carolina House of Representatives who, with Barnwell Senator Edgar Brown, pretty much ran the State of South Carolina during the middle part of the 20th century.

To your right at 483 Main Street is the renowned **Miller's Bread Basket**, offering home-style Mennonite cooking and a shop featuring antiques and handmade Mennonite crafts and quilts.

Heading east, cross Lartigue Street. At 429 Main Street is the delicate **Simon Brown House**, built around 1849.

Continue southeast on Main Street 0.2 mile to the intersection with Dexter Street. Turn right (west). On your left at 3151 Dexter Street is the **Hagood House** (1850). Built by William H. Hagood, who served as a surgeon in the Confederate army, this home was used by Union troops as an infirmary for their wounded soldiers.

Cross Lartigue Street westward and turn right (north) onto SC 3/Solomon Blatt Avenue. Drive 3 blocks to 19420 North Solomon Blatt Avenue to see the **Old Depot Library**. A circular drive allows you to park in front of the red-shingled, green trimmed, Victorian-style former train depot that was moved to this location, the grounds of the old Blackville High School.

*If you'd like to visit Healing Springs, exit the library driveway, turn right again onto Solomon Blatt Avenue, and head north 2.4 miles to **Healing Springs**. Turn right on Healing Springs Road/S-6-32. Travel 0.3 mile and turn right onto*

Springs Court/S-6-358. Healing Springs Baptist Church (1853) is adjacent to the springs. Native Americans were the first to believe in the artesian water's healing powers, and they brought wounded Revolutionary War soldiers here to drink. In 1944 Luke Boylston deeded the property to God. Now the area is called "God's Little Acre." Visitors come here to wash, drink, and carry home the elixir's ailment-curing properties. You can drink directly from any of the well's 12 naturally flowing spouts.

Exit Healing Springs and head south back into downtown Blackville on SC 3/ Solomon Blatt Avenue.

Depart from downtown Blackville heading southward on SC 3/Solomon Blatt Avenue. Just after you cross Dexter Street, leaving town, slow down and look to your right. The **Mathis House** (332 S. Boundary St.) built in 1889 is barely visible now behind thick vegetation and trees. Charles Mathis, who lived here, is said to have been the first to plant cantaloupes in the area.

Continue 1.5 miles southwest on SC 3/Solomon Blatt Avenue past gardens and fields of cantaloupes in the summer to visit **Barnwell State Park** (223 State Park Rd.). At the stop sign, turn left to continue on SC 3/Solomon Blatt Avenue. The park is 0.9 mile ahead. To enter the park, turn right (west) on State Park Road to enter the modest 307-acre park constructed by the Civilian Conservation Corps in the 1930s.

The park has two small lakes and an interpretive nature trail winding around them through pine and hardwood forest. The woods are full of woodpeckers and warblers; pied-billed grebes and ospreys inhabit the lake environs. The picnic and playground area is adorned with dogwoods, oaks, pines, poplars, hollies, and lots of magnolias. You may fish for bass, bream, and catfish off a dock or along the lake shoreline. Restrooms are available.

Exit the park by turning right onto SC 3 and heading southwest toward your final destination, the town of Barnwell 7 miles away. Along the way, pass woodlands, small churches, and modest farms and homes before entering historic, picturesque **Barnwell** on SC 3/Marlboro Avenue.

In town, turn right on Main Street. On your left is Collins Park, a shady space with benches and tables perfect for a picnic.

Pass beautiful old homes and travel 0.3 mile to the town square locally known as "The Circle." This is a great 1950s-style downtown area with shops and eateries. Turn right (north) onto Wall Street. Park on the northern side of the square to take a stroll in this quaint downtown and to get a closer view of the **Barnwell County Courthouse** at 141 Main Street rebuilt in 1879. In front of the courthouse is a vertical sundial, erected in 1858 and said to keep perfect time. Nearby are statues of children at play.

Barnwell County Courthouse plaza Patricia Pierce

Leave the downtown center heading north on Wall Street. Cross over Allen Street to see **Bethlehem Baptist Church** on your left at 177 Wall Street. The original structure on this site was built in 1829 and donated to African American Baptists in 1860. This is one of only a handful of pre–Civil War churches in the South organized by and for people of color. It was rebuilt in 1889 using some of the original materials from the first church.

Lake Edgar Brown is also nearby. To visit the lake, bordered by greenery and a paved walking trail, from Wall Street, turn left (west) on Gilmore Street and drive a couple of blocks to Bryan Street/S-6-43. Turn right (north) to ride a few yards to a dam that shores up the lake.

Backtrack on Wall Street. Turn right (southwest) onto Allen Street and then left again (southeast) on Dunbarton Boulevard/Pechman Street to return to the downtown area. Continue around "The Circle" on Jefferson and McDonough Streets to exit southward on Burr Street. Drive three blocks south.

Directly ahead is the **Episcopal Church of the Holy Apostles** at 1706 Hagood Avenue. This beautiful cypress-wood church was completed in 1857. It is said that the Church members hid the stained-glass windows in the well, located behind the church, and now covered by a white wooden gazebo, from Union troops in 1865, when they quartered cavalry horses in the building. Sherman's horses were also said to have drunk water from the baptismal font that sits near the altar if you are able to tour the quaint wooden church. You may want to stroll in the lovely old cemetery, which holds the remains of a number of well-known statesmen and other notables.

From the church's grass parking lot on the corner of Burr and Hagood, head west on Hagood Avenue and turn right (north) on Jefferson Street, almost directly across from the church cemetery road. This residential area is filled with homes from the early 1800s, so take time to meander through the streets.

Turn right (east) onto Academy Street, a tiny lane. Travel one block to cross Burr Street. Here, on the corner to your right at 100 Madison Street, is the quaint **St. Andrews Roman Catholic Church** (1831). Cross over Franklin Street. On your left is the **Old Barnwell Presbyterian Church** (1848) at 325 Academy Street. After Union troops burned the county courthouse, the church was used as a temporary courthouse. Now the Circle Theatre and the Barnwell Performing and Cultural Arts Center use the old church building for a playhouse.

Continue one block east on Academy Street to the intersection with Marlboro Avenue. Turn right on Marlboro Avenue (south) and drive one block. On your left, at the corner of Marlboro and Hagood Avenues, is the **Barnwell County Museum** (9426 Marlboro Ave.). Stop here to learn more about the city of Barnwell and to end your drive.

Nearby Attractions

Aiken Gopher Tortoise Heritage Preserve, Beech Island Historical Society, Dupont Planetarium, Edisto Memorial Gardens, Misty Lake State Park, Redcliffe Plantation State Historic Site, Savannah River Site Museum.

7

Midlands Towns, Woodlands, and Waters

Historic Newberry to Pomaria

General Description: A 90-mile journey highlighted by charming little towns, delightful old churches, and the waterways and woodlands of the Enoree/Tyger District of Sumter National Forest.

Special Attractions: Historic Newberry, Newberry Opera House, Newberry College, Enoree/Tyger District of Sumter National Forest, Whitmire,

Enoree River, Rose Hill Plantation State Historic Site, Tyger River, Broad River, Monticello Reservoir, Peak, Pomaria.

Location: North central part of the state, northwest of Columbia.

Services: Newberry offers full services and accommodations. Metropolitan Columbia is nearby.

The Drive

A charming old college town, pastures, forestlands, mighty rivers, an idyllic lake, venerable country churches, and rustic villages highlight this drive. Begin in beautifully restored downtown Newberry with its splendid old opera house. From here, you pass through the edge of Enoree/Tyger District of Sumter National Forest toward the former textile mill town of Whitmire to the majestic Rose Hill Plantation State Historic Site. Cross the Broad and Tyger Rivers and multiple creeks to visit tranquil Monticello Reservoir and old country churches before winding through the remote, peaceful villages of Peak and Pomaria.

Historic Newberry

The **Newberry** area was settled in the mid-1700s; the town was established in 1789. A community of delightful old homes and tree-lined streets that has become something of a middle-class retirement mecca in recent years, the town's German settler heritage remains strong.

Begin at the town green, Memorial Park, bounded by Main, Nance, Caldwell and Boyce Streets. Enjoy the beauty of the Gothic-style **Newberry Opera House** (1201 McKibben St.) on the north side of the town green. Built in 1882 and splendidly restored in the 1990s, this redbrick structure, with a steeple that houses the town clock, hosts an impressive array of big-name performances throughout the year. Tours are available.

Midlands Towns, Woodlands, and Waters:
Historic Newberry to Pomaria

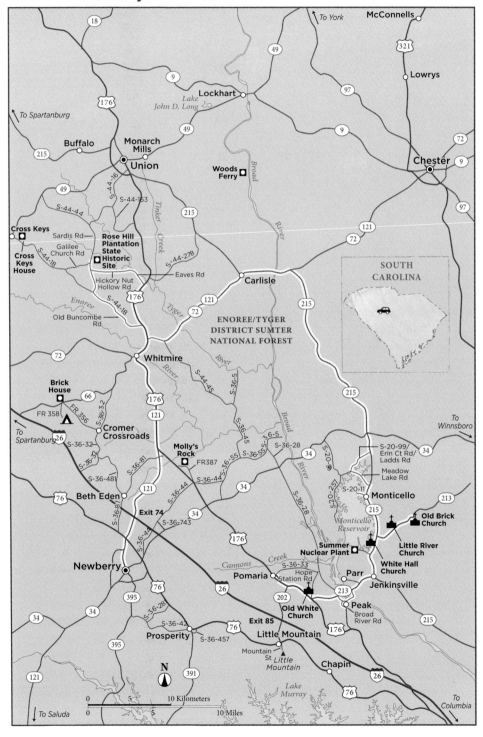

Newberry Opera House MARIE GOFF

Memorial Park is decorated with monuments honoring World Wars I and II, the Vietnam and Korean conflicts, and the Civil War adding to the ambience of the delightful shops, office buildings, and eateries that adorn Main and adjoining side streets.

The **Old Newberry County Courthouse** (1109 Main St.), built in 1852, is on the east side of the green. Drive east on Main Street to admire the bas-relief on the front gable of the building. It was added in 1876, at the end of the state's post–Civil War Reconstruction period. It shows an American eagle with the scales of justice in its beak beside an overturned palmetto tree, representing South Carolina. On the eagle's scales are South Carolina's feisty gamecock on one side and a dove of peace, holding an olive branch, on the opposite side. The Newberry Visitors Center is here inside the Chamber of Commerce office on the first floor.

Travel east on Main Street for a half-mile to see more of the beautiful century-old homes that adorn Main and nearby streets. Turn left (north) on Summer Street to head back downtown. Drive two blocks to Harrington Street and turn left (west). Travel 0.6 mile and turn right (north) on Lindsay Street.

On your right after 2 blocks is tiny, picturesque **Wells Japanese Gardens**, created in 1930 by the H. G. Wells family as a private garden with exotic plants set among ponds. It is open to the public.

Continue north on Lindsay Street one more block and turn left (west) on Calhoun Street. Travel one block to College Street and turn right (north). On your right is **Newberry College** (2100 College St.). Established by Lutherans in 1856, the college retains its close church ties to this day. Drive by the main entrance and the college's oldest buildings, and the football stadium on your right about the length of 4 blocks.

Newberry to Rose Hill Plantation

Head north out of town on College Street/SC 121 past Rosemont Cemetery on your right towards Whitmire 15 miles away.

A mile after crossing I-26, enter the **Enoree/Tyger District of Sumter National Forest**. The Enoree and Tyger Rivers flow west to east through this 168,000-acre land of forests and streams, emptying into the Broad River on the border between Newberry and Fairfield Counties. Opportunities for hiking, mountain biking, fishing, hunting, birding, camping, canoeing, and kayaking abound in this wildlife-rich area, where the proximity of dry upland forest to swampy river bottomland provides an appealing mix of habitats. Always be on the lookout for the forest's numerous deer as they bound across roads.

As is the case with South Carolina's other national forest tracts, the Enoree/Tyger property was mostly acquired from economically distressed landowners in the 1930s, and federal property is interspersed serendipitously with private holdings throughout northern Newberry County, southern Union County, and western portions of Chester and Fairfield Counties.

Proceed 5 miles northward through rolling countryside where US 176 merges with SC 121. Cross Indian Creek after 0.2 mile and travel 7 more miles on SC 121/US 76, crossing Duncan Creek and entering Whitmire, a town once bustling with textile mill activity, but facing hard times after the mill closings.

Proceed slowly through the edge of town past old mill homes about 0.3 mile and follow the road to the right when you reach the junction of 72/West US 176/SC121 North. The road takes you across the **Enoree River** where you enter Union County, named in 1785 for Union Church, an amalgam of Episcopalians, Presbyterians, and Quakers.

Travel a mile to bear left to continue on US 176. Then drive another mile on US 176 towards Union and turn left (west) onto S-44-18/Old Buncombe Road. A brown sign directing you to Rose Hill Plantation State Historic Site marks the left-hand turn.

Journey through lush forestlands, at least those that have not recently been clear cut, on Old Buncombe Road. After 2.6 miles from your turn, look to your left to see a restored plantation home (circa 1790) atop Flint Hill.

Continue 2.2 miles to the right-hand turn onto Sardis Road/SC-44-16. Drive 2 miles to the intersection with Galilee Church Road/S-44-63. Turn right to continue on Sardis Road/S-44-16 for 0.3 mile to reach the entrance to **Rose Hill Plantation State Historic Site** (2677 Sardis Rd., Union).

This beautifully situated 44-acre park in the heart of the national forest centers on the old home place of South Carolina's 68th governor, often referred to as the "Secession Governor," William H. Gist.

Made wealthy by cotton, Gist finished this Federal-style mansion in 1832. It served as both his private home and as the governor's mansion between 1858 and 1860, when the fiery secessionist worked ceaselessly to bring about South Carolina's withdrawal from the United States of America. He achieved his goal at the end of his term in December 1860, and four months later Confederate troops in Charleston fired the first shots of the Civil War.

Furnishings and clothing belonging to the Gist family adorn the inside of the white stuccoed brick mansion, fronted with a four-columned double porch facade. The attractive grounds, bordered by a healthy stand of hardwoods, are laced with ornamental plants and the heirloom rose gardens that gave the plantation its name. A number of original plantation outbuildings complement the main house. A delightful 1.5-mile nature trail leads from the picnic area through the oak/hickory forest down to the banks of the enchanting Tyger River.

Admission to the park grounds is free, but there is a small charge for tours of the mansion. It is recommended to call ahead if you want to join a tour. Modern restrooms are located in an old log cabin with a tin roof and large brick fireplace.

Rose Hill Plantation to Monticello Reservoir

Exit the park by turning left (south) on Sardis Road/S-44-16 and backtrack for 0.3 mile toward the intersection with Galilee Church Road. Turn left to remain on Sardis for 1.2 miles before turning left on Hickory Nut Hollow Road/S-44-136 to experience more of the thick forest. You might even see deer and turkey cross the road in this quiet, wooded area.

After 3 miles, turn right on Eaves Road. Continue just one more mile to connect with Whitmire Highway/US 176 East. Turn right. After a mile, cross Padgetts Creek and continue for 2 miles to reach the left turn (east) onto SC 72/SC 121 Carlisle/Whitmire Highway. Carlisle is 9 miles ahead.

Travel over rolling hills and past lush forests and modest homes scattered along the way. After 3 miles, cross the **Tyger River** and then Cane Creek after another 4.5 miles. Continue 1.5 more miles to pass through the community of Carlisle, where you bear right at an intersection to follow SC 215/SC 72 eastward.

Continue 2.5 miles to cross the William Farr Memorial Bridge over the **Broad River**, dark brown and, well, broad. Ride over the bridge and enter Chester

County. Just a mile after the bridge slow down to veer right (south) onto Fairfield Road/SC 215.

After quickly crossing Sandy River and Johns Creek, you enter, after 2 miles, Fairfield County, settled by Scots-Irish Presbyterians in the 1740s. According to local lore, it was named by Lord Cornwallis, who, while encamped here for several months during the American Revolution, admired the area's "fair fields."

Travel 12 more miles southward on SC 215/Old Cherokee Road over rolling hills and past lush forests to reach Salem Crossroads. Cross over SC 34 and continue south 1.4 miles before turning right (southwest) on Erin Court Road/Ladds Road/S-20-99. The turnoff is marked by a sign pointing toward 99 Boat Ramp. The exit for the swimming area of Monticello Recreational Lake Beach and a boat ramp, managed by Dominion Energy, is 2 miles down the road. There are rudimentary restroom facilities and a short mile nature trail connecting the swimming and fishing area with the boat ramp, the major northern access to the lake.

Monticello Methodist Church and cemetery, beside Monticello Reservoir JOHN CLARK

At the intersection 0.1 mile farther, bear left (south) on Meadow Lake Road/S-20-99. Clear signage marks the right (west) turn for 99 Boat Ramp 0.3 mile past the intersection.

Continue southeastward to traverse a causeway on the northern end of **Monticello Reservoir**, a lake constructed a half century ago to provide cooling water for a nuclear power plant built at the southern end of the lake. Look to your right for great views. A lakeside parking area is on the southeast side of the causeway.

A little over a mile past the causeway, turn right (south) onto SC 215 and ease into the tiny, charming community of **Monticello**, 0.7 mile from the intersection. Slow down to turn right (west) onto Monticello Street and the center of this quaint, ancient settlement of abandoned country stores, farmhouses, and fields. The scene you encounter is all that remains of a much larger community which

Monticello Reservoir JOHN CLARK

was flooded in order to construct the reservoir needed for the nuclear power plant.

Turn left on S-20-11 Spur and rejoin SC 215 by turning right (south). Almost immediately on your right is beautiful **Monticello United Methodist Church** (5100 SC 215, Monticello) and its old cemetery, set on a hillside that gently slopes down to the east bank of the lake. Trek down the long inviting entranceway and stop in the shade of oak trees in the parking area. Wander behind the church for an absolutely idyllic vantage point. If you are lucky, you will see cows grazing in verdant pastureland and wading into the water, as Canada geese laze around the lake. A comfortable old barn rests to one side.

Exit the Monticello church property and continue southward. A few yards along the way on SC 215 is the attractive oak-lined entrance to Plainview Farm on the right.

Monticello East Boat Landing is 2 miles farther on SC 215. This is a great spot to snap photos and take a break. Alternately, travel a few yards farther on SC 215 and turn right into Lake Monticello Park, which offers an observation pier, picnic facilities, and a small beach.

Monticello Reservoir to Pomaria

Continue south on SC 215 as you begin to pass through the community of Jenkinsville. The intersection with SC 213 is a little more than a mile past the landing.

Turn left (northeast) here, and ride 0.6 mile to **Little River Baptist Church** (343 Little River Church Road, Jenkinsville), organized in 1768. Turn left onto Little River Church Road. The present one-story, 4-columned structure was completed in 1856 and features a great stained-glass window of Jesus with a flock of sheep. An old cemetery surrounded by granite walls and an attractive picnic area with granite tables frame the sanctuary.

Exit the Little River Church property. The **Old Brick Church** (11235 SC 213, Jenkinsville), built in 1788 by a congregation dating from colonial days, is 1.1 miles up the road, on your right. The Associate Reformed Presbyterian Church of the Carolinas got its beginning here in 1803, as a theologically conservative denomination breaking away from the mainstream Presbyterian Church. This church building was used regularly until 1920. A great cemetery with ancient tombstones is found here, too.

Backtrack 1.6 miles to SC 215 and take a left (south) on what is now SC 215/SC 213. **White Hall African Methodist Episcopal Church** (8594 Monticello Rd., Jenkinsville) is 0.6 mile down the road, on the right, with its pleasant cemetery across the street. Built in 1867 as the first African American church in

Fairfield County, White Hall offers another shady parking area with a nice view of the lake.

Off to your right and out of sight as you continue is the one-unit V.C. Summer Nuclear Plant, one of the oldest of South Carolina's seven nuclear plants. In the first two decades of the 21st century, an attempt was made to construct two more nuclear units at this site. Cost overruns eventually ballooned out of control, and management attempts to hide the financial disaster ended in civil financial judgements against the electric power company, the major design and construction company, and top management individuals. Some top management officials were also convicted of criminal charges, and ratepayers were stuck with billions of dollars in costs for facilities that never produced a single kilowatt of electricity. At the Jenkinsville community crossroads, 2.1 miles farther south, turn right (southwest) on SC 213, toward the Broad River. Signage indicates this stretch of SC 213 has been designated the "Slick McMeekin Nuclear Highway."

After you drive 2.3 miles, you may choose to turn left onto Alston Road. A brown Palmetto Trail sign marks the turn. After 0.3 mile the pavement ends. Continue 0.2 mile farther to the fork and bear right, cross the railroad track, and go under the trestle. You have arrived at the Alston Trailhead of the Peak to Prosperity Passage of the **Palmetto Trail***.*

The picnic area is a great place to enjoy a view of the Broad River. You may want to access the trail and walk the first several hundred feet, which take you over a railroad trestle-turned-footbridge across the river. The span offers several scenic perspectives of the waterway. If more exercise appeals to you, the trail skirts the town of Peak on the other side of the river and goes all the way to Pomaria, 6.5 miles farther up the way.

Cross over the Broad River after 2.6 miles from the Jenkinsville crossroads and head back into Newberry County. After 0.8 mile farther, turn left (south) onto S-36-28/Broad River Road. Travel a half mile to cross Crims Creek, turn left (east), and ease another half mile down a winding road, River Street, into delightful, sleepy, tiny **Peak**. The town's little stores, old schoolhouse, homes, post office (10 River St.), and churches are set on a hillside around a hairpin turn that converts S-36-28 from River Street into Mulberry Street and then into Church Street. As you climb back uphill for one block, turn right (north) on Suber Street. Ride another block and take a left (west) back onto River Street.

After 0.4 mile, turn right (north) at the stop sign, continuing on S-36-28/Broad River Road for a half mile to return to SC 213/Parr Road at another stop sign, where you turn left (west).

After 2 miles, turn right (northwest) at another stop sign onto US 176. Drive 0.1 mile to Hope Station Road/S-36-170 and turn right (north) to go 0.4 mile to the **Old White Church** (622 Hope Station Rd., Pomaria), on your left. Across the

Lutheran "Old White Church" built near Pomaria by Swiss-German settlers, around 1810 JOHN CLARK

street is a much larger church in use today. The Old White Church was built as St. John's Lutheran Church between 1800 and 1810. Organized by Swiss-German settlers and constructed on king's grant land given to John Adam Epting and Peter Dickert in 1763, the church has solid wood shutters and arched panels above the doors and windows. It is adjacent to one of the area's oldest cemeteries.

About 1.2 miles farther up the road is the Hope Rosenwald School (1917 Hope Station Road), constructed in 1926. This facility was one of more than 500 rural African American schools in South Carolina funded in part by the Julius Rosenwald Foundation between 1917 and 1932. This two-room school, with grades 1-8 taught by two teachers, closed in 1954.

Return to US 176 and turn right (northwest), toward **Pomaria**. The John Summer House/Pomaria Plantation/Summer-Huggins House (4177 US 176, Pomaria) built around 1825, is 1.1 miles along the way, on the right.

Travel northwest 1.7 more miles to cross Crims Creek again and enter the tranquil little village of Pomaria. Turn right on Holloway Street to ride past the rustic, partially deserted town center.

Conclude with views of lovely old homes, including the Oakland House (411 Holloway St.) built in 1821, on your left at the intersection with Glymph Street, and the **Folk-Holloway House** (561 State Rd. S-36-107) built around 1835 on your left just before the junction of Holloway and Folk Streets. Life here is slow, as perhaps it should be.

Nearby Attractions

Battle of Musgrove Mill State Historic Site, Blackstocks Battle State Historic Site, Brick House former stagecoach stop, Buncombe Trail, Cross Keys House, Dreher Island State Park, Little Mountain town and monadnock, Padgett's Creek Baptist Church, Pine Island State Park, Town of Prosperity (where Erskine Caldwell once lived), Presbyterian College in attractive town of Clinton, Union County Carnegie Library.

8

Battlefields and Yesteryear

Kings Mountain to Historic Brattonsville and Chester

General Description: A 45-mile journey that begins at the site of a major American Revolution battlefield and takes you along bucolic back roads to the well-preserved Brattonsville living-history complex, before visiting serene lakes and ending in the picturesque town of Chester.

Special Attractions: Kings Mountain National Military Park, Kings Mountain State Park, Historic Brattonsville, Lake Oliphant, Chester State Park, Historic Chester.

Location: North central part of the state, north of Columbia and southwest of Charlotte.

Travel Season: All year.

Services: Rock Hill has full services, and Chester and York have most services.

The Drive

Begin near the North Carolina state line at Kings Mountain National Military Park, a shady, rolling setting that was the site of a major turning point in the American Revolution. Continue through Kings Mountain State Park, with its thousands of acres of outdoors opportunities, and then ride through forests, rolling pasturelands, and the land of big, green lawns. Along the way, you pass through Historic Brattonsville, visit placid Lake Oliphant and peaceful Chester State Park before viewing numerous historic homes and other buildings in fascinating old Chester.

Kings Mountain to Brattonsville

Kings Mountain National Military Park (2625 Park Road, Blacksburg) is in the southern portion of the Kings Mountain Range, a small series of granite outcroppings straddling the border between South Carolina and North Carolina. The park covers the chief locations of the Battle of Kings Mountain (October 7, 1780), an important confrontation in the American Revolution that was pivotal in turning the tide of war in favor of the Patriots. Here, a ragtag amalgamation of rugged frontiersmen overwhelmed militia forces loyal to the British Crown, beginning a series of setbacks for the British in the southern theater of the war that culminated with the surrender of Lord Cornwallis's army at Yorktown a year later.

Battlefields and Yesteryear: Kings Mountain to Historic Brattonsville and Chester

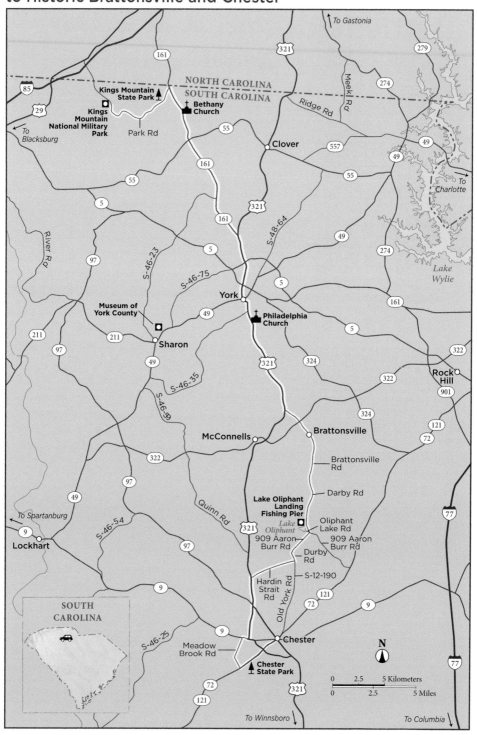

To Gastonia

279

321

274

161

85

NORTH CAROLINA

SOUTH CAROLINA

Meek Rd

Ridge Rd

49

29

Kings Mountain
State Park

Bethany
Church

49

To
Blacksburg

Kings
Mountain
National Military
Park

Park Rd

55

Clover

557

55

161

49

To
Charlotte

55

5

161

321

S-48-64

49

River Rd

S-46-23

5

274

97

S-46-75

5

Lake
Wylie

Museum of
York County

49

York

Philadelphia
Church

161

211

211

5

97

Sharon

322

49

S-46-35

324

Rock
Hill

901

S-46-91

322

322

324

McConnells

Brattonsville

121

72

322

Brattonsville
Rd

97

Darby Rd

49

To Spartanburg

S-46-54

Lake Oliphant
Landing
Fishing Pier

Oliphant
Lake Rd

77

9

Lockhart

Quinn Rd

321

Lake
Oliphant

909 Aaron
Burr Rd

909 Aaron
Burr Rd

97

Durby
Rd

S-12-190

9

Old York Rd

Hardin
Strait
Rd

72

121

9

SOUTH
CAROLINA

9

Meadow
Brook Rd

S-46-25

Chester

N

72

Chester
State Park

0   2.5   5 Kilometers

121

0   2.5   5 Miles

To Winnsboro

77

To Columbia

Entrance to Kings Mountain National Military Park JOHN CLARK

Begin your drive at the **Kings Mountain National Military Park Visitor Center**, 3.7 miles from SC 161/York Road (2625 Park Rd., Blacksburg). The park is about 3 miles south of I-85 North Carolina exit 2.

The facilities at the visitor center are excellent, including exhibits, an interpretive film theater, a bookstore, and picnic areas. Rangers are available to assist you with questions. A 1.5-mile interpretive loop trail around and through the ridgetop battlefield includes a variety of monuments and markers, as well as the grave of British Major Patrick Ferguson, who was killed here. Also passing close to the center is a shady, rolling 14.5-mile loop trail that circles through both the military park and adjacent Kings Mountain State Park.

Turn left (east) out of the visitor center parking lot and ride through shady, hilly forestland. You cross into 6,885-acre **Kings Mountain State Park** after 2 miles. About 2 miles farther are a living history farm and state park headquarters on your right (1277 Park Rd., Blacksburg), and a campground and day-use area to the left.

This park, one of many constructed by Civilian Conservation Corps in the 1930s, has a number of attractive amenities, including a small fishing lake and numerous streams, miles of hiking and equestrian trails, canoe and boat rentals, a store and gift shop, restrooms, and thousands of acres of cool, shady forestland.

Exit the park between rows of zigzag log fences by continuing eastward another mile on Park Road/S-46-705. Turn right (south) on SC 161/York Road and ride past pastureland, farm fields, rolls of hay, patches of forest, modest homes, and the first of many large, green manicured lawns.

Pretty **Bethany Associate Reformed Presbyterian Church** (1454 SC 161, Clover) and its old cemetery are located on your left 2.7 miles down the way, where Maynard Grayson Road/S-46-235 intersects from the east. A stoplight at the intersection with SC 55 is a half-mile farther south. Cross SC 55 and continue on SC 161 for 3.5 miles.

SC 161 veers to the right and becomes US 321/Filbert Highway. Travel 3.7 miles and then Filbert Highway becomes US 321 Bypass. Continue 7.2 more miles past verdant pastures dotted with rural homes and some commercial establishments all the way to the left turn to Brattonsville Road. A brown sign marks the turn, so you can't miss it. Turn left on Brattonsville Road.

Brattonsville Road is scenic, shady, and narrow. After a mile you come to a stop sign and cross over McConnells Highway/SC 322. The visitor center at **Historic Brattonsville** is 1.7 more miles, on your left at 1444 Brattonsville Rd., McConnells.

Brattonsville, which operates as part of the nonprofit Culture and Heritage Museum, is an 800-acre site featuring over 30 colonial and antebellum structures, 2 house museums, heritage breed farm animals, a variety of trails, and a Revolutionary War site that present the history of the Scots-Irish and African American struggles in the upstate during the late 18th and 19th Centuries. Docents in period costumes give demonstrations and are available for questions at many venues.

The Bratton family, of Scots-Irish origin, settled in the area in the mid-1700s and farmed here until about a half century after the Civil War. The area was used as a setting for much of the filming of **The Patriot**, an American Revolution epic starring Mel Gibson. In fact, it was the actual site of Huck's Defeat, a July 12, 1780, confrontation between Patriots led by Col. William Bratton and a small force of British regulars and Loyalists under the command of Captain Christian Huck of the British Legion. This was the first defeat of regular British forces after the fall of Charleston in May of that year, and gave the American revolutionaries new hope.

Brattonsville is also known for a violent attack on an African American sharecropper, Jim Williams, who lived and worked on the Bratton property and was fighting for voters' rights. Led by a descendant of the Bratton family, James Rufus Bratton, the KKK attacked and hung Williams and later took his body to a store owned by the Bratton family. Today there is a plaque outside of the store, which has been restored to its original appearance at the time of Williams's death, depicting the attack and ultimate horrendous death precipitated by the KKK in March 1871.

A cabin in Historic Brattonsville, settled by Scots-Irish in the mid-1700s Patricia Pierce

The visitor center contains a gift shop full of interesting items from the old days. There are modest admission fees to explore the grounds, and guided and self-guided tours are available throughout the year.

From the visitor center area, turn left and continue southward on Brattonsville Road/S-46-165. After 3 miles you cross into Chester County, and the road becomes Darby Road/S-12-190 as you ride through forest and idyllic, rolling pastureland.

Lake Oliphant is 2 miles farther. Turn right (west) on S-12-569/Oliphant Lake Road. A few yards up the entranceway is a restful little lake, pier, and picnic area with plenty of shade. Lake Oliphant is maintained by the South Carolina Department of Natural Resources, and it is a great place to take a break, have a picnic, and relax in a bucolic setting.

Chester State Park and Town of Chester

Exit Oliphant Lake Road and turn right on (south) on Darby Road. After just 0.2 mile, turn right (southwest) on Aaron Burr Road/SC 909. Drive 1.5 miles, turn

Lakeside in Chester State Park JOHN CLARK

left (southeast) on Old York Road/SC 909, go 0.2 mile and turn right (west) onto Hardin Strait Road.

Follow Hardin Strait for 2.9 miles, through forestlands and across a wetlands until you reach the intersection with US 321/Lowrys Highway. Turn left to follow US 321 southward. Cross over Sandy River after 2.7 miles and arrive at an Intersection with SC 9/Pinckney Road after 1.9 more miles. Here you turn right, go 0.2 mile, and turn left (south) on Meadowbrook Road.

After 1.9 miles on Meadowbrook, you reach a stop sign at an intersection with SC 72/SC 121/West End Road. A cemetery, Chester Memorial Gardens, is directly in front of you. Turn left (northeast) and drive 0.2 mile to the entrance to **Chester State Park** (788 State Park Rd., Chester), on your right.

This 523-acre facility was built by Franklin Delano Roosevelt's Civilian Conservation Corps in the 1930s and sports an archery range, in addition to campgrounds, picnic areas, hiking trails, boat rentals, and a 160-acre fishing lake. Motor slowly for a mile along a curving road through shady pines and take it easy beside the restful serenity of the peaceful lake.

Exit the state park and turn right (northeast) on SC 72/SC 121/West End Road, toward Chester. Cross US 321 after 1.5 miles, as West End Road becomes West End Street. Wiley Park (107 Dewey St.) is on your right a half mile farther. Just past Wiley Park, as you travel northeast along West End Street toward the center of town, you pass by several gracious structures.

Take note of the **Coleman/Simpson House**, built around 1907, at 149 West End Street, a Queen Anne Victorian design with a second-story smoking porch.

Next are the **Balser House** (1880) at 145 West End, the **David Hemphill House** (1885) at 137 West End, the **David Hamilton House** (1910) at 133 West End, and the **Whitlock House** at 129 West End, built immediately after the end of the Civil War.

Brotherly love is in evidence at 124 and 126 West End, sites of the **Thomas White House** (1890) and the **John G. White House** (1891). The **Nancy Whitlock House** at 120 West End was constructed around the beginning of the Civil War.

Saint Joseph's Catholic Church, on your right at 110 West End Street, was built as a Presbyterian facility in 1839 and acquired by Catholics in 1854.

Sporting a 3-story clock tower, the jewel of downtown is **Chester City Hall**, on your right, at the corner of Main and Center Streets, at the edge of the west end of town, where West End Street becomes Main Street. It is a renovated opera house originally constructed in 1891 in the Romanesque Revival style.

The old-timey downtown area is so well preserved that it was used as the early 1900s filming set for the *Chiefs* TV miniseries in the 1980s.

Chester City Hall MARIE GOFF

One block past City Hall, where Main and Gadsden Streets form a fork in the heart of downtown, is **Monument Square**, a pocket park home to a Confederate monument, an old Civil War cannon, an ancient cistern, and the Aaron Burr Rock, upon which the former vice president stood in 1806 to plea for help from capture by federal authorities wanting to try him for treason. Chester citizens did not heed his plea, but he was tried and eventually acquitted.

On your left at 114 Main Street is **Chester Hardware Building**, constructed in 1904. The first part of the old **McAliley-Chester Hotel**, completed in 1854 in a Classical Revival style, is at 118 Main Street.

The **Eaves-DaVaga Building** at 126 Main Street, built by an attorney around 1843, has seen many uses over its 180 years, but today it still includes offices for lawyers. Next door is the **Agurs-Wiley Building**, a Romanesque Revival structure built in 1905 at 134 Main Street as a drugstore and telegraph office, with upstairs business and professional offices. Last in this complex is the

Graham-Hardin Building, built in 1853 as a general merchandise store at 136 Main Street.

Next, as you head downhill, are the monuments and grounds of **Chester County Courthouse**, constructed at 140 Main Street between 1852 and 1854 in the Jefferson Classical style. Beside the courthouse is the War Memorial Building, with monuments honoring locals who died In World Wars I and II, the Korean and Vietnam Wars, and the War on Terrorists. A monument honoring World War I deceased is directly in front of the courthouse.

The **Henry-McLure Building** (ca. 1884) is across the way at 139–141 Main Street.

As you proceed downhill, the **Chester Associate Reformed Presbyterian Church**, built in 1898, is on your right, at 159 Main Street. The congregation was organized in 1869. On your left, at 158 Main Street, is the Old Post Office, constructed in 1908 and now home to several county offices.

At the next intersection, the **Bethel United Methodist Church**, an example of Gothic-Romanesque architecture completed in 1897, is directly ahead at 101 York Street. Bear left (northeast) on York Street. The **Matthew Henry White House** (1884) at 100 York Street is on your left.

Among the numerous notable residences along this lovely thoroughfare are the **Robert Gage House** (1913) at 108 York, the **William T. Robinson House** (1855) at 124 York, the **Curry-Owen House** (1873) at 125 York, the **John L Albright House** (1837) at 127 York, the **Albright-Heyman House** (1870) at 131 York, the **Gaston-Gage House** (185) at 143 York, the **S. M. Jones House** (1908) at 144 York, the **Key House** (late 1880s) at 151 York, the **Giles J. Patterson House** (1890) at 154 York, and the **Raney-Lindsay House** (1875) at 155 York.

After 4 blocks on York, take a right (southeast) on Foote Street. The **Leard-Latimer House** (1890) at 160 York is on your left as you make the turn. After one block on Foote Street, go right (southwest) on Saluda Street/SC 72.

As you cruise along Saluda back toward downtown, enjoy views of more gracious southern homes, including the **McDonald-Mobley House** (1851) at 143 Saluda and the **Hafner-Rudisill House** (1890) at 120 Saluda.

Saluda merges into Main Street 4 blocks from Foote Street, and here you turn left (southeast) on Hudson Street. Travel one block and take a right (west) on Gadsden Street for one more foray through the historic downtown. Chester Is called "A City on a Hill," and you are now in a business area called **"The Valley."**

The Classical Revival **Rodman-Brown Building** at 167–179 Gadsden Street was constructed for a large mercantile company around 1915, a few years after the **Samuels Building** was constructed at 163–165 Gadsden Street as a dry goods establishment around 1909.

Virtually all of the edifices along this way are of vintage heritage. These include **Elliott's Market Building** (ca. 1909) at 161 Gadsden Street, the **Low-rance Brothers Building**, **Pundt's Building**, and the **T. J. Irwln Building** at 153–157 Gadsden, all built around 1880; the **Coleman Building**, built before 1877 at 147–149 Gadsden; the **Lindsay Merchantile Company Building** constructed in the early 1870s at 145 Gadsden; and the **F. M. Nail** and **Leitner Buildings** at 137 and 135 Gadsden, both erected around 1880.

Ezell Hardware at 157 Gadsden is one of the oldest hardware stores in South Carolina, established in 1886. You're sure to find something you need here from nails and a hammer to pickled vegetables and iron skillets.

Gadsden Street merges with Main Street at Monument Square. Bear left (southwest) onto Main Street, pass Center Street and City Hall again, and continue as Main Street becomes West End Street. After 2 blocks, turn right (northwest) on Reedy Street and proceed for 2 blocks past old bungalows to Pinckney Street/SC 9, where you turn right (northeast) again.

Enjoy more lovely homes as you follow Pinckney 2 blocks to Center Street. These homes include the **Bell House** (1886) at 128 Pinckney and the **J. J. McLure House** (1850) at 110 Pinckney.

At Center Street/SC 9/US 321, turn right (southeast). **Saint Mark's Episcopal Church** (1879) is at 135 Center Street, and the **Old Jail**, built in 1842 and now a law office, is at 128 Center Street.

Turn left (northeast) after one block onto McAliley Street. The **Chester County Historical Society Museum** is a half block down the way, housed in a 1914 jail building at 107 McAliley Street.

After one block, turn left again onto Wylie Street. Along this street are the **DaVega-Barron House** (1892), now a funeral home, at 133 Wylie, **Puritan Presbyterian Church** (1854) at 135 Wylie, and the **Dr. A. P. Wylie House** (1840s) at 145 Wylie.

After four blocks on Wylie, you reach the old **Seaboard Freight Depot**, a warehouse built in 1890 and now a transportation museum at 157 Wylie Street, and the old **Seaboard Passenger Station**, built in 1920.

Turn around at the train station, drive one block, and turn left (northeast) on Academy Street. Among the old homes on this street are the **Joseph Walker House** (1892) at 114 Academy and the **Clark-Patterson-Lalli House** (1910) at 120 Academy.

Directly ahead at 111 Pine Street, is the **Hamilton House** (1903). Turn right (southeast) and ride one block to York Street to conclude your tour of Chester. Along the way you pass the **Agurs-Byars House** (ca. 1841) at 104 Pine.

(For the most part, we avoid touting commercial establishments in this book. However, we wish to make an exception for the Cyclone Restaurant, a down-home southern eatery at 249 Columbia Street in Chester. Places like the Cyclone were commonplace back in the middle of the 20th century, but are a rarity today. It isn't fancy, but the food is great. And so are the folks who operate their restaurant in a converted motel building.)

Nearby Attractions

Catawba Cultural Center, Lake Wateree State Recreation Area, Museum of York County, Museum of Western York County, Ridgeway, South Carolina Railroad Museum, Winnsboro, Winthrop University.

Catawba River Basin and Old Carolina

Historic Camden to Andrew Jackson State Park

General Description: A 90-mile journey that begins in historic Camden and then moves through horse country and forests to the banks of Lake Wateree, and the Catawba River Valley, concluding at a state park honoring the birthplace of the seventh US president.

Special Attractions: Historic Camden and its Revolutionary War Visitor Center, National Steeplechase Museum and Springdale Race Course, National Historic Landmark Battle of Camden Site, Lake Wateree, Beaver Creek, Liberty Hill, Fishing Creek Dam, Fishing Creek Reservoir, Landsford Canal State Park, Catawba River, Andrew Jackson State Park.

Location: North central part of the state, northeast of Columbia and directly south of Charlotte.

Travel Season: All year. The spider lilies are in bloom at Landsford Canal mid-May through mid-June. Celebrations of historic events, battles, and figures are plentiful at Camden's Revolutionary War Center and Andrew Jackson State Park throughout the year. Camden's Springdale Race Course hosts the Carolina Cup Races in spring and Colonial Cup Races in the fall.

Services: Camden, Lancaster, and Rock Hill have full services. The drive begins on the northeastern edge of the Columbia metropolitan area and ends on the southeastern edge of the Charlotte metropolitan area.

The Drive

This drive begins at Camden's Historic Revolutionary War Site, where the town was first settled, and then passes many of the historic sites in Camden significant during the Revolutionary War. The route wanders through the town's eclectic arts and antiques district and eases past some of the beautiful antebellum homes in downtown Camden. After crossing a bridge beside Fishing Creek Dam and taking in views of Fishing Creek Reservoir, you pass through Fort Lawn before visiting the enchanting waters of Landsford Canal State Park. You then cross a high span over the Catawba River to experience the locale of Andrew Jackson's boyhood home and a shady state park devoted to his heritage.

Catawba River Basin and Old Carolina:
Historic Camden to Andrew Jackson State Park

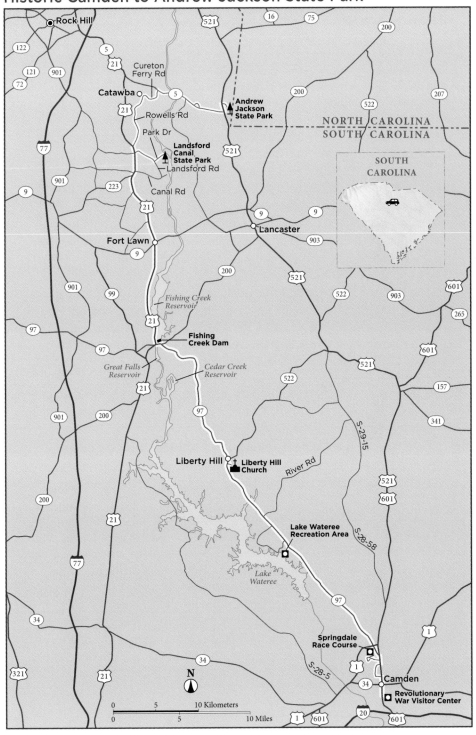

Historic Camden

Camden's rich history dates back more than a thousand years, when the Catawba, Cherokee, and Wateree tribes lived in this region. In 1730 King George II ordered Camden's original township to be planned, and around 1750, Scots-Irish immigrants, many of whom were Quakers, moved here from northern colonies and named the area Fredericksburg Township. The Quakers built the first saw and gristmills and established a thriving market town along today's Broad Street, the old Catawba trading path.

In 1758 Joseph Kershaw, said to be the founding father of Camden, arrived from Yorkshire, England, and established a store in the Fredericksburg Township, which further helped develop commerce in the area and made the settlement a significant trade center. The area's name was changed to Pine Tree Hill around this time, and then, upon Kershaw's suggestion, the name changed for a third time to Camden, in honor of Lord Camden who championed colonial rights.

By the early 1770s Camden had established a courthouse, stores, and mills. Between 1780 and 1781, Lord Cornwallis moved here and occupied Camden for the British government during the American Revolution conflict. Camden eventually became the central supply post for the British forces, and approximately 2,500 British soldiers camped at this location. Today Camden is best known for the battles that were fought here, including the Battle of Camden on August 16, 1780, which the British won, and then the Battle of Hobkirk's Hill on April 25, 1781, which the Patriots won. In May 1781 the British retreated in defeat and burned Camden to the ground. In the early 1800s, however, the town was rebuilt north of its original site, and it continues to thrive today.

Begin your drive at the **Revolutionary War Visitor Center at Camden** (212 Broad St.), located 1.3 miles from exit 98/I-20 on the right (east) side of US 521 North/Broad Street. A large wooden sign marks the turn into the Visitor Center parking lot.

Once in the parking lot, the **Public House** is on your left. It is Camden's visitor center and includes a permanent exhibit about the American Revolution, the Southern Campaign, the real turning point in the war, and the role South Carolina played. In the gift shop found inside the Public House you can purchase tickets for guided and self-guided tours of the adjacent Historic Camden Revolutionary War Site and the reconstructed Kershaw-Cornwallis House. Beside the gift shop is a wall of free brochures that detail many of the historic homes, structures, and sites to visit in Camden, as well as festivals and events in and around Camden and Kershaw County, and the unique shopping available in Camden's Antique and Arts District.

Two other buildings at the Visitor Center are **Liberty Hall**, which includes a meeting space and public restrooms, and the **Market Building at Pine Creek**, crafted after an 18th century tavern and also serves as a meeting space.

The adjacent **Historic Camden Revolutionary War Site** (222 Broad St.) is a 3.4-acre outdoor museum complex that covers a portion of the original town site of Camden.

Some of the historic structures found at the property are the **Bradley House** (1800), a wooden settlers' cabin, the **Drakeford House**, built around 1812 by Richard Drakeford, a former Patriot soldier, and the tiny **Bonds Conway House** (1812), believed to have been constructed by the first African American in Camden to purchase his own freedom which occurred around 1793. The home serves as headquarters for the **Kershaw County Historical Society** and was recently moved to the Revolutionary War Site from 811 Fair Street.

The **Cunningham House** (1835), the Historic Camden Exchange, serves as a gift shop and information center for the Revolutionary War Site. Here you can also pick up brochures on Camden and its historic sites, walking and driving tours, books, souvenirs, and tour tickets for guided tour of the **Kershaw-Cornwallis House**, a reconstruction of Joseph Kershaw's home that served as the headquarters for Cornwallis during the British occupation in 1780 and 1781. You can walk the grounds at your leisure free of charge, and pamphlets identify the many sites you will see here, including forts, reconstructed town walls, a powder magazine, a blacksmith shed, and a handful of home structures.

Consider walking the 0.6-mile loop nature trail that begins at the blacksmith shop and the Revolutionary War Powder Magazine and takes you to Big Pine Tree Creek, the waterway that supported the mills in the 18th century, and sites of the eastern British fortified redoubts constructed and reconstructed.

Exit the Revolutionary War Site by turning right (north) on US 521/Broad Street and then making a quick turn left (west) on Meeting Street/S-28-27 after only a few yards. Head west on Meeting Street. On your right is the site where Major General Baron Johann de Kalb was buried after his death during the historic Battle of Camden on August 19, 1780. He was later disinterred and reburied at Bethesda Presbyterian Church on DeKalb Street in downtown Camden. Also on your right are the original sites of 18th Century stores (no remnants are found now) and the remains of the **Camden oak tree**, believed to have been planted in 1790. The **Old Presbyterian Burial Ground** and **Revolutionary War Memorial** are on your left.

Continue west another block, past Church Street/S-28-235, the western boundary of 18th Century Camden, and then Campbell Street/S-28-115, the southwestern site of a British fortified redoubt, to enter the historic **Quaker Cemetery** (713 Meeting Street) established in 1759, on the corner of Meeting and Campbell Streets. The cemetery was established by Samuel Wyly, a Quaker who gave four acres of property for 999 years for "one pepper corn per year" rent. Today the cemetery encompasses 50 acres. The town of Camden deeded the property to the Quaker Cemetery Association in 1874.

Circle through the beautiful burial site. Head west on North Quaker Avenue. A kiosk to the left of North Quaker Avenue has pamphlets that provide a history of the cemetery and the notable people who are buried here, including American Revolution and Confederate veterans.

Turn left (south) on Memorial Avenue. Just before you turn left onto South Quaker Avenue, look to your right for the triangular stone that marks the site of the original Quaker Meeting House. Follow the road to the left again to end on South Quaker Avenue. The loop is less than a half-mile.

Exit the cemetery by turning left (north) on Campbell Street, entrance to Camden's Historic African American Corridor. Go one long block, passing the **Beth El Jewish Cemetery** (1877) on your left, and turn right (east) on Bull Street/S-28-217. This corner was formerly the northwestern side of British fortified redoubts. Drive 2 long blocks, crossing over Church Street. On your left is the site of Old Episcopal Cemetery and the graves of Joseph Kershaw, Camden's founding father and his family enclosed by a brick wall in the distance. On your right was early Camden's Cricket Field.

At the intersection with Broad Street/US 521, turn left (north). This intersection was the site of Camden's original town square in the 1770s. After turning on Broad Street, look to your right to see the site where President George Washington addressed citizens of Camden on May 25, 1791, during his tour of the South.

Travel 2 blocks on Broad Street into Camden's historic district. On your left is the restored Kershaw County Courthouse (1826), designed by famed South Carolina architect Robert Mills at 607 South Broad Street.

On your right directly across from the courthouse is a gravel lot believed to be the site of the old Camden jail, where Andrew Jackson was imprisoned around the age of 14 and is said to have watched the Battle of Hobkirk from the jail's second-story window. A historical marker marks the area.

Drive one more block to York Street. On your right at the corner of Broad and York Streets, at 724 Broad Street, is the **Price House** (1830). The early-1800s structure once had a store on its first floor and a home on the second floor. Today the building is used for community social events. On the western side of Broad and York Streets is Mount Moriah Baptist Church, established by and for African Americans in 1866. The current structure was erected in 1889, and renowned substantially after a fire in the 1950s.

To visit the African American Cultural Center of Camden (517 York St.), turn right here, and the Center is immediately on your right in a small white wooden house. The Center highlights the history of African Americans in Camden through exhibits, artifacts and documents.

As you continue 2 more blocks to Rutledge Street, passing many eclectic antiques and art shops, look up to see the weather vane atop the **Old Opera House Tower** (1886) at 950 Broad Street. This is a replica of the original vane crafted in 1825 to honor a Catawba chief who befriended early settlers in Camden during the mid-1700s. He was given the name King Haiglar and is considered the "patron saint of Camden." The original weather vane is housed in the Camden Archives and Museum.

If you'd like to explore Camden's downtown historic district on foot, turn left (east) on Rutledge Street and on your right is free public parking and the rear entrance to the Galleria (1101 Broad St.), a refurbished warehouse that includes a restaurant, art galleries, and clean public restrooms. Stop here to wander through the art shops, stop for a bite to eat and exit on Broad Street to explore more of Camden's varied downtown eateries, art, and antique stores.

Turn right (east) on Rutledge Street and pass more art galleries, restaurants, and unique stores. Two blocks directly ahead is **Camden City Hall** (1000 Lyttleton St.), on the corner of Rutledge and Lyttleton Streets. Look up at the cupola here to see another replica of the Catawba chief striking his bow.

Turn right (south) on Lyttleton and then ride a long block to pull into the parking lot of the **Fine Arts Center of Kershaw County** on your left, at 810 Lyttleton Street. Marble horse heads atop brick columns cast by Constance Bassett in 1983 mark the entrance to the two parking areas. Camden celebrates art, music, and theater here and houses a library of steeplechase memorabilia. The Bassett Building hosts theatrical events, and the **Douglas-Reed House** (1812) on the property hosts cultural events.

Exit the parking lot, turn right (north) on Lyttleton Street to backtrack past City Hall, and continue one more block to the intersection with DeKalb Street/Jefferson Davis Highway. **Hampton Park**, a pretty open space, named for General Wade Hampton, Civil War hero and governor of South Carolina from 1877 to 1879, is across DeKalb Street to the right of Lyttleton Street.

Turn left (west) on DeKalb Street and look to your right to see lovely **Bethesda Presbyterian Church** (1822) at 502 DeKalb Street. The church structure and the monument in front of the church were designed by Robert Mills. The monument honors Revolutionary War hero Baron Johann de Kalb, who was reinterred here in 1825 from the Meeting Street burial site.

Continue about a block west past an old-fashioned theater, banks, and downtown storefronts to Broad Street. On the corner of DeKalb and Broad is the Camden **Post Office** (1915) at 105 East DeKalb Street.

Ahead to the left on the corner of Broad and DeKalb Streets is the Dibble Building, a 19th-century building owned by a prominent African American business family.

Turn right onto Broad Street and head one block north. On your right at the corner of Walnut Street and Broad Street is the 3-story brick **Bishop Davis House** at 1202 Broad Street, named for Rev. Thomas Frederick Davis, who was raised here and was bishop of South Carolina from 1853 to 1870. Constructed around 1817, the Charleston-style home is now an antiques store.

Next on your right is the **Geisenheimer House** at 1204 Broad Street, believed to have been used as a hospital for Confederate soldiers during the Civil War. On your left at 1301 Broad Street is **McCants House**, built in 1813, and "Greenleaf Villa" (1815) at 1307 Broad Street.

Just past Laurens Court, on your right, is the **Camden Archives and Museum** (1915) at 1314 Broad Street. Pull into the circular drive to get a good look at the building that originally served as the Camden library, a gift from the Carnegie Foundation, until 1973, when it was converted into the Archives and Museum. The museum collects and preserves important historical documents and artifacts relating to the history and genealogy of Camden and Kershaw County. It also houses the South Carolina Daughters of the American Revolution and the South Carolina Society of Colonial Dames XVII Century Libraries.

Exit the Archives and Museum by turning right on Broad Street (north) and then left (west) onto Laurens Street. On the west side of Broad Street is **Memorial Park** (1798) at the corner of Broad and Laurens Streets. You may want to linger in the park and see the two monuments here. One commemorates Confederate soldiers and the other honors Lieutenant Colonel James Polk Dickinson, who died in the Mexican War.

The first house on your right is **Tanglewood** at 612 Laurens Street, where Federal troops are said to have used the home's well water while camping in the square. Turn right on Monument Square just before the Tanglewood home.

On your left at 1315 Monument Square is a home that was used as a schoolhouse from 1903 to 1919. You'll pass beautiful old homes on your left along this small lane. As you near Broad Street, look to your left to see **Aberdeen** (1810) at 1409 Broad Street. The small, red, wooden structure at the rear of the house is thought to be the original kitchen.

When you reach Broad Street, turn left (north). Notice **Camden House** (1502 Broad St.), the third house on your right, a great example of an antebellum mansion that used to be an "in-town" plantation home.

To see more historic homes, travel another block and turn right (east) on Hampton Street. Ride to the end of Hampton Street, passing neat bungalows with pretty manicured yards and gardens, to Lyttleton Street. Turn left (north) and on

Aberdeen, a Camden home constructed in 1810 PATRICIA PIERCE

your left at 1515 Lyttleton Street is a stately 2-story home built around 1832. At 1613 Lyttleton Street is a one-story home built in 1839 and believed to have been the site of a bachelors' club, Stag Hall. Notice the park on your right and the Rectory Square Pantheon. The six columns of the pantheon represent the six Confederate generals from Kershaw County.

The enormous home at the corner of Lyttleton and Chestnut Streets, ahead to your right, at 314 Chestnut, was built around 1848. Cross over Chestnut Street and continue a half mile to Greene Street, past more historic mansions. Turn left (west) on Greene Street.

On your right at 406 Greene Street, set back from the road, is a home that used to be a log cabin but was rebuilt around 1880 into the present mansion. The next home on your right, built in 1830, was once the residence of Judge Thomas Jefferson Withers, a signer of the Ordinance of Secession and a delegate to the Confederate Convention.

Continue one block to Broad Street. Ahead is **Hobkirk's Hill**, site of the Battle of Hobkirk's Hill on April 25, 1781. Within a month after this battle, the British withdrew from Camden.

Turn right (north) on Broad Street and travel a half mile to Knights Hill Road/S-28-35. A white wooden sign to the left of Broad Street marks the turn to Springdale Race Course. Turn left (northwest) and travel almost a mile, passing the Camden Country Club on your left, to visit the **National Steeplechase Museum and headquarters for the Springdale Race Course** (200 Knights Hill Rd.), home of the annual spring Carolina Cup and fall Colonial Cup Races, on your right. The Steeplechase Museum is the only one of its kind in the United States, dedicated solely to the history of steeplechase racing. You will be treated to photography, memorabilia, documents, and trophies. A timber racing gallery and an educational film room and library highlight the history of steeplechase and its relationship to foxhunting. The museum also exhibits memorabilia on timber fence racing and a gift shop.

While outside, be sure to look around the grounds of the 600-acre steeplechase training facility, notice the life-size bronze of steeplechaser Lonesome Glory, and check out the viewing stand across the street from the museum. If you are lucky, you may glimpse a thoroughbred horse racing around the track.

Exit the museum and race course and head southeast almost a mile on Knights Hill Road to return to Broad Street. Turn left (north) onto Broad Street/US 521/601 and drive 0.3 mile to bear left at the fork onto Liberty Hill Road/SC 97/John G. Richards Road.

*If you would like to visit the **National Historic Landmark Battle of Camden Site**, where one of the most disastrous battles of the American Revolution for Patriot troops took place on August 13, 1780, continue straight on US 521/US 601/*

The Carolina Cup held at Springdale Race Course Marie Goff

Kershaw Highway 3.7 miles to bear left on Flat Rock Road/SC 58. Continue 2 miles, and the 6-acre park will be on your right. Fourteen soldiers' graves were found here and reinterred at the Site. You'll find several walking trails in the park.

Backtrack southeast to Camden on US 521/US 601/Kershaw Highway and turn right (northwest) onto Liberty Hill Road/SC 97 North/John G. Richards Road toward Liberty Hill.

Camden to Liberty Hill

Continue 10 miles past modest homes along the country road and look for the left-hand turn onto Baron DeKalb Road/S-28-40 that takes you to Shaw Air Force Base Lake Wateree Recreation Area and a public boat landing, White Oak Creek Access Area (2014 Baron DeKalb Rd.). A brown sign on the right-hand side of the road marks the left turn. The boat landing is 0.8 mile down this road and offers great views of **Lake Wateree**.

Backtrack to SC 97/Liberty Hill Road/John G. Richards Road and turn left (northwest) to travel 5 miles along a forested road to cross expansive Beaver Creek. Just before and after the bridge are restaurants, local hangouts where you can stop for a steak, fresh seafood, ice cream, or drinks. The restaurants offer views of a creek that looks more like a lake.

Liberty Hill Presbyterian Church, constructed in 1880 PATRICIA PIERCE

As you cross **Beaver Creek** on the Senior Trooper Michael J. Rao Bridge, you are sure to see all sorts of boats riding up and down the water and jet skis cutting a wake.

Travel 2.7 miles north on SC 97 to **Liberty Hill**. Just as you enter the village, look to your left for the charming, old-fashioned, white wooden Liberty Hill Post Office (4049 John G. Richards Rd.).

About 0.3 mile farther on your right is Meeting Lane. Turn right (east) here, just before **Liberty Hill Country Store** (4118 John G. Richards Rd.), to view pretty **Liberty Hill Presbyterian Church** at 20 Meeting Lane. The church was founded in 1851, and the present structure dates from 1880. Notice the interesting woodwork and the old cemetery. An old bell still hangs in the steeple. The flowers adorning the grounds invite visitors to sit on the bench around the oak tree or linger in the green space beside the parking area.

Head west back to SC 97/John G. Richards Road. Across the street is Peay's Ferry Road, named for Austin Ford Peay, a prominent planter and politician from Fairfield County who served the state as a representative and then a senator from 1812 to 1839. Peay owned ferry rights on the Wateree River. Peay's Ferry Road extended from the Wateree River to Liberty Hill from the early 19th century until the early 20th century, when the nearby dam flooded it.

Turn right (north) on SC 97/John G. Richards Road. After 2 miles you leave Kershaw County and enter Lancaster County, and SC 97 becomes Cedar Creek Road. Continue 9.6 miles through forests, rolling hills, and winding roads toward Great Falls to the intersection with SC 97/SC 200 Francis Avenue. Turn left here on SC 97 North/SC 200 West. Cross the Tom G. Mangum Bridge, spanning the Catawba River. Look to your right for a terrific view of Fishing Creek Dam.

The dam is the reason there are no longer any great falls near the old mill town of Great Falls, just south of here. The dam does, however, provide a nice recreational body of water, Fishing Creek Reservoir, north of the water barrier.

Fishing Creek Dam to Andrew Jackson State Park

After you cross Tom G. Mangum Bridge, take the first right (north) onto US 21/Catawba River Road toward Rock Hill and Charlotte. **Fishing Creek Landing** (5700 Fish Camp Rd, Great Falls), a great turnout to view the beauty of largely unspoiled **Fishing Creek Reservoir**, is on your right on Fish Camp Road, about 1.4 miles after you turn.

A half mile farther up the road, beside Battlefield Drive, are a stone monument and historical marker noting the Battle of Fishing Creek on August 18, 1870, a Revolutionary War encounter in which Patriot General Thomas Sumter's forces

Fishing Creek Dam, where the Catawba River is transformed into the Wateree River PATRICIA PIERCE

were caught by surprise and routed by a unit of Cornwallis's British army led by Colonel Banastre Tarleton.

Drive 6 more miles through forestland and right-hand turnouts to the reservoir until you reach **Fort Lawn**, a crossroads community straddling US 21 and SC 9, the road connecting Chester and I-77 on the west with Lancaster in the east. Before the construction of I-77 just west of here, US 21 was the longtime chief artery connecting Columbia and Charlotte, and highway commerce in this area, remnants of which you see today, was quite significant.

From Fort Lawn continue 7 miles north on US 21/Catawba River Road toward Landsford Canal State Park, past modest homes and businesses, forestland, pastures, and a fair amount of red dirt.

Turn right on Landsford Road. A brown sign marks the turn. Travel 1.6 miles to enter the 448-acre **Landsford Canal State Park** (2051 Park Dr., Catawba). Turn left (west) on Park Drive/S-12-690 and drive about a mile to the main parking area.

Landsford Canal was built in the early 1800s to bypass rapids on the Catawba River at "Land's Ford." The canal was in use from 1820 to 1835 but had been completely abandoned by 1846. The site's history is much broader, however. The property was long an important place to ford the Catawba River because the stream is wide and shallow at this point. Cornwallis's British troops crossed here, and Patriot general Thomas Sumter used the area as a camp and meeting place.

Landsford Canal is famous for wildflowers, and its crown jewels are its rare rocky shoals water lilies. During their peak blooming season from mid-May to mid-June, the largest concentration of these flowers in the world converts the waterway into a sea of white. Other blooms found in the park include cardinal flower, Jack-in-the-pulpit, crane-fly orchid, spicebush, spiderwort, Solomon's seal, fire pink, and yellow passionflower.

In the vicinity of the parking area are an interpretive display, park headquarters and log cabin, restrooms, a picnic area and playground, the old, stone lock-keeper's house, the short Eagle Point Trail, and the shore of the canal, interspersed with shoals. A half-mile nature trail and 1.5-mile Canal Trail run southward.

Birds are in abundance here, making the area attractive for eagles and assorted hawks. Ospreys, green-backed herons, purple martins, ruby-throated hummingbirds, and a great many varieties of warblers can be encountered.

Backtrack out of the park on Park Road and take a right on Seegers Road/Landsford Road/S-12-327 to ride 1.6 miles through undulating horse country before reaching the intersection with US 21/Catawba River Road.

After 0.2 mile, fork right (north) onto Rowells Road/S-12-465 in the Rowell community and head toward the Native American settlement of Catawba, 4.2 miles away. You soon cross into York County, and Rowells Road changes designation to S-46-832 as you ease past modest homes and community buildings and cross a railroad track before coming to a stop sign at the intersection with Cureton Ferry Road. Turn right (east) on Cureton Ferry Road/S-46-697 and ride 1.8 miles past a plethora of railroad tracks and a giant forest-products industrial facility on the right before coming to an intersection with SC 5.

At SC 5/Rock Hill Highway turn right and journey eastward, crossing after a mile a high bridge spanning the Catawba River, with great views in both directions. Continue another 4 miles to the intersection with US 521/Charlotte Highway, turn left (north), and follow signs to the entrance of 360-acre Andrew Jackson State Park (196 Andrew Jackson Park Rd., Lancaster) a half mile up the road. Turn right (east) onto Andrew Jackson Park Road. The headquarters area of the park is 0.3 mile farther.

Andrew Jackson State Park features a museum detailing the boyhood of our nation's seventh president, who grew up here in what was then called the Waxhaws of the South Carolina backcountry. At the park you'll find a stunning boyhood statue of the president, **"Old Hickory,"** sculpted by Anna Hyatt Huntington, and an historic orchard and herb garden. The garden features fruit trees, herbs, and vegetables that were important to early settlers and Native Americans. Apple, peach, plum, and fig trees date back to the 17th and 18th centuries. Flax, used to create linen, is also grown here, as an example of one of the crops planted by settlers

Among the most interesting features of the park are its living-history programs. Docents dress in period clothes as they guide you through the museum. Be sure to visit the replica of a late-18th-century one-room schoolhouse while you are here. Camping, picnic facilities, restrooms, fishing, and hiking trails are also available. A small lake provides a soothing backdrop for relaxing in this cool and shady oasis at the doorstep of the Charlotte metropolitan area.

Nearby Attractions

Ann Springs Close Greenway, Catawba Cultural Center, Fort Mill History Museum, Goodale State Park, Hartsville, Lake Wateree State Recreation Area, Rock Hill, Springs Farm Market, Winthrop University.

10

Sand Hills and the Great Pee Dee Basin

Carolina Sandhills National Wildlife Refuge to Bennettsville

General Description: A 75-mile journey through forested sand hills, peach orchards, and cotton fields, and picturesque old towns in the Great Pee Dee River Basin.

Special Attractions: Carolina Sandhills National Wildlife Refuge, Sand Hills State Forest, Historic Cheraw, Great Pee Dee River, Quaint Society Hill, Charming Bennettsville.

Location: Northeast part of the state, a little bit north of Florence.

Travel Season: All year. Early summer to mid-autumn is best for observing crop fields in their full glory. Late fall, winter, and early spring are best for wildlife. Flowers peak in early spring.

Services: Cheraw and Bennettsville have accommodations and most basic services. Florence has full services.

The Drive

Highlights of this drive are fascinating small towns, peach orchards, cotton fields, public forests and nature preserves, remnants of an ancient seashore known as the sand hills, and a majestic waterway.

You begin in the Sandhills National Wildlife Refuge, ride through Sand Hills State Forest, crisscross through the shinning jewel of historic Cheraw, amble through an old village with ancient buildings, visit a pair of superb venues for viewing the Great Pee Dee River, and end up in Bennettsville, with beautiful old homes and a 1950s-era charm.

Carolina Sandhills National Wildlife Refuge to Cheraw

Begin in Chesterfield County at the entrance to **Carolina Sandhills National Wildlife Refuge** (23734 US 1, McBee).

The county was settled by Welsh Baptists from Delaware in the mid-1700s and named for the Earl of Chesterfield, an English statesman. This entire area is called the **Sandhills** (also spelled "*Sand Hills*"), remnants of an ancient seacoast that now form a sandy belt stretching southwest to northeast across South Carolina's midriff, from North Augusta through Columbia and Camden all the way to Cheraw and into North Carolina.

Carolina Sandhills NWR to Bennettsville and the Great Pee Dee Basin

Wetlands in Sandhills National Wildlife Refuge JOHN CLARK

A brown sign marks the entrance to the delightful Wildlife/Refuge Visitors Drive, a narrow, paved, winding roadway through the heart of the refuge.

There is no admission for Carolina Sandhills National Wildlife Refuge, which is open daily, sunrise to sunset. Hiking, hunting, fishing, and mountain biking opportunities abound. Restrooms and picnic facilities are located at the entrance off US 1 and at the Lake Bee Recreation Area off SC 145.

Carolina Sandhills National Wildlife Refuge was established in 1939 on 45,000 acres of land exhausted and eroded by farming. Through careful management, it has been restored to a rich, varied environment for many kinds of wildlife. Traversing the property is historic Wire Road, a route used by General Sherman's army on its rampaging Civil War march through South Carolina. The longleaf pine and wire grass ecosystem characteristic of the refuge's habitat once covered 90 million acres across the southeastern United States, from Virginia to Texas. Today, only scattered patches remain, mostly on public lands.

Rolling beds of deep sandy soils play host to an extensive longleaf pine forest, with an understory of scattered scrub oaks and a wire grass ground cover. Numerous small creeks and tributaries flow through the tract, providing corridors for hardwood species such as blackjack and black oaks, alder, bald cypress, southern red oak, dogwood, and sourwood, as well as dense stands of evergreen shrubs. The refuge also has 30 man-made ponds, numerous springs percolating through sandy soil, and 1,200 acres of fallow fields, forest openings, and cultivated fields, contributing to the land's richly diverse habitat.

At least 190 bird species, 42 mammal species, 41 kinds of reptiles, and 25 types of amphibians have been identified within the refuge's boundaries. The refuge is an important inland stopover for migratory waterfowl. Wood ducks, Canada geese, and great blue herons are found here year-round, and great egrets and anhingas are usually in the ponds in spring and fall.

Also, the refuge provides habitat for the endangered red-cockaded woodpecker. Trees housing woodpecker nests are identified by white rings painted around the trunks. Red-tailed hawks, northern harriers, and American kestrels are common, and bald eagles and ospreys occasionally fly overhead.

Opossums, raccoons, fox squirrels, beavers, bobwhite quail, songbirds, wild turkeys, white-tailed deer, cottontail rabbits, fox, yellow-bellied slider turtles, and buckeye and spicebush swallowtail butterflies are frequently spotted. Pine barrens tree frogs, listed by the state of South Carolina as "threatened," inhabit boggy areas.

Wildflowers go wild in the spring and include trailing arbutus, orange milkwort, yellow jessamine, sweet pepperbush, wooly mullein, sensitive brier, lizard's tail, prickly pear, mountain laurel, and Saint-John's-wort. Both the yellow and purple varieties of pitcher plants capture and devour insects.

Pool A and the 1-mile Woodland Pond Trail that loops around its edges are 0.8 mile ahead. Ferns and wildflowers decorate the edges of the picturesque, stump-filled pond, and beavers are sometimes in evidence. Continue one mile uphill along Wildlife Drive, passing Wire Road, trees, more ponds, clearings, and lots of sand. A number of parking pullovers dot the way.

After 2.5 miles **Martin's Lake Recreation Area** is on your right. The parking area is less than a mile from the right turn. Beside the lake are both a photo blind and an observation tower. In winter this is a special place for observing migratory waterfowl. Food plots are on the other side of the lake, creating additional opportunities for wildlife viewing. This is the southern trailhead for Tate's Trail, which runs northwest through sandy terrain for 2 miles, past Pool D and looping around Lake 12 to Lake Bee. The Martin's Lake end has lengthy boardwalks running through bald cypresses and briers.

Return to Wildlife Drive and continue northeastward. You cross between Pool D on your left and Martin's Lake 0.2 mile along, with great views of wetlands. At 0.6 mile past the wetlands, turn left (northwest) at the stop sign to stay on the paved road, rather than going right on the gravel road toward Mays Lake.

Pass Pool G on your right and, about 0.4 mile along, reach a left (south) turn toward Lake 12, where a kiosk provides a great deal of information about the refuge. Among many other interesting tidbits, you learn that beavers mate for life.

You reach SC 145 after 0.6 mile. Cross over SC 145, and continue 0.1 mile to the **Lake Bee Recreation Area** on your left. For more delightful ponds, observation towers, forests, and meadows with great viewing opportunities, continue over gently rolling countryside for another 2 miles westward on Wildlife Drive. Pools H and J and Honkers and Oxpen Lakes provide great habitat, and side roads provide a number of sightseeing options.

Return to SC 145, turn right (south), and travel 6.2 miles to the intersection with US 1. The countryside is punctuated with cotton fields and peach orchards. South Carolina is a huge grower of peaches, producing twice as much as Georgia, and Chesterfield County is one of the Palmetto State's largest producers.

Turn left (northeast) on US 1, toward Patrick (13 miles ahead) and Cheraw (26 miles). For a while, Carolina Sandhills NWR is on your left and on your right, and then also on your left, is the **Sand Hills State Forest**, consisting of 46,000 acres. The federal government purchased the largely infertile land of the current state forest between 1935 and 1939 and turned it over to the state for management, before finally deeding it to South Carolina in 1991. Reforestation has been successful, and the once barren sand hills support productive stands of pines and a variety of wildlife and plant life.

You can enter the heart of the state forest by turning left at Middendorf Road (5 miles past your turn onto US 1) or at several other left turns farther along. Crisscrossed mainly with sandy dirt roads, the state forest offers substantial mountain biking and equestrian opportunities, along with fishing, hunting, birding, and picnicking.

*The forest contains primitive camping areas, a small lake with a nature trail and picnic facilities, and **Sugar Loaf Mountain Recreation Area**. Sugar Loaf Mountain is a monadnock, a granite outcropping remaining on flatter land that was worn away by climatic events eons ago. Covered with sand and once capped with ferrous sandstone, Sugar Loaf rises steeply about 100 feet above surrounding terrain. An 8- to 12-minute trek to the top is worth the effort. A viewing area allows visitors a 360-degree view of the surrounding forestlands.*

Drive 7.4 miles past Middendorf Road to enter **Patrick**, a village entirely surrounded by the Sand Hills State Forest. Now reliant on timber trade, the community was once a distribution center for tar, resin, and turpentine. Note, on your left, Patrick Depot, a timeworn former train station situated in the town park alongside the railroad tracks.

Heading out of Patrick you reach the edge of Cheraw State Park after 3 miles.

Continue northeast to the intersection of US 1 and US 52, 9.8 miles from Patrick. Here, bear left (north) on merged US 1/US 52 toward Cheraw. Pass by the wetlands of Thompson Creek to enter lovely old Cheraw after 2 miles.

Historic Cheraw

Cheraw, which bills itself as "The Prettiest Town in Dixie," was settled in 1740 as the site of a small trading post and water mill. Named for a nearby Native American tribe, the town was laid out with wide streets, and a town green is the nucleus of a 218-acre historic district. Rich with gardens, parks, and the architectural legacy of more than two centuries, the area has a multitude of antebellum and Victorian structures.

The community was once the head of navigation for the Great Pee Dee River, used by steamboats in the 19th century to carry merchandise to Georgetown and the Atlantic Ocean. Local products sent downstream included cotton, indigo, tobacco, corn, rice, and cattle products. This commerce made Cheraw relatively wealthy, and the community once boasted the largest bank in South Carolina outside of Charleston.

Its more recent claim to fame is as the hometown of Dizzy Gillespie, whose legacy is bebop, the fast, intense form of jazz he helped create.

Upon entering Cheraw, turn right (northeast) on Market Street. After a block along the way, note on your left a gray, classic Queen Anne house built in 1825 (700 Market St.). On the opposite corner of Market and Christian Streets, is a home built around 1850 (617 Market St.). Next on your left, at 602 Market Street is **Saint Peter's Catholic Church** (ca. 1840).

In the next block, at 504 and 505 Market Street, on your left, are houses built around 1850. At the intersection with Huger Street is the deep red brick "new" Saint David's Episcopal Church on your left, built in Gothic style in 1916 (420 Market St.). The homes at 320, on your left, and 317 Market Street on your right were both built around 1822.

In the next block is the lovely, inviting town green area. The **Greater Cheraw Chamber of Commerce** (221 Market St.) houses a visitor center. Here also you'll find the tiny Greek Revival **Inglis-McIver Office** (ca. 1820), a statue of the musical great, Dizzy Gillespie, a historic water pump, and the steepled **Market Hall** (ca. 1837). The **Lyceum Museum** (ca. 1825) and **Town Hall** (1858) sit at the corner of Market and 2nd Streets, across from Market Hall. The **Merchant's Bank Building** (1835) is at 232 Market Street.

From the town green area, continue east on Market Street one more block, crossing over 2nd Street, and ride into a pretty little downtown shopping area flanked by many late 19th century buildings. At the end of Market Street, straight

Statue of native son Dizzy Gillespie at Cheraw town green Marie Goff

ahead on Front Steet, is the original **B. C. Moore and Sons** department store building. This store was once the cornerstone of a major retail chain throughout small towns in the Carolinas.

Turn right (southeast) on Front Street and go about two blocks, where Front Street bears left to cross a railroad track before ending at Church Street. Cross Church Street and enter the grounds of **Old St. David's Church and cemetery** (91 Church St.).

Constructed around 1770, this was the last Anglican "state church" built in South Carolina under King George III. It was used by both Patriot and British forces in the American Revolution, and by Confederate and Union soldiers during the Civil War. Veterans from every American war are buried in the venerable cemetery. In front of the cemetery is the first Confederate monument in South Carolina, erected in 1867 while the state was still under occupation by Federal troops.

From the churchyard, take a right and ride 0.2 mile northeast on Church Street to **Riverside Park**, at the east end of Church Street. The park overlooks the majestic **Great Pee Dee River**, and it once was the site of a steamboat landing and a covered bridge. This is the perfect place to take a break under the tall oak trees that shade picnic tables. Easy walking trails begin near the parking area.

The Great Pee Dee, which originates in the North Carolina mountains as the Yadkin River, is still passable by small boats for 175 winding miles downstream

View from park alongside Great Pee Dee River, Cheraw PATRICIA PIERCE

to Georgetown. Stephen Foster originally called his famous song "Way Down upon the Pee Dee River," but he was somehow later persuaded that "Suwannee" sounded more melodious. South of Cheraw, the river, teeming with catfish, bream, and redbreast, flows through lowland swamps and flood plains.

Backtrack on Church Street to Front Street. Turn right (northwest) on Front Street, go just one block crossing the railroad tracks, and turn left (southwest) back onto Church Street. Travel to the next corner and turn right (northwest) on 2nd Street to ride four blocks through more downtown before turning left (west) on Kershaw Street to see some of Cheraw's lovely, historic homes.

On your right at 212 Kershaw Street is a small bungalow, built around 1830. Cross over 3rd Street and view the 2-story white wooden house at 310 Kershaw Street built about 1826. Next on your right, a 1902 neoclassic frame Victorian house with massive columns is at 314 Kershaw Street. Turn left on Greene Street to get a full view of the stately **Prince-Stevenson House** (ca. 1824) at 223 Greene Street with its many columns and wide wraparound porch.

Turn around to head northwest again. At 307 Greene Street on your left is the brick **Wesley United Methodist Church**, which Dizzy Gillespie attended in his youth in the early 1900s. Notice the beautiful stained-glass windows.

On your left at 323 Greene Street is a late Queen Anne house, built in 1895, and an even older home at 327 Greene Street, constructed around 1860. Across the street at 328 Greene Street, is a cheerful looking old farmhouse built around 1815. Surprisingly, it is said to be haunted.

In the next block are antebellum houses at 406 Greene Street (ca. 1800) and 416 Greene Street (ca. 1855). Turn right (north) on Boundary Street, right (northeast) on North Street, and right (southeast) again on 3rd Street.

The first house on your right after you turn at 427 3rd Street is a more modern Georgian Revival home built in 1905 and enclosed with a stucco wall. On your left, farther along at 412 3rd Street, is a house built prior to 1856, and at 404 3rd Street, a home built around 1837.

At the next block at 335 3rd Street is a Dutch Colonial Revival house erected in 1901 that resembles a Quaker barn. On your left at 324 3rd Street is a brick neoclassic structure built in 1919.

On the next corner at Kershaw and 3rd Streets is the **Lafayette House** (ca. 1823), where the Marquis de Lafayette of American Revolution fame was entertained (235 3rd St.). Slow down to be sure to take in this very fancy white home. It does look like it was made for entertaining.

"The Teacherage," built prior to 1790 and the oldest house in town, is on your left at 230 3rd Street. A Charleston Box house (ca. 1800) is also on your left at 226 3rd Street, and the old **Presbyterian Manse** (ca. 1836) is at 219 3rd Street.

Cross over Market Street to see the beautiful **First United Methodist Church** (ca. 1851), built in Greek Revival style with four Doric columns, on your right at 113 3rd Street.

Continue a half block, turn right (southwest) on Church Street, go one block and turn right on Greene Street. After one more block, turn left on Market Street to head out of Cheraw by retracing your way back to US 52/US 1 South, crossing back over the Thompson Creek wetlands.

Cheraw to Bennettsville

When you reach the intersection where US 52 and US 1 split, bear left to continue southward on US 52 toward Society Hill, 11 miles away through farmlands and forest.

*One mile down the road, on your right, is the entrance to 7,361-acre **Cheraw State Park** (100 State Park Rd.). South Carolina's oldest state park, it has a golf course, a swimming and boating lake with bathhouse facilities, equestrian stables and trails, picnic areas, and nature trails. The idyllic lake is shaded by abundant bald cypress trees.*

The **Society Hill** area was settled in the early 1730s by Welsh Baptists migrating down from Pennsylvania and creating homesteads on both sides of the Pee Dee River. They built a society out of wilderness, and the area became known as Welsh Neck. Welsh Neck Baptist Church was established in 1738. By the time of the American Revolution, the area uphill from the river had become a trading village called Long Bluff.

The present name of the town derives from Saint David's Society, a group formed in 1777 to promote education in the area. They founded Saint David's Academy, which many years later was absorbed into the public school system.

After entering Society Hill, turn right (southwest) on US 15/US 52/Main Street. Most of the old structures in town are strung out along and just off Main Street.

A cluster worth a stop is around the ancient **Coker and Rogers General Store** (299 S. Main St.). The original portion was built in 1832. Next door and behind the store is the **Caleb Coker House** (309 S. Main St.), also built in 1832. Across the street, on the grounds of Main Street Park and Town Hall (280 S. Main St.), is the tiny Old Society Hill Library, built in 1826.

A half block farther, on the left, is the **Sompayrac Store** (323 S. Main St.), a portion of which dates to 1815. Travel a couple of blocks more to see the **Adam Marshall House** (454 S. Main St.), a Greek Revival home built around 1800. It is set back from the highway, on your right, just past Townsend Drive.

From here, turn around and head northeast on US 15/US 52/Main Street. After 0.4 mile, turn left (north) on Burns Street to visit **Trinity Episcopal Church**, at 171 Burns Street, just 0.1 mile farther. No longer in use, this impressive edifice was built in 1834 and remains structurally unchanged.

Return to the main highway and turn left (northeast). After 0.1 mile, US 52 forks left, but you continue straight ahead on US 15.

Less than a half mile farther you pass the **Society Hill Depot** (on your left, 400 N. Main St.), the town's rail station back when passenger trains actually came through Society Hill. It was constructed in 1866, a year after Sherman's Union troops burned the original structure.

As you continue northeast out of town on US 15, look for a right turn (east) to head downhill into the **Society Hill Boat Landing**, a pleasant, shady park with picnic tables on a deck providing your second overlook of the relaxing waters of the **Great Pee Dee River**.

The Great Pee Dee, named for a mostly-extinct Native American tribe, originates in the North Carolina mountains as the Yadkin River and is passable by small boats all the way to Winyah Bay and the Atlantic Ocean, at Georgetown. It is the main artery for northeastern South Carolina's broad coastal plain water basin emptying into Winyah Bay. A 70-mile stretch just south of here has State Scenic River status. The Pee Dee River Basin also includes the Little Pee Dee, Lynches, Black, and Waccamaw Rivers, among others.

Return to US 15 and turn right (northeast). Cross the bridge over the Great Pee Dee and over 4 miles of causeway and 4 more bridges before reaching high ground in Marlboro County. **Marlboro County** was formed in 1785 and named for colorful British General John Churchill, the first Duke of Marlborough. Here, cotton was and still is king.

Four more miles along US 15/US 401 brings you to **Bennettsville**, a charming town with stately old homes and a splendidly-preserved downtown area. It was established in 1819 specifically to serve as the Marlboro County Seat and is named for the state governor at that time. Bennettsville is the hometown of Marian Wright Edelman, an activist for civil rights and children's rights, and the founder and president emerita of the Children's Defense Fund.

At a fork where US 15/US 401 Bypass goes right, you stay left and travel straight ahead 1.7 miles on West Main Street to arrive at the **Bennettsville Visitor Center**, housed in the D. D. McColl House (1884), a Queen Anne-style, turreted house at 304 West Main Street, on your right. Park, step into this helpful venue, and enjoy the grounds and front porch rocking chairs. Next door at 300 West Main is an earlier D. D. McColl house, built in 1826 and now also a public facility.

D. D. McColl House, constructed in 1884 and now used as the Bennettsville Visitor Center John Clark

Leaving the visitor center, turn right, travel one block, and turn right (southwest) on Liberty Street. Drive one block, turn left (northwest) on McColl Street, and then one more block and turn left once again, on Broad Street. You are in the middle of beautifully preserved downtown Bennettsville, with quaint shops and loft apartments.

Soaring one block straight ahead is the **Marlboro County Courthouse**, at the intersection of Broad and Main Streets. It was completed in 1885 and sports a wide edifice and grand clock tower.

Turn right (northeast) on East Main, and ride past the **Kinney Building**, a 1909 retail structure at 200 East Main, and **First United Methodist Church** (ca. 1900) on your left with its impressive four-story bell tower at 311 East Main.

On your right at 402 East Main is the **Moore House**, dating from 1860, and the **Breeden House Inn**, an inviting bed and breakfast facility constructed around 1886, at 404 East Main. **"Magnolia"** is an 1853 clapboard house at 508 East Main, and the Whitney-Evans Funeral Home occupies a Victorian-style house built around 1879, across the street at 507 East Main.

Continue one more block and then turn right (south) on South Cook Street. Ride 0.3 mile through a pleasant Ozzie-and-Harriet era neighborhood, and then turn right (southwest) on Fayetteville Avenue. After 0.4 mile, note on your left, at 100 Fayetteville Avenue, **"Shiness,"** an impressive 1903 Georgian Revival-style house named for an ancestral home in Scotland and now occupied by the *Marlboro Herald-Advocate* newspaper and a gift shop.

Turn right (northwest) on South Marlboro Street. On your immediate right is the imposing Murchison School, a Romanesque Rival-style structure built in 1902 to house the town's white public school.

Halfway up the block, on your left at 122 South Marlboro, is the **Matheson Building**, built as a hotel in 1915. Across the street (123 S. Marlboro) are the **Dr. J. F. Kinney Home** (ca. 1902), now home to the **Marlboro County Historical**

Broad Street in downtown Bennettsville John Clark

Museum, as well as a small Doctor's Museum. The **Jennings-Brown House** (1826) and the old **Bennettsville Female Academy** (1833) are also located on the museum's grounds.

Conclude your journey by crossing East Main and circling the courthouse square. Palmetto trees and various historical markers and monuments punctuate the grounds, including the obligatory (in this neck of the woods) monument to fallen Confederate soldiers.

Beginning on the northwest corner of the courthouse square and extending to Cheraw Street is a block of Market Street once known as "The Gulf." For about a hundred years after Reconstruction, The Gulf served as a "Colored Business District" in this segregated town. Integration marked the eventual demise of this once vibrant shopping, entertainment, and professional office district.

Nearby Attractions

Bishopville and the South Carolina Cotton Museum, Blenheim, Coker College and Kalmia Gardens in Hartsville, Darlington International Raceway, Lake Wallace, Lee State Natural Area.

11

Old Conway and Country Roads

Conway to Dillon

General Description: This 65-mile country drive takes you through farmlands, forests, and wetlands, punctuated with a few small towns, representative of the rural South Carolina of the old days.

Special Attractions: Historic Conway, Kingston Lake, Little Pee Dee State Scenic River, Little Pee Dee State Park, Little Pee Dee Bay Heritage Preserve, and Dillon.

Location: Northeast part of the state.

Travel Season: All year.

Services: Accommodations and all other services are plentiful in and near Conway, Dillon, in addition to Myrtle Beach. Various food offerings and other supplies are available here and there at country stores along the way. Downtown Conway especially has high quality restaurants.

The Drive

This drive is about the South Carolina that used to be and the rural and small-town heritage that defined South Carolina from the 1700s until the latter part of the 20th century.

Begin in the old downtown of Conway, on the banks of the Waccamaw River and its Kingston Lake tributary. The city's well-preserved homes and live oak trees are magnificent. Next, you ride through miles full of tobacco, corn, soybean, hay, and cotton fields; forestlands, wetlands, and pastures with grazing cows; crossroads country stores and rustic villages and hamlets. Finally, you ride beside and over the Little Pee Dee State Scenic River and into the delightful nostalgia of historic Dillon.

Historic Conway

Conway was first settled as Kingston Village in 1735. In order to put distance from the British, its name was changed to Conwayborough in the early 1800s, after local political power Robert Conway. The town name was shortened to Conway in 1883.

Many old homes in this city of Spanish moss–draped live oak trees date from the 1800s, while most of the historic commercial buildings were constructed in the early 1900s after a major fire. Long before the 1950s, when tourism blossomed on

Old Conway and County Roads: Conway to Dillon

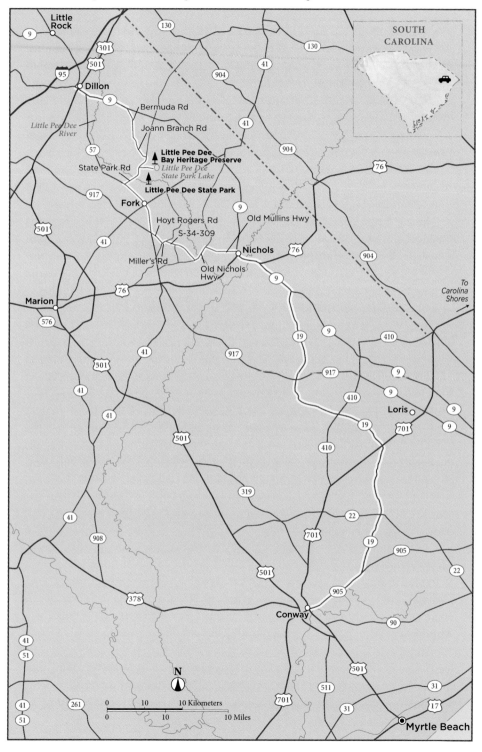

the coast 10 miles to the east, Conway flourished as a trade center for forest products and tobacco.

Begin at enchanting **Kingston Presbyterian Church** (1858) and **Old Village Burial Ground** at 800 Third Avenue.

Ride one block southwest to the corner of Third Avenue and Main Street to admire the Old Horry County Courthouse, now **Conway City Hall** (229 N. Main St.), an 1825 structure designed by famed South Carolina architect Robert Mills. It is across the street, to your left.

Turn right (northwest) on Main Street and peruse the many enticing shops in this block of old mercantile buildings and the Art Deco old movie theater at 335 Main Street, before turning right again (northeast) on Fourth Avenue.

Go one block and take a left (northwest) on Kingston Street. At the end of the block, look to your right to see the **Beaty-Spivey House** (ca. 1848) at 428 Kingston, also known as **"The Oaks."**

Live oaks, in fact, are treasured in Conway. There are more than 200 large specimens in Conway, all of which are protected and nine of which have their own names. Streets are altered to give them growing space.

Make a left (southwest) on Fifth Avenue and take a break at the Conway Visitor Center on the corner of Main and Fifth in the old post office building at 428 Main Street. The Wade Hampton Oak grows on the grounds.

Travel one more block on Fifth Avenue and turn right (northwest) on Laurel Street. The **Burroughs-Kleine House** (ca. 1870) at 509 Laurel and the **Norton-Nye-Williams House** (ca. 1910) at 511 Laurel are on your left. Turn right (northeast) on Sixth Avenue, and ride one block to the corner of Sixth and Main. The **Beaty-Little House** (ca. 1849), the **C. J. Epps House** (1902), and the **Sessions-Woodward-Shelley House** (1889), are at 507, 514, and 601 Main Street, respectively.

Turn left (northwest) on Main Street and drive one block. Then turn right (northeast) on Kingston Lake Drive, noticing the **Bryan House** (ca. 1912) at the corner at 606 Main Street.

This beautiful section of town down by the river includes **Sherwood Hill** (ca. 1910) at 504 Kingston Lake Drive and the **Arthur Burroughs House** (1903) at 500 Lakeside Drive, both on your left. Round the left corner (northwest) onto Lakeside Drive, ride one block and turn left (southwest) onto pretty little Applewhite Lane. On your right are the **Barnhill-Weston House** (ca. 1847) and the **Abbott House** (ca. 1880), at 905 and 907 Applewhite Lane.

Stay on Applewhite Lane as it turns northwest and then turn left (southwest) onto Lakewood Avenue. Go one block and admire, directly in front of you, the **Old Burroughs School**, built in 1905 at Main Street and Ninth Avenue. This building at 805 Main Street now houses the Horry County Museum which

Arthur M. Burroughs House, constructed in 1904 in Conway JOHN CLARK

features local artists and the prehistory, history, and culture of Horry County. It includes an aquarium where visitors can view living natural history exhibits and encounter a variety of fresh water fish found in local waters. The Conway Library is to the left of the museum.

Turn right (northwest) on Main and then left (southwest) on Ninth Avenue. Take a left (southeast) after one block on Laurel Street to view the **J. W. Holliday House** (1910) at 701 Laurel, the **McDermott-Mathis House** (ca. 1882) at 610 Laurel, and the **Causey House** (ca. 1876) at 605 Laurel.

At Sixth Avenue take a right (southwest), and you will immediately notice the **Confederate Oak**, protected in a little median at the end of the block. The simple granite marker at the foot of the oak is inscribed with a poem by Archibald Rutledge.

Turn right on Elm Street and ride 2 blocks northwest to the intersection with Ninth Avenue. The **Gully Store-Burroughs Hospital** (ca. 1870), now an abandoned residence, is on your left at 805 Elm Street. Continue one more block to enjoy the **Gurganus-Collins-Wilson House** (1864) at 902 Elm and the **Bell-Marsh-Pinson House** (ca. 1850) at 1001 Elm.

Turn left (southwest) on Tenth Street, go one block, and then take another left (southeast) on Pine Street. At the end of Pine Street, turn right (southwest) and enjoy the **Calhoun-McIver House** (ca. 1850) at 1300 Ninth Avenue, the

McNeil-Bell House (ca. 1870) at 1301 Ninth, and the **S. P. Hawes House** (1918) at 1309 Ninth.

At the intersection with Burroughs Street, turn left (southeast) and ride 3 blocks to Sixth Avenue. Take a left (northeast), go 2 blocks, and turn right (southeast) on Elm Street. Travel 3 blocks to the corner of Elm and Third Avenue. Look to your right to see the current **Horry County Courthouse** (1201 Third Ave.), built in 1908.

Ride one more block on Elm Street, turn left (northeast) on Second Avenue, and ease along 2 blocks, passing under the US Highway 501 Bridge to Myrtle Beach and arriving at one of several access points to the **Conway Riverwalk**, which offers terrific views of the Waccamaw River and its Kingston Lake tributary.

Conway Riverwalk, alongside the Waccamaw River JOHN CLARK

From the parking lot, turn right (northeast, then northwest) on Kingston Street. On your left is the **C. P. Quattlebaum House** (ca.1807) at 219 Kingston Street and the **Paul Quattlebaum House** (ca. 1850) at 225 Kingston Street. The **Old Village Burial Ground** and the **Kingston Presbyterian Church** (1858) will be in front of you at 800 Third Avenue.

Continue on Kingston Street as it jogs along the side of the church and turn right (east) on Fourth Avenue/SC 905, crossing a scenic section of the **Kingston Lake** tributary of the Waccamaw River and passing the old **Conway Train Depot** on your left. It was built in 1928 by the Atlantic Coast Line.

Rural Horry County to Little Pee Dee State Park

From the old Conway Train Depot, continue northeast on SC 905 through a fairly densely populated commercial and residential rural area toward the Hickory Grove community, about 4.6 miles away. Pass **Hickory Grove Baptist Church** (2710 SC 905, Conway), and 0.3 mile farther turn left (north) onto East Highway 19/S-26-19.

You are now entering the large rural section of Horry (pronounced "oh-ree") County, less than 15 geographic miles from the Myrtle Beach Grand Strand. It is named for Peter Horry, son of French Huguenot parents, a Patriot officer in the American Revolution, and state legislator after independence was won.

Horry County is the largest county in South Carolina geographically, and one of its fastest growing. Of course, most of the growth is in the coastal area and in the inland communities serving as bedrooms to coastal commerce. But here in the middle and western portions of the county, the agrarian culture is in many ways largely unchanged. In vast contrast to the coastal area, the rural population of Horry County is largely composed of families, black and white, that have lived here for generations.

Horry was never a large plantation county, but rather one of small farms. Many of those farms exist to this day, and the rural values of land, self-sufficiency, church, and the great outdoors seem prevalent. The crops you see as you ride through the countryside are tobacco, soybeans, corn, hay, cotton, and vegetables. Cattle and horses graze in pastures, and woodlands abound.

Ride through forest and farmland, crossing over the limited-access SC 22/Veterans Highway/Conway Bypass after 5 miles and continuing another 5 miles to the Allsbrook crossroad community at the intersection of SC 19 and SC 701.

Continue northwest on SC 19 for 10 more bucolic miles, passing through Sarvis Crossroads at the intersection of SC 19 and SC 45 and Play Cards Crossroads at the intersection of SC 19 and SC 410/Green Sea Road, eventually arriving in the Pleasant View community, at the intersection of SC 19 and SC 917.

Your next stop in this journey through the South Carolina of yesteryear is Nichols, 12 miles away. Cross SC 917 and ride north on SC 19 for more than 7.6 miles, before you take a slight left onto SC 9, which takes you northwest 4.7 miles into the hamlet of **Nichols**.

SC 9 coincides with US 76 just before you cross the lazy Lumber River to leave Horry County and enter **Marion County**, named for Revolutionary War hero General Francis "The Swamp Fox" Marion. Slide onto South Nichols Street/SC 9/US 76, passing the Nichols Post Office (206 S. Nichols St.), on your right after 3 blocks.

Nichols was almost entirely destroyed in South Carolina's great flood of 2015. Insurance and federal and state assistance have provided some recovery relief, but the tiny town's best days appear to be all in the past.

Go 2 more blocks on SC 9/US 76/South Nichols Street and then stay on SC 9 as it veers left off South Nichols for a block and then right (north) onto South Main Street, while US 76 heads southwest, to the left. Cross North Railroad Street and Floyd Street, before turning left (west) on Old Mullins Highway/S-34-30.

Ride 2.5 miles, passing Pineland Country Club on your right, before turning left (southwest) on S-34-60/Old Nichols Highway. Cruise 1.3 miles through the wetlands of the Little Pee Dee River, crossing the river and arriving at another classic country store, **Allread's Bait and Tackle and Groceries** (7538 Gilchrist Rd., Mullins), at the intersection with Gilchrist Road/S-34-309.

Turn right (northwest) here and drive 2.8 miles, to **Miller's United Methodist Church** (3571 Gilchrist Rd., Mullins), at the intersection with Miller's Road/S-34-21.

Turn left (southwest), go 0.3 mile, and turn right (northwest) on Hoyt Rogers Road/S-34-29. Ride 1.2 miles and turn right (north) on SC 41 North/David Bethea Memorial Highway. Drive 2.5 miles toward Fork, crossing the wetlands of Buck Swamp to enter Dillon County and the village of **Fork**.

Dillon County, whose motto is "Quietly Progressive," was formed in 1910 from the upper portion of Marion County because of local dissatisfaction with governance from the dominant lower part of the county. When formed, it took its name from its largest town, which, in turn took its name from James W. Dillon, an area merchant who had engineered a land deal for the local railroad line and depot. Historically, its economy was based on cotton. Cotton is still important, as you can see on the drive, but not as important as chickens, manufacturing, and the service industry along I-95.

When you reach the intersection in Fork where SC 41 goes right and SC 41 Alternate goes left, drive straight ahead (northwest) onto SC 57. *If you want to explore the Fork village, go right on SC 41 for a block or 2 and then circle around back to this intersection.* The modest little Fork Post Office is just 0.2 mile ahead, on the right at 4114 SC 57.

Pass hay fields and grazing cows on SC 57 until you reach the right-hand turnoff for State Park Road/S-17-22, 2.1 miles farther. Turn right (northeast). Carmichael's Bridge over the enchanting **Little Pee Dee State Scenic River** is slightly less than a mile farther along, as you enter 835-acre **Little Pee Dee State Park**. There are actually two bridges here, because the river branches around a wetland island. If you want to take pictures of this idyllic setting, pull off the road between the two bridges.

This crossing is part of a 48-mile section of the Little Pee Dee River that has State Scenic River status. It is characterized by tea-colored water, cypress-tupelo swamps, and white-sand stream bottoms and beaches. Fish include bluegill, large-mouth bass, redbreast sunfish, crappie, and catfish.

Next, you ride through stunningly white sand reminiscent of what you might find on Caribbean beaches. On your left are 301 acres of the **Little Pee Dee Bay Heritage Preserve**, acquired by the state's Department of Natural Resources to protect a medium-size Carolina bay on the edge of the river floodplain.

Carolina bays, mainly concentrated in the coastal plains of South and North Carolina, are shallow oval dents in the earth's surface, all oriented in the same northwest to southeast direction. They range in size from a few acres to more than 1,000 acres. Their origin is unknown. Typically, the bays collect rainwater and hold it slightly above normal water tables, thus giving rise to freshwater wetlands that support an abundance of plants and wildlife.

Scrub oaks and short pines punctuate the rolling sand hills. You may want to take a right (east) 0.4 mile farther along and ride down dirt-surfaced Blowhorn Place for a half mile or so to experience more of this natural oddity. When you reach Turkey Ridge Road, you are out of the State Park.

Park Access Road, which, as the name implies, gives you access to park facilities, is a mile from Carmichael's Bridge on your right. Turn (east) here and ride 1.1 cool, winding miles to the center of the park, on the shore of 54-acre Lake Norton. The facilities here are among the most modest of any in South Carolina's state park system, but if you are looking for peaceful solitude, you will find it here.

The park features **Beaver Pond Nature Trail** and has fishing boats, canoes, and kayaks for rent. Fishing for bream, bass, and catfish from the lake's dam is a pastime enjoyed by a few locals, and the park has restrooms, a small playground, and picnic and camping facilities.

Little Pee Dee River in Dillon County JOHN CLARK

Quaint Dillon

Backtrack on Park Access Road, turn right (north) on State Park Road/S-17-22, and exit the park 0.2 mile farther along. After another 0.7 mile, turn left (northwest) at Carmichael's Crossroads onto Joann Branch Road/S-17-155. Proceed 1.7 miles, bear left (northwest) onto Bermuda Road, and ride another 2.7 miles before merging into SC 9.

Next, drive northwest and cross the Little Pee Dee River and its wetlands again after 2.2 miles. An old bridge blocks views on your left, but there is a nice vista on the right as you cross.

Continue 2 more miles to downtown **Dillon**, entering on SC 9/East Main Street. Dillon was founded in 1888 as a railroad depot stopover, after landowners in the long-established, nearby settlement of Little Rock refused to grant rights of way to the railroad.

About a block after East Main crosses Old Marion Highway/Lockemy Highway and merges with SC 57, you are on a thoroughfare of attractive historic, early-20th-century homes. More are found in the neighborhood along South 14th Avenue, to your left. Note the **Columns Bed and Breakfast** on your right at 601 East Main Street, a circa 1903 Greek Revival residence with a wraparound porch supported by 34 columns.

The downtown historic district, composed mostly of buildings from the first half of the 20th century, begins in the 200 block of East Main Street. After you cross MacArthur Street and the railroad track to begin West Main Street, consider parking on Railroad Avenue, at the Amtrak station on your right, and looking around a bit.

Historic structures line North MacArthur Avenue, North Railroad Avenue, and the first 2 blocks of West Main Street, in addition to the stretch on East Main you have just passed. On MacArthur Avenue, note the **Chamber of Commerce** in the old bank building at 100 MacArthur and the community playhouse in the old Dillon Theatre.

Adjacent to the train station is the town clock, and across Main Street is a mural depicting Ben Bernanke, former chairman of the US Federal Reserve, who grew up in Dillon as the son of a local pharmacist and was educated in the local public schools.

Continue northwest on West Main Street for 2 blocks until you come to the intersection with Martin Luther King Boulevard/Third Avenue. The **Dillon County Courthouse**, completed in 1911, sits across the way, to your left, at 301 West Main Street. The spacious green in front of the courthouse and its numerous steps are a great place to take a stroll and enjoy the slow pace of Dillon.

Mural in downtown Dillon, depicting native son Ben Bernanke, former Chief of the Federal Reserve of the United States JOHN CLARK

Nearby Attractions

Gallivants Ferry, Latta, Lake View, Loris, Marion, Mullins, Myrtle Beach and the Grand Strand, L.W. Paul Living History Farm, Myrtle Beach State Park, South of the Border tourist stop complex on I-95, Waccamaw National Wildlife Refuge, Waccamaw River Park.

12

Tobacco Road

Williamsburg County

General Description: Visitors enjoy a 70-mile loop in the heart of South Carolina's coastal plain farm country, starting in live-oak-laden Kingstree beside the enchanting Black River, and crisscrossing the river several times as they travel past tobacco fields and green pastures, numerous churches, tin-roofed homesteads and shanties, pine forests and hardwood swamps, and ancient barns and old settlements while glimpsing the rural South of yesteryear.

Special Attractions: Black River, Kingstree, Williamsburg County Courthouse, Cooper's Country Store, Indiantown Presbyterian Church, Springbank Retreat Center.

Location: Eastern part of the state, midway between Georgetown and Florence.

Travel Season: All year.

Services: Kingstree and Lake City, have most basic services. For a full array of options, go to Florence, Sumter, or Georgetown.

The Drive

This drive begins in Kingstree, settled in 1732 by Scots-Irish immigrants. Change has come slowly since then. You pass by live oaks, old homes surrounded by Spanish moss–laden trees, and a courthouse designed by Robert Mills, and you visit the dark, mystical Black River. Travel through rich farmland filled with tobacco, cotton, corn, and soybeans, past pastures full of hay, cows, and horses, through pine forests and hardwood bottomlands, and over creeks and swamps. You see country stores, numerous small churches, farmhouses and shanties, and abandoned structures of many types as you pass through one of the most agrarian counties in the state. The tiny communities of Salters, Millwood, Cedar Swamp, Nesmith, Indiantown, Cades, and Hebron await as you visit the true Old South, one of miles and miles of country roads, with its rustic charm and beauty.

Kingstree to Salters

Begin in picturesque **Kingstree**, the county seat and largest town in the heavily agrarian county of Williamsburg. The town and county were settled by Scots-Irish Presbyterians from Ulster beginning in 1732, and the names in the phone book attest to their continuing heritage. McBrides, McClams, McClarys, McCreas, McCulloughs, McCutchens, McElveens, McFaddens, McGills, McIntoshes, McKenzies, McKnights, and many similar names abound.

Tobacco Road: Williamsburg County

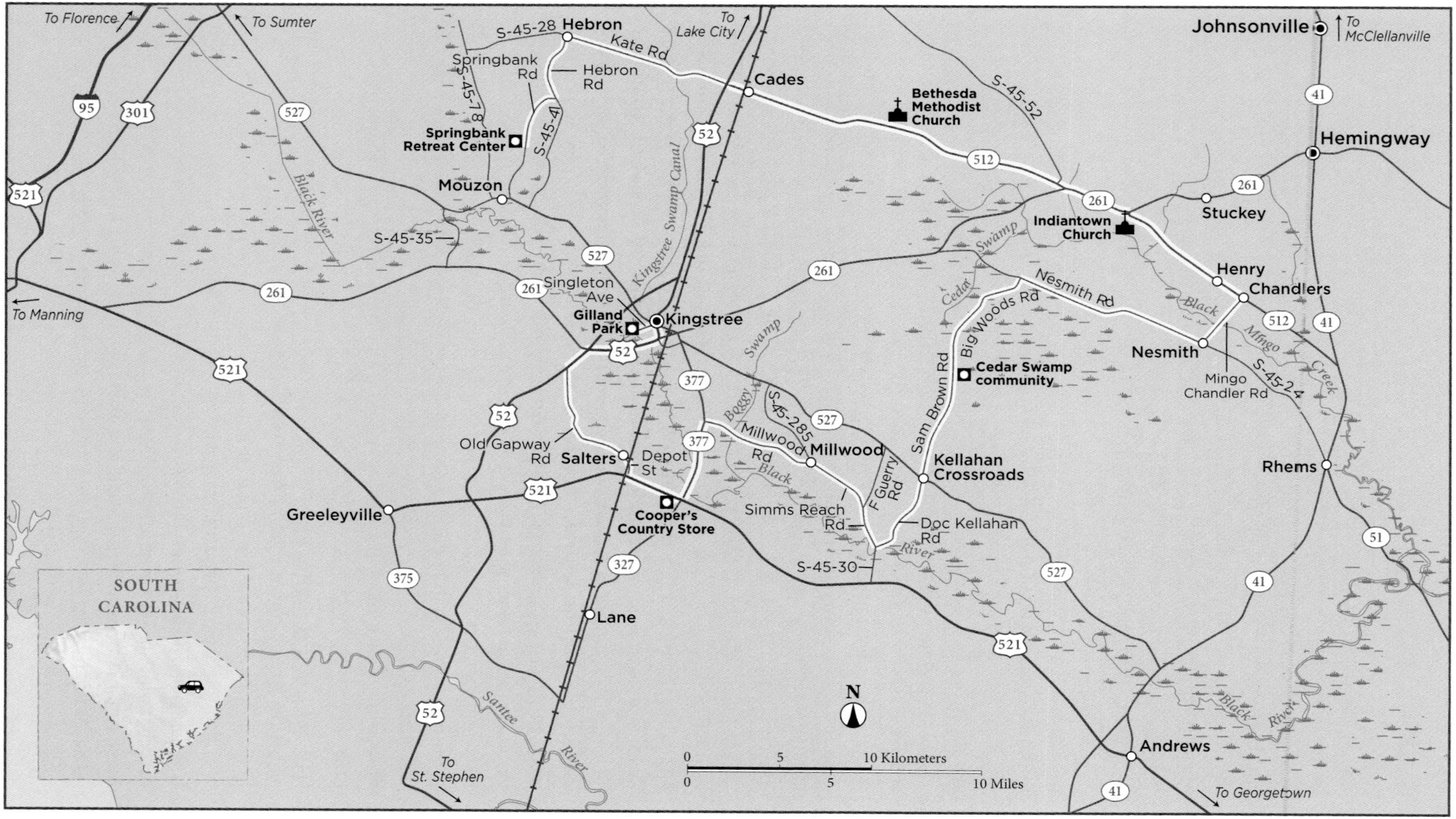

Williamsburg County remained largely rural and agricultural as other areas began to industrialize during the 20th century. For the most part, its inhabitants like things just as they are, away from the hustle and bustle of interstate highways and industrial smokestacks. When citizens think of the benefits of their locale, they think of hunting, fishing, and eating the world's best barbecue. In Williamsburg "barbecue" refers only to vinegar-based pork barbecue, but barbecue chicken is also popular. The word *"chicken"* is always attached to distinguish it from good ol' regular barbecue, which is pork, of course.

Williamsburgers also think heritage. A number of Revolutionary War skirmishes were fought throughout the county, and many citizens remain proud of the contributions of locals to the Confederate war effort. Because so many original families remain rooted here, genealogy and church history are of great significance.

One reason Williamsburg County and Kingstree are scenic is they have been spared from, or deprived of, depending on your point of view, economic development. Both have decreased in population about 25 percent over the past several decades—the county from 38,000 to about 30,000, and the town from 4,100 to about 3,300. The economy once depended on tobacco farming. Tobacco is still grown here, but its financial rewards are greatly diminished.

Begin your tour at **Gilland Memorial Park** (698 Singleton Ave./S-45-104), a municipal recreation area on the Black River a half mile from US 52, at the southwest end of Singleton Avenue in Kingstree. This site is one of 12 riverside properties that compose the 70-mile **Black River State Park and Water Trail**.

The Black River is free-flowing through undisturbed swamp forest. Low water levels provide white sandbars amid the inky black water which is produced by tannins leaching from leaves. The undeveloped land provides a home for endangered species such as the herb American chaffseed and the raptor swallow-tailed kite. The winding river is navigable for canoes and fishing boats many miles northward, and boaters can travel downstream all the way to Winyah Bay and Georgetown.

Gilland Park has a boat ramp, a picnic shelter, a playground, and a swimming area. The snowy white, sandy beach area contrasts beautifully with the black, mysterious river. For many years before the park was established, this area was known as the Scout Cabin, and generations of Kingstree area young folks learned to swim here.

From the park, proceed northeast about a half mile, crossing a bridge over the Kingstree Swamp Canal to reach the intersection with US 52/North Longstreet Street (named after Confederate General James Longstreet). Turn left (north), drive one block on US 52/North Longstreet Street and then turn right (east) on West Academy Street.

Black River at Gilland Park in Kingstree JOHN CLARK

Notice the many lovely homes and churches in this quiet, graceful town decked with live oak trees and Spanish moss. The Gothic Revival-style John Gotea Pressley House Is on your left, at 216 West Academy Street. It was constructed in 1855.

After two blocks, West Academy Street takes a right (south) turn and becomes North Academy Street. **Williamsburg Presbyterian Church**, on your right at 411 North Academy Street, was organized in 1736. The present structure was built in 1890. The M.F. Heller House at 405 North Academy was built in 1845 and then enlarged in 1895 into a late Victorian-style structure.

After four blocks on North Academy, you reach Mill Street, which begins the small downtown section.

Turn left (east) on East Mill Street and drive one block to see the **Williamsburgh Historical Museum**, in the old Carnegie Library building at 135 Hampton Avenue, on the corner of Mill Street and Hampton Avenue. Catty-corner to the county museum, on your left, is the C. Williams Rush Museum of African American Arts and Culture, at 200 Hampton Avenue.

Take a right (south) on Hampton and go one block to once bustling but now serene Main Street, which is also SC 261.

Across the street to your left is the old Kingstree Train Depot, still used by Amtrak. For half a century one of the mainstays on Main Street was a department store operated by the father of Dr. Joseph Goldstein, a Nobel Prize winner for medicine in 1985 and product of 12 years of education in the Kingstree area public school system.

Go right (west) on Main Street/SC 261 and ride 1.5 blocks. On your left, take in the **Williamsburg County Courthouse** (125 W. Main St.), designed by famed South Carolina architect Robert Mills and constructed in 1823, with its stately raised columned entrance. On the east side of the courthouse, a Confederate monument stands tall, with a soldier on top facing north to forever guard against invaders. There is a slight problem, however. The insignia on the soldier's apparel indicates that he is a Union man. It seems there was a mix-up when local folks ordered their statue from a manufacturer in Pennsylvania at the turn of the 20th century. The mystery of what happened to the Confederate soldier ordered by Williamsburg was solved a few years ago when people in York, Maine, realized they had a Rebel on their monument.

The Confederate monument is nicely balanced on the west side of the courthouse, where memorials to former US Supreme Court justice Thurgood Marshall and Dr. Martin Luther King Jr. have been erected. In 1954, Marshall represented parents in neighboring Clarendon County, who won their Supreme Court decision outlawing school segregation. King visited here in 1966 to launch eventually successful voting rights efforts in South Carolina.

Also on the courthouse grounds are markers honoring Revolutionary War, World Wars I and II, Korean War, and Vietnam War veterans, as well as a Liberty Bell recovered from the belfry of a demolished schoolhouse.

Proceed west on Main Street one more block, and then turn right (north) on North Longstreet Street, passing the **Greater Bethel African Methodist Episcopal Church** on your left (300 W. Main St.). After one block, turn left (west) and follow West Mill Street one block to its terminus at the Mill Street Landing, another segment of the **Black River State Park and Water Trail**. Park and walk to the water's edge to enjoy a quiet, lush, sylvan setting for the Black River and its backwaters.

Next, backtrack one block on West Mill, turn right (south) onto US 52/North Longstreet Street, ride one block, and then turn right (west) on US 52/West Main Street, in the direction of Charleston.

*You may wish to detour by going straight ahead (southeast) on South Longstreet Street/South Nelson Boulevard/SC 527 for 0.5 mile to visit **Thorntree**, a restored plantation house originally built in 1749 at a remote rural location and moved in 1969 to Fluitt-Nelson Memorial Park (5 Nelson Blvd.). It is the oldest surviving residence in the Pee Dee region of South Carolina.*

Main Street in Kingstree, one of South Carolina's oldest towns John Clark

One block after following US 52 as it heads southwest out of town, a small granite monument near the edge of the flowered median on your left marks the spot where the original **King's Tree** was located. When Scots-Irish Presbyterians sailed up the Black River from Georgetown in 1732 looking for a place to disembark, they noticed a tall white pine, rare in this area, towering above a low bluff. At the time, white pines were reserved for use as masts on the king's ships. The settlers landed and settled the area around the King's Tree, which eventually became the seat of government for the new county of Williamsburg, named after William of Orange, hero to the Ulstermen.

Continue a few yards past the median and cross the Lamar Nathan Johnson Bridge over the beautiful, serene **Black River**, protected as a State Scenic River.

Drive along a causeway above the ponds and wetlands that border the Black River. After 2.3 miles past the Black River crossing, pass by a road sign indicating SC 261 and Manning to the right as you continue left (southwest) to stay on US 52/Williamsburg County Highway.

About 0.8 mile farther, on your left, is a large cotton processing facility (5288 South Williamsburg County Highway, Salters). Just beyond, at 0.2 mile farther, turn left (southeast) on Old Gapway Road/S-45-197 to travel past tiny churches, modest rural homes, farm fields and pastures, and a patch of wetlands, toward Salters, 4.4 miles away.

When you pass by a large, charming dwelling on your right, you have reached the quaint railroad village of **Salters**. Turn right (southwest) on S-45-145/Depot Street, split from the east side of town by a still heavily used double railroad track. Carolina Street/S-45-146 runs parallel to Depot Street on the other side of the track. Continue 0.3 mile on Depot Street.

Salters is a throwback to early 20th-century rural South Carolina. Mostly African American folks live in the modest cottages on the east side of the tracks, and mostly white folks live in the homes on the west side. In the case of both races, most inhabitants are descendants of families that have lived in the area for almost two centuries.

Bright flowers adorn the attractively manicured railroad median as you ease your way 0.3 mile down Depot Street. Stately moss-hung oaks canopy the roads on both sides of the train tracks, and pecan trees shade the yards. You pass the **Salters Post Office** (33 Depot St.) and comfortable old country homes, including a rambling Victorian house (5 Depot St.) on your right at the end of the street.

Where Depot Street ends, turn left (east) onto Glad Street/S-45-19. Pass the long-abandoned **Salters Depot Railroad Station**, and, after crossing the train tracks, a small volunteer fire department (161 Glad St.).

Salters to Nesmith

Continue southeast and merge into US 521/B. J. Gordon Highway after 0.4 mile and continue eastward 1.5 more miles, past kudzu and the wetlands of Thorntree Swamp to arrive at Cooper's Country Store at the intersection of US 521 and SC 377 (6945 US 521, Salters).

Cooper's Country Store is an emporium of eclectic delights. Famous for its smoked ham and fresh Williamsburg County barbecue, it also sells boiled peanuts, Exxon gasoline, hunting and fishing licenses, pit and English bulldogs, guns and ammo, fishing canes, lawn mowers, kitchenware, men's underwear and ladies' "quality" lingerie, plumbing fixtures, tools, oil burning lamps, laundry scrub boards, and a variety of snacks and groceries.

This is a great place to take a break. Enjoy a cold, tangy Blenheim Ginger Ale along with a Moon Pie or a pack of Nabs while relaxing at an adjacent picnic table under the shade of old pecan trees. Clean restrooms are attached to the exterior of the building. Behind the main building is a screened-in structure where cured hams hang.

Several generations of the Burrows and Cooper families have operated this significant cultural and architectural example of an early-20th-century country store. It started with the motto "We Serve the Needs of the Neighborhood." Originally, the owners lived on the second story, above the white wooden store. The home's enclosed front porch stretches over the gasoline pumps.

Leave the store and head east a few yards to a stop sign. Turn left on SC 377/ Martin Luther King, Jr. Highway at the Bryan's Crossroads intersection and head north in the direction of Kingstree. On your left is a historical marker noting the Battle of Lower Bridge during the American Revolution, where Patriot general Francis Marion and his irregulars defeated the British in 1781 and thwarted their attempt to cross the Black River and invade the heart of Williamsburg County.

You again cross the beautiful, winding Black River, with attractive views east and west. Three more bridges carry you over sprawling wetlands as you travel 2.9 miles to S-45-142/Millwood Road, where you turn right (east).

Drive 4 miles, passing Boggy Swamp, farm fields, and hunt clubs to reach the heart of the old **Millwood** community. A comfortable old farmhouse, Millwood Methodist Church (9 Millwood Rd., Kingstree), the Millwood Community Center, and remnants of once-thriving commerce compose "downtown" Millwood.

Bear right (southeast) on S-45-285/Simms Reach Road, which becomes S-45-30/Simms Reach Road after 2.5 miles. Tobacco, corn, soybeans, and pine trees are plentiful, and this route includes a few old-timey tobacco curing barns, rickety buildings about 2 stories high, topped by tin roofs, with their sides often wrapped in green roofing material. Advertising on these back roads is thankfully scarce, and the few signs you see are often suggestions for saving your soul or directions to nearby churches.

About a mile and a half farther along S-45-30/Simms Reach Road (4 miles from Millwood), you cross the Black River again, this time along one of its most scenic stretches. There are small boat landings on both sides of the river, and you can often see locals lolling in small boats, practicing the official pastime of Williamsburg: goin' fishin'. Bass, redbreast, crappie, catfish, and bream await baited hooks. Moss-laden trees overhang the stream, and lily pads decorate the shallows. Tupelos, cypresses, and live oaks frame the bucolic scene, while birds of prey circle lazily above, searching for victims in the dense wetlands below.

After you reach the far (west) side of the river, turn around and recross the bridge, heading east. Just beyond the east side of the river, turn right (northeast) on S-45-584/Doc Kellahan Road toward Kellahan Crossroads, 3 miles away; the first mile is an unpaved, single lane road through mysterious wetlands on both

Tobacco field ready for harvest MARIE GOFF

sides. When you reach Kellahan Crossroads, cross over SC 527 and continue north toward the **Cedar Swamp** community on S-45-254/Sam Brown Road.

(If recent rains have muddied the road, or if you just want to avoid a dirt road, go north from the bridge 1.3 miles on S-45-30/Sims Reach Road. At the fork, bear right (northeast) on S-45-30/F. Guerry Road to SC 527. Turn right (southeast) and go 1.6 miles on SC 527 to reach Kellahan Crossroads, and then turn left on S-45-254/Sam Brown Road.)

This rich crop and pasture land is amid some of the earliest land cleared and settled by Scots-Irish colonials in the first half of the 18th century. Horses, hogs, tobacco, and soybeans reign here, and the community was a longtime hotbed of a sport called lancing, in which riders use jousting lances not to attack each other, but to spear small rings dangling from cross-arms. Renowned financier and presidential adviser Bernard Baruch owned nearby Little Hobcaw Plantation in this area and sometimes attended local lancing tournaments.

After 4.6 miles, turn left (northwest) onto S-45-218/Big Woods Road to cross through the middle of the Cedar Swamp community. Immediately after you turn, **Cedar Grove Baptist Church** is on your left (3905 Big Woods Rd., Kingstree). Continue northeast 3.8 miles on S-45-218, which becomes Kennedyville Road after a short distance. Pass the **Kennedyville United Methodist Church** (1293 Kennedyville Rd.), and the road dead-ends at S-45-24/Nesmith Road. Turn right (southeast) toward the Nesmith community, 6.7 miles away.

After passing wetlands and more rich farmland, you enter **Nesmith**, which boasts a few ramshackle homes, a volunteer fire station, a modest little post office (11 Mingo Chandler Rd.), and abandoned buildings. A railroad track splits the bleak settlement that once thrived, many years ago. Cross the tracks and turn left (northeast) on S-45-121/Mingo Chandler Road, toward Henry.

Nesmith to Springbank

Cross Black Mingo Creek, and its scenic wetlands to reach an intersection with SC 512/Henry Road, 2.2 miles from Nesmith. Take a left (northwest) toward Indiantown, about 5 miles away. Pass over the railroad tracks in Henry after a half mile and continue through countryside full of modest farmhouses, cotton, tobacco, corn, and soybeans. As you approach Indiantown, the farmhouses become more impressive.

Pass over wetlands to an intersection with SC 261, 4.3 miles from the Henry railroad tracks. Turn left (west) on SC 512/SC 261/Hemingway Highway. A sign points toward Kingstree. Travel only about 0.2 mile, crossing more wetlands, and pull into the parking lot of lovely **Indiantown Presbyterian Church** on your left (4865 Hemingway Hwy., Hemingway). This congregation was organized in

Indiantown Presbyterian Church, built in 1830 by Scots-Irish settlers of Williamsburg County JOHN CLARK

1757, and its first building was destroyed by British troops in 1780. The present structure, the third on this site, was completed in 1830. The old cemetery beside the building is especially appealing, and includes the grave of Major John James, a hero of the Revolutionary War.

Leave Indiantown Presbyterian Church and continue west through farmland on SC 512/SC 261, past the old Indiantown School, the community school for whites during the first two-thirds of the 20th century, and the old Battery Park School, once the community school for African Americans. After 2.1 miles, bear to the right (northwest) on SC 512/Cade Road toward Cades, as SC 261 veers southwest in the direction of Kingstree.

This 11.5-mile stretch to Cades is an exceptionally pretty roadway. After crossing more swamp wetlands, you pass through gently rolling, verdant pastures, forests, and crop fields. Horses and cows graze in the shade of hardwoods and drink from scattered creeks and ponds. Cowbirds, whose ancestors migrated from Africa on slave ships, stand watch over the cattle in their search for bugs. Attractive farm dwellings can be spotted among the trees.

About 5 miles along the way, look for a stone memorial marker for the old **Cooper Academy**, on your right, just before you pass the modern **Bethesda Methodist Church** building (2000 Cade Rd., Cades). The academy was built in 1905 as a private boarding school for African American children and served this purpose until 1926, when it was absorbed into the public school system. Continue eastward 6.6 miles, past the old, white frame Bethesda Methodist Church building on your left, tin-roofed farm homes, and more tobacco and cotton fields until you reach the village of **Cades**, left behind when the railroad stopped bringing passengers and US 52 blossomed a half mile away.

Cross the railroad tracks and continue a half mile to the junction with US 52.

"Grandmother Oak" at Springbank Retreat Center for Eco-Spirituality and the Arts JOHN CLARK

Cross US 52 and continue westward on SC 28/Cade Road toward the Hebron community, 5.9 miles away. Pass by more attractive farm structures, cotton and tobacco fields, pastures, and woodlands. At the crossroads settlement of **Hebron**, you'll see the old Hebron School on your left. A few homes dot the area, along with the steepled white frame **Hebron United Methodist Church** (2273 Hebron Rd., Cades).

Turn left (south) on S-45-47/Hebron Road. After 2.5 miles, turn right onto S-45-114/ Springbank Road. This is a pleasant lane through magnolias, dogwoods, oaks, and pines. You begin a long stretch past the walls of Springfield Plantation on your left as the **Springbank Retreat Center** (1345 Springbank Rd., King-stree) unfolds on your right, with the back entrance gate 0.6 mile from the turn onto Springbank Road.

Formerly a rice and cotton plantation, begun in 1782, and then a quail-hunting reserve, Springbank became a monastery in 1955, known for its social outreach programs. In the 1980s, it was deeded in trust to an ecumenical board of directors. Today it is an 80-acre retreat facility that offers seminars, workshops, and other healing and renewal experiences, as well as hiking trails.

A sign marks the back entrance. Pull into Springbank and enjoy the natural beauty of the lush grounds. The landscape features live oaks and flowering camellias, as well as a swamp wilderness filled with stately gums. Your drive takes you past an enormous, sprawling live oak known as "The Grandmother Tree," estimated to be about a thousand years old.

After a few yards farther, you are in front of the lovely white-columned mansion headquarters, attached to a chapel constructed of cypress by Dominican priests who previously lived here. You can stop and admire the grounds before concluding your scenic drive by exiting through the soothing, magnolia-lined front drive.

Nearby Attractions

Black River Preserve, Lake City, Ramsey Grove State Park, Waccamaw National Wildlife Refuge, Williamsburg Presbyterian Cemetery, Woods Bay State Park.

13

Waccamaw Neck

Murrells Inlet to Pawleys Island

General Description: This 25-mile coastal drive begins in the restaurant-laden fishing village of Murrells Inlet and takes travelers to salty Huntington Beach State Park, exquisite Brookgreen Gardens, and the dark Waccamaw River before ending at the beaches of rustic Pawleys Island.

Special Attractions: Murrells Inlet Marsh Walk and eclectic seafood restaurants, Huntington Beach State Park, Atalaya, Brookgreen Gardens, Waccamaw River, Sandy Island, Litchfield Beach, Pawleys Island.

Location: Northern coast.

Travel Season: To enjoy the marsh walk, beaches, and gardens, this drive is best enjoyed during the spring, summer, and fall. Brookgreen Gardens is especially beautiful in spring when the colorful azaleas are in bloom, and fall is the perfect time to feast on oysters at the beach.

Services: Accommodations and all other services are plentiful, especially in Myrtle Beach, but also in Surfside Beach, Garden City, Murrells Inlet, Litchfield Beach, Pawleys Island, and Georgetown.

The Drive

This drive begins in the midst of the lush tidal, salt marsh creeks of the Murrells Inlet fishing village, taking you past the numerous and eclectic seafood restaurants and harbor vistas that make Murrells Inlet the seafood capital of South Carolina. Next, pass by stately oaks to visit Huntington Beach with its rolling sandy dunes and Moorish old seaside mansion, before stopping at Brookgreen Gardens, home to the largest and most comprehensive collection of American figurative sculpture in the country, set in exquisite botanical gardens. You glimpse isolated Sandy Island, the largest undeveloped tract remaining in the Waccamaw Neck area, continue past touristy Litchfield Beach, and wind up at rustic Pawleys Island, once a resort island for wealthy South Carolina plantation owners and now "arrogantly shabby."

Murrells Inlet

Begin this ride in the heart of Murrells Inlet, South Carolina's Seafood Capital, at the Murrells Inlet Marsh Walk on US 17 Business where it intersects with Maclean Avenue in the gravel parking lot that serves the south end of the Marsh Walk and popular seafood restaurants such as the Claw House (4097 US 17 Business) and the Dead Dog Saloon.

Waccamaw Neck: Murrells Inlet to Pawleys Island

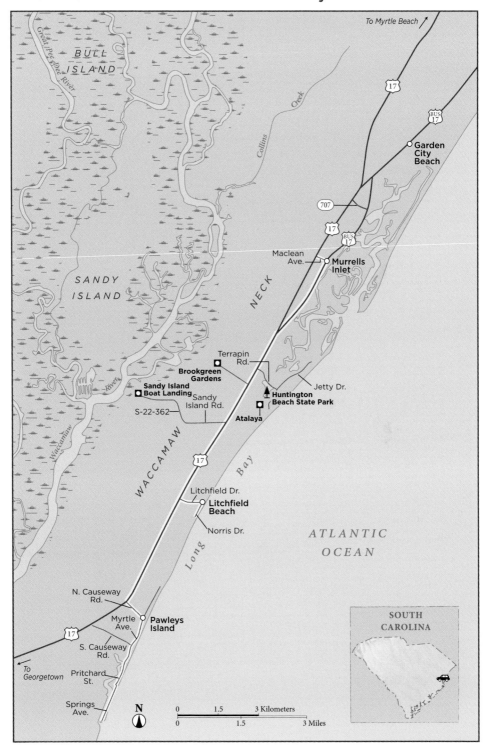

To Myrtle Beach

Great Pee Dee River

BULL ISLAND

Collins Creek

17

BUS 17

Garden City Beach

707

17

BUS 17

Maclean Ave.

Murrells Inlet

NECK

SANDY ISLAND

Terrapin Rd.

Brookgreen Gardens

Jetty Dr.

Sandy Island Boat Landing

Huntington Beach State Park

Sandy Island Rd.

S-22-362

Atalaya

River

Waccamaw River

WACCAMAW

17

Bay

Litchfield Dr.

Litchfield Beach

Norris Dr.

ATLANTIC OCEAN

Long

N. Causeway Rd.

Myrtle Ave.

Pawleys Island

17

S. Causeway Rd.

To Georgetown

Pritchard St.

Springs Ave.

SOUTH CAROLINA

N

0   1.5   3 Kilometers
0   1.5   3 Miles

Park here and walk northward along the boardwalk to take in views of the marsh, shrimping and recreational boats, and restaurant decks to your left along the marsh. The boardwalk offers educational information along the way about the history of Murrells Inlet, the ecology of the salt marsh, as well as the fish, birds, and other wildlife you may encounter here in the coastal waterways.

Founded in the late 18th century by a Captain Morrall, **Murrells Inlet**, built beside tidal and salt marsh creeks, has supplied the Waccamaw Neck area with fresh seafood for more than 200 years. This quaint fishing village remains a port for commercial fishing boats and home to many deep-sea fishing charter vessels even to this day.

"Waccamaw Neck" is the name of the peninsular area south of Myrtle Beach between the Atlantic Ocean on the east side and the Waccamaw River and its wetlands on the west side. It extends from the south side of Myrtle Beach to the mouths of the Waccamaw, Great Pee Dee, and Black Rivers flowing into Winyah Bay and separating the Waccamaw Neck from Georgetown.

Waterside wedding at Murrells Inlet John Clark

Part of the intrigue of Murrells Inlet is its interesting folklore. **Drunken Jack Island**, off the coast of Murrells Inlet, is said to have been the site where an old pirate, Jack, was accidentally marooned with no provisions save his shipmates' rum supply. When the ship returned to the island months later to retrieve the rum cargo, the crew found case after case of empty rum bottles all along the shore, as well as the bones of Jack. This same island is believed to be where Blackbeard's treasure is buried, and it is the first recorded site of the Hot Fish Club clubhouse. Formed before 1816 by the planters of All Saints Parish and dedicated to epicurean pursuits, this social club most likely dissolved before the Civil War. A nearby restaurant now has this name.

Murrells Inlet is also home to the ghost of Alice Flagg. The legend, which began in 1849, tells the story of Alice, who fell in love with a man of a different social class. Because he did not meet with her parents' approval, he and Alice became secretly engaged. When Alice's mother discovered the engagement ring, Alice was sent to a school in Charleston to separate the pair. Alice became ill in Charleston, so her brother was sent to retrieve her. On their journey home to Murrells Inlet, Alice died and was buried in the **All Saints Church Waccamaw Episcopal cemetery** (10172 Ocean Hwy. 17 South, Pawleys Island), but without her engagement ring. It is said that Alice is still sighted today in the cemetery, searching for her ring.

If the ghosts of Murrells Inlet don't tickle your fancy, then perhaps the dozens of restaurants found here, most of which are arranged along US Business 17, will delight you and your taste buds. You can't go wrong at any of the village's eating establishments.

Exit the parking lot and drive south on US Business 17.

To your left are the beach and a series of marsh creeks—Whale, Parsonage, Allston, and Woodland. Homes, some belonging to writers and other mild celebrities, are tucked behind old oaks, amid the numerous restaurants and pubs. The drive down "restaurant row" to the stop sign at US 17 South is only 2.5 miles.

When you arrive at the end of US Business 17, cross over US 17 North and merge onto US 17 South toward Huntington Beach State Park.

Huntington Beach State Park

Huntington Beach State Park (16148 Ocean Hwy., Murrells Inlet) is on your left (east), approximately 1.2 miles from US Business 17. Turn into the park on Terrapin Road. There is a small admission fee.

Huntington Beach is in an area where rice plantations flourished in the 18th and 19th centuries. The park's 2,500 acres are remarkable for their range of habitats, including sandy ocean beachfront, freshwater and saltwater marsh, dunes, shrub thickets, freshwater lagoons, maritime forest, rock jetties, and inlets, not to mention the Atlantic Ocean. Saltwater marsh is considered the most productive habitat in the world, so this park is an exceptional example of a natural beach-dune-estuary system.

Much of Huntington Beach's marsh is now registered under the state's Heritage Trust Program to preserve the park's pristine nature. More than 300 bird species are found here, and Huntington Beach is probably best known for its public bird-watching, perhaps the best not only in South Carolina but on the entire East Coast.

Follow Terrapin Road, the main park road, 0.7 mile to the first stop sign. The stand of hardwoods near the park entrance is home to a variety of birds, including warblers year-round, chickadees, titmice, nuthatches, sapsuckers, solitary vireos, brown creepers, northern parulas, and eastern screech owls.

Cross over a causeway where oyster beds bulge from the saltwater mud on your left and alligators bask in the sun to your right. Egrets wade in the marsh near the wooden walkways that stretch deep into the marsh. The causeway divides freshwater marsh on the south side from saltwater marsh on the north side. Turn left onto Jetty Drive to drive toward the northern end of the park.

Stop in at the **Environmental Education Center**, a few yards along, on your left. It offers a wide variety of programming, including the chance to see loggerhead turtles and other endangered plant and animal species up close. A boardwalk offers a great view of the salt marsh. To the right of the road is the south entrance to the Sandpiper Pond Nature Trail.

Continue northward along Jetty Drive, lined with thick shrubs, pines, live oaks, wax myrtle, red cedar, tamarisk, groundsel, yaupon holly, yellow jessamine, smilax, Virginia creeper, black needle rush, and salt marsh aster. Birds found here include common ground dove, prairie warbler (spring and summer), gray catbird, rufous-sided towhee, Carolina wren, yellow-rumped warbler, cedar waxwing, robin, sparrows, hawks, and painted bunting (in spring and early summer).

The road dead-ends, 1.7 miles from Terrapin Road, into a large paved parking area where picnic tables, vending machines, restrooms, a large grass meadow, a long expanse of wide beach, and two nature trails can be accessed. This is a great place to get out of your car and take in terrific views of the Atlantic Ocean to your right and Oaks Creek and marshlands to your left. The salt marsh is dominated by cordgrass (spartina). Birds in the marsh area include herons (tricolored and great blue), egrets (snowy and great), willet, American oystercatchers, plovers (black-bellied and semipalmated), sandpipers, clapper rails, boat-tailed grackles, seaside sparrows (sharp-tailed sparrows in winter), and marsh wrens.

Both birds and birders flock on and near the jetties protecting the sea entrance to Murrells Inlet, a 2-mile walk northward from the parking area. Some birds seen here include ruddy turnstones, purple sandpipers, double-crested cormorants, horned grebes, and scooters. Rare birds found are old squaws, eider and harlequin ducks, greater cormorants, greater black-backed gulls, and brants. Offshore are gannets, common loons, and black skimmers.

On the lagoon and in the dunes, live gulls, terns, snow buntings, longspurs, short-eared owls, ground doves, marsh wrens, and, in winter, sedge wrens. Sparrows that make their home here include seaside, rare Savannah, Le Conte's sharp-tailed, and Ipswich varieties.

If you happen to visit the park late into the evening, you may get a glimpse of the ghost of Theodosia Burr Alston, married to a local plantation owner and daughter of American founding father Aaron Burr. Theodosia disappeared after boarding the *Patriot* in Georgetown on December 30, 1812. After the ship left Georgetown, it was never seen again. On foggy nights Theodosia is sometimes sighted suspended above the waves of the Atlantic Ocean.

Courtyard of Atalaya, former beachside of sculptor Anna Huntington, at Huntington Beach State Park JOHN CLARK

Backtrack on Jetty Drive (south) to Terrapin Road intersection. Continue southward as Jetty Drive becomes Seashore Drive. Just past the intersection is a parking lot on your left. This is also a good place to stop and take in the natural beauty of this area.

A dock on the right (west) side of the road, across from the parking lot, extends into the freshwater lagoon full of ducks, tundra swans, coots, common moorhens, pied-billed grebes, anhingas, bald eagles, sedge wrens, yellowthroat warblers, sora rails, scaup, mergansers, buffleheads, least bitterns, and black-crowned night herons. In summer, least terns and white ibis are found here. Alligators in large numbers and pond sliders represent the reptiles here, swimming with bass and bream.

Continue south on Seashore Drive 0.2 mile more to a large parking area and **Atalaya**. This National Historic Landmark, long called "The Castle" by locals, is the Moorish-style former vacation home and studio of philanthropists Archer and Anna Hyatt Huntington, the creators of nearby Brookgreen Gardens. You are welcome to stroll through the complex on your own, but guided tours are also available.

The park offers picnic areas with shelters, boardwalks, surf fishing, crabbing, and bird-watching, as well as a visitor center and gift shop. Two camping areas offer RV and primitive camping as well as a 200-person group site. The beach is easily accessible from this parking area, where restrooms, shower facilities, and picnic grounds are also located.

From the south-end parking area, backtrack on Seashore Drive and turn left on Terrapin Road to exit Huntington Beach State Park. Turn left (south) onto US 17 South.

Brookgreen Gardens

Brookgreen Gardens (1931 Brookgreen Dr., Murrells Inlet) is 0.4 mile down the highway on your right (west). You can't miss Anna Hyatt Huntington's magnificent statue, *Fighting Stallions,* at the entrance.

Brookgreen Gardens, a National Historic Landmark, was established in 1931 by Archer and Anna Hyatt Huntington to preserve the beauty of the area and to display sculpture in an outdoor setting. Brookgreen was the first public sculpture garden in America, and it was constructed on the site of four colonial rice and indigo plantations covering more than 9,000 acres of savannah, marshes, and beaches.

Brookgreen charges an admission fee and is open daily year-round. If you choose to visit, plan to allocate at least a couple of hours.

Famous "Fighting Stallions" sculpture, created by Anna Huntington, at entrance to Brookgreen Gardens PATRICIA PIERCE

Beautiful live oaks, formal gardens, sculpture gardens, and botanical gardens are found here, as well as a Low Country Zoo and a butterfly sanctuary. A serpentine boardwalk around a half-acre cypress swamp takes you to an impressive aviary featuring herons, egrets, ibis, bald eagles, owls, and red-tailed hawks. In addition, a herd of about 40 deer roam a 20-acre enclosed savannah. The nature trail passes a native plant garden, which features insect-eating Venus-flytraps and pitcher plants, as well as other plant life.

A place of great natural beauty, Brookgreen Gardens has the largest and most comprehensive outdoor collection of American figurative sculpture in the world. Developed first as a showplace for the works of Anna Hyatt Huntington, today more than 1,200 19th- and 20th-century sculptures are on display. Huntington designed the original gardens in the shape of a butterfly wing. Visitors can now enjoy additional gardens, such as the Fountain of Muses, Dogwood, Palmetto, Lowcountry Center, and the Cultural Gardens showcasing a variety of flora and fauna. The 250-year-old **Live Oak Allee**, which leads from the former site of the Brookgreen Plantation mansion, is a particular attraction.

The gardens are a good bird-watching area, especially in autumn and winter. The birds move in mixed flocks, comprising red-bellied and downy woodpeckers, yellow-bellied sapsuckers, eastern phoebes, Carolina chickadees, tufted titmice, white-breasted nuthatches, Carolina wrens, golden-crowned and ruby-crowned kinglets, blue-gray gnat-catchers, eastern bluebirds, hermit thrushes, American robins, brown thrashers, solitary vireos, and warblers of many varieties, including the orange-crowned, yellow-rumped, pin, palm, black-and-white, and common yellowthroat. Sparrows found here in winter include chipping, field, song, swamp, and white-throated.

Birds of prey in the neighborhood include American kestrel and sharp-shinned, red-tailed, red-bellied, and Cooper's hawks, as well as turkey vultures, ospreys (common in spring), bald eagles, Northern harriers, and the rare peregrine falcon and merlin. Great horned owls can sometimes be heard or glimpsed at closing time.

The best bird viewing at Brookgreen Gardens is along the Waccamaw River and Brookgreen Creek, at the back of the park. The latter has an observation deck. One might find rails, which are more readily heard than seen, marsh wrens, least and American bitterns, common moorhens, wood ducks, American wigeons, American black ducks, Canada geese, and bald eagles.

Brookgreen to Pawleys Island

Exit Brookgreen and turn right (south) onto US 17/Ocean Highway. Ride a mile through maritime forest and then turn right (west) onto S-22-362/Sandy Island

Road. After 1.6 miles Sandy Island Road becomes Allston Boulevard. Continue another 0.8 mile to the boat landing on the **Waccamaw River** at the end of Allston Boulevard. Across the water is forested **Sandy Island**, a pristine piece of property between the Waccamaw and Pee Dee Rivers.

The island is the largest undeveloped tract remaining in the Waccamaw Neck, and the largest freshwater island in the east. At 4 miles wide and 6 miles long, the property is a welcome contrast to the highly developed communities north of Pawleys Island. No bridge spans the waters of the Pee Dee or Waccamaw River to reach the island, and, happily, none ever will, thanks to the one hundred or so residents of the Gullah community of Sandy Island, most of whom are descendants of freed slaves in the area.

If you want to visit, you need to bring your own boat or make arrangements with several of the local tour guides offering ferry trips across to the island. Residents work and attend school on the mainland, but at the end of the day, they retreat by boat to a serene existence on the island. They came together in the early 1990s, when their way of life was threatened by possible development and construction of a bridge from the mainland. The community united and, with assistance from public agencies, local environmental groups, and the business community, they preserved their island's sensitive ecosystem and protected their community from future development.

The South Carolina Department of Transportation purchased a majority of the 12,000-acre island with the financial assistance of the Nature Conservancy, which now holds that land in trust. More than 9,000 acres of longleaf pines, cypress trees, marine forests, endangered wildlife, and wetlands are being protected. Hiking trails and sandy roads lace the property, in addition to several boat landings.

Along the Waccamaw River on the eastern side of Sandy Island are 1,100 acres of wetlands filled with bald cypresses, tupelos, and swamp pocosins. Freshwater swamps supported rice plantations during the 1800s. Along the Pee Dee River that abuts the western portion of the island are approximately 3,000 acres of bottomland hardwood forests. Some of the longleaf pines are more than a century old. The island's forests protect a number of endangered species, including the red-cockaded woodpecker. Eagles, ospreys, bears, deer, and turkeys can also be found here. In addition to natural attractions, visitors are often delighted by **New Bethel Baptist Church**, a picturesque white stucco structure sitting atop a high sandy ridge, shaded by longleaf pines and symbolizing the strength and integrity of this community. Built in 1818, the church serves as the social and spiritual center of the island.

Backtrack 2.4 miles (east) to US 17 and turn right (south) to visit **Litchfield Beach**. To drive through the oceanfront part of the Litchfield Beach community, turn left on Litchfield Drive/S-22-302. After 0.3 mile the road curves to the right and becomes Norris Drive/S-22-44. Public parking is on your right.

Private houses line the one mile of beachfront. On your left are public beach access paths. The first one is 0.2 mile down the road across from Lazy Lane.

Backtrack to Ocean Highway/US 17 and turn left (south). The Pawleys Island community begins about 3 miles down the road. You will see a string of popular "beachy" shops offering abundant shopping opportunities.

Plan to turn left (east) onto North Causeway Road, which takes you to **Pawleys Island** proper, at a stoplight 4 miles from Litchfield Drive. No road sign is visible, but you can trust the green sign to the right of US 17, directing you to turn left.

Cross a bridge over the marsh, and the barrier island is directly in front of you. Turn right onto S-22-46/Myrtle Avenue to visit the historic district of Pawleys Island. This narrow road is lined with historic homes, sand dunes, and lovely trees on your left, with marsh on your right. Travel at a leisurely pace; the drive to the end of the island is only about a couple of miles.

Pawleys Island, once a refuge for rice planters who sought to escape the malaria epidemic, is one of the oldest beach resorts in the state. The island was originally developed as a summer retreat for rice and indigo planters during the 18th and 19th centuries, and its heyday was during the 1930s and '40s. Pawleys describes itself as "arrogantly shabby," which sums up the situation nicely. Its longest-staying visitor is a famous ghost, "the Gray Man." Legend has it that the Gray Man first appeared on the beach at Pawleys Island before the great hurricane of 1822. He is said to have given warnings of severe storms ever since.

As you approach the marshlands, you will see on your right the venerable interdenominational **Pawley Island Chapel** at 391 Myrtle Avenue. Three tenths of a mile farther on your left is the beginning of the historic district.

The **Joseph Blythe Allston Pawley House** at 441 Myrtle Avenue stands on land once owned by Robert Frances Withers Allston (1801–1864), a successful rice planter and South Carolina's governor from 1856 to 1858. His nephew, Joseph Blythe Allston, obtained the land in 1866, and it is thought that he then moved this circa 1800 house onto this property.

Just past the Joseph Blythe Allston Pawley House is the **South Causeway**. Robert Frances Withers Allston is also responsible for building the causeway between 1845 and 1856, connecting the island to the mainland.

P. C. J. Weston, who served as lieutenant governor of South Carolina from 1862 to 1864, built the house at 506 Myrtle Avenue. Named the **Pelican Inn**, it is a superb bed and breakfast accommodation.

Pawleys Island creekside dock Marie Goff

Farther along is the **All Saints Summer Parsonage**, at 516 Myrtle Avenue Built by 1848, it served as the summer parsonage for All Saints Episcopal Church for many years.

The **Ward House**, or Liberty Lodge, at 520 Myrtle Avenue, one of the oldest buildings on Pawleys Island, was reportedly moved here around 1858. It stands on land once owned by area rice planter Joshua J. Ward (1800–1853), who was lieutenant governor of South Carolina from 1850 to 1852.

The LaBruce Lemon House at 546 Myrtle Avenue was built around 1858. Two small dwellings on the property were slave cabins.

The **Nesbitt/Norburn House** at 560 Myrtle Avenue (1842) was owned by Robert Nesbitt (1799–1848), a native of Scotland and a rice planter in this area. The house is hidden behind thick vegetation.

The **All Saints Academy Summer House** at 566 Myrtle Avenue was built between 1838 and 1848 as summer lodging for the academy's headmaster, future governor Robert F. W. Allston.

Continue 0.8 mile down Myrtle Avenue and veer left onto Doyle Drive/S-22-48 where the road forks and Myrtle Avenue goes right. Turn left onto Pritchard Street/S-22-265 and then right onto Springs Avenue. Drive almost a mile to a small parking area near the end of the island where you can take a relaxing walk on this quiet, secluded seashore.

Nearby Attractions

Franklin G. Burroughs-Simeon B. Chapin Art Museum, Mansfield Plantation, Myrtle Beach State Park, Myrtle Beach Colored School Museum, North Myrtle Beach Area Historical Museum, South Carolina Hall of Fame (at Myrtle Beach Convention Center), Vereen Memorial Historical Gardens, Waccamaw National Wildlife Refuge.

14

Winyah Bay and Santee River Delta

Georgetown to McClellanville

General Description: Beginning at Hobcaw Barony just north of historic Georgetown, this 40-mile tour takes visitors through plantation-dotted coastal marshland and the northern edge of Francis Marion National Forest before ending in the quaint fishing village of McClellanville.

Special Attractions: Hobcaw Barony, Winyah Bay, historic Georgetown, Sampit River, Tom Yawkey Wildlife Center Heritage Preserve, Hopesewee Plantation, Santee River, Santee Delta Recreation Area, Francis Marion National Forest, Hampton Plantation State Historic Site, St. James Santee Parish Church, McClellanville, St. James Santee Episcopal Chapel of Ease, Jeremy Creek.

Location: Northern coast.

Travel Season: All year.

Services: Conventional accommodations and other services are abundant in Georgetown and Pawleys Island. Limited services are available in McClellanville.

The Drive

The Carolina Coastal Plain area around Georgetown sits astride Winyah Bay, where the Waccamaw, Great Pee Dee, Black, and Sampit Rivers empty into the Atlantic to form one of the finest natural harbors in the United States. A few miles south of Winyah Bay are the wetlands of the sprawling Santee River delta, home to several important wildlife reserves because of its great ecological significance, especially for ducks and other shorebirds. This drive takes visitors through the lands surrounding these great outlets to the Atlantic Ocean, and ends in a delightful old fishing village.

Hobcaw and Historic Georgetown

Here in 1526, almost two centuries before Georgetown was occupied by British settlers, the Spanish made the first European settlement on the North American mainland. They were driven out by Native Americans and disease within a year. The English arrived in 1705 and began the Georgetown settlement. The town plan was laid in 1729, making Georgetown the third oldest town in the state.

Begin at **Hobcaw Barony Discovery Center** (22 Hobcaw Rd.).

Winyah Bay and Santee River Delta:
Georgetown to McClellanville

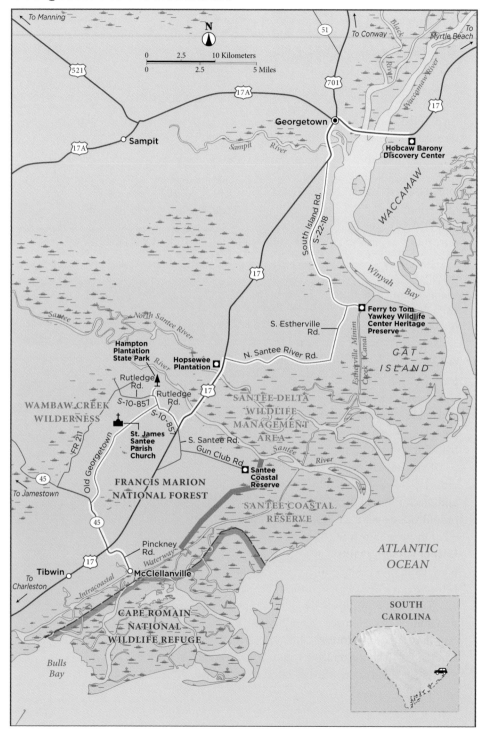

Here you can view exhibits about the history and ecology of the salt marshes, swamps, maritime and upland forests, cypress swamps, freshwater ponds, rice fields, Carolina bays, and other natural areas that support an abundance of fish and wildlife on the 16,000-acre nature and research reserve on the Waccamaw Neck, a peninsula which extends from Horry County to the southern end of the Barony. The area was named "hobcaw" by Native Americans because it was "between the waters" of the Waccamaw River, Winyah Bay, and the Atlantic Ocean.

The land was originally granted by King George I of England as a barony in 1718. The plantation shows evidence of Native Americans, European settlers, and indigo plantations. In 1905 Bernard M. Baruch, a native of Camden, South Carolina, who was a successful financier and adviser to seven presidents, purchased the property, covering more than a dozen plantations, to serve as a winter hunting retreat for his family and friends. Fifty years later, his daughter, Belle W. Baruch, acquired the land and ensured that after her death it would be preserved in perpetuity for future generations to enjoy. Today the Belle W. Baruch Foundation, Clemson University, and the University of South Carolina manage the property and allow visitors access to explore the area through guided tours and programs throughout the year. The Barony's primary use, however, is for coastal research.

The Discovery Center is open Monday through Friday and admission is free. Guided tours are available, including a bus tour that highlights Hobcaw's history, the Hobcaw House, Belle Baruch's home and stables, Friendfield Village, an 1800s slave village with cabins dating back to the 1940s, and the coastal ecology and wildlife found in the Barony. Other scheduled programs throughout the year include guided birding trips, beach walks, trail rides with horses, nature camps, fly-fishing adventures, and flower festivals.

Exit Hobcaw Barony by turning left (south) on US 17 and travel 2.5 miles to cross L. H. Siau Bridge, first over the Waccamaw and then over the Great Pee Dee and Black Rivers. Enter Georgetown and turn left (southwest) after a half mile onto Broad Street/S-22-379 into the heart of **historic Georgetown**.

On Broad Street to your right, just before you reach Duke Street, is the **Bethel African Methodist Episcopal Church** (417 Broad St.), the first separate black church in Georgetown County, built in 1882. Across the street on your left is the second oldest Jewish cemetery in the state, established in 1722.

Turn right (northwest) on Duke Street and then immediately left (southwest) on Orange Street. On your left at 334 Orange Street/S-22-93 is the white wooden **Augustus T. Carr House** (1855), named for the founder of the Bethel AME Church you just saw on Broad Street. Go one block southwest to High Market Street.

At the northwest (far right) corner of Orange Street and High Market is the **Duncan Memorial United Methodist Church** at 901 High Market Street. In 1785, the Methodist congregation was formed in Georgetown by William Wayne, nephew of the Revolutionary War general Anthony Wayne. On the far left (southeast) corner is Duncan Memorial Chapel, site of an early cemetery, parsonage, and church that was in use from 1833 until 1903.

The tan house with black shutters to your immediate left at 834 High Market Street (corner of Orange and High Market) is the **Childermas Croft House** (1765). The house is said to have been occupied by the British during the Revolutionary War and used as a hospital.

Turn left (southeast) onto High Market Street/S-22-156. Drive one block and on your left at the corner of High Market and Broad Streets is **St. Mary's Catholic Church** (317 Broad St.), built in 1901, a beautiful brick structure with a statue of the Virgin Mary at its front.

Continue southeast on High Market across Broad Street. On your left is **Prince George's Winyah Episcopal Church** (300 Broad St.), established in 1721 by the Church of England. The parish church was built between 1745 and 1750, and the tower and chancel were added in 1824. Notice the weathered brick wall enclosing the church. Markers in the cemetery date to the 1760s.

Drive southeast on High Market Street. On the corner of Screven and High Market Streets, to your left, is the **Prince George Winyah Parish Hall** (1845), which was formerly used as a jailhouse and a library. On your right is the white wooden **John Ernest Poyas House**, built around 1790.

Cross Screven Street and on your left at 630 High Market Street is the **Martha Alston Pyatt House** (1790), named for the widow who lived here for almost 50 years. On your right is **Temple Beth Elohim** (1949). The next house on your left is the **Eleazer Waterman House** (1770) at 622 High Market Street.

The **James Baxter House** (1770) is on your right at 601 High Market Street, just before Queen Street. Baxter was one of the earliest settlers in Georgetown. Cross over Queen Street and on your right the tan house with black shutters is the **Richard Dozier House** (1770). Dozier was a local politician who owned the house during and after the Civil War. On your left at 510 High Market Street, the small yellow home with a brick base is the **Thomas Jefferson House** (1825). The former owner is said to have been a boot maker.

Cross Cannon Street. The house to your right enclosed by a white picket fence is the **Bradford Sherman House** (1830). Continue to St. James Street and turn right (southwest). The house on your left at 212 St. James Street is the **Mary Gilbert House** (1737).

Turn right (northwest) onto Prince Street. On your left at 417 Prince Street is the **Thomas Hutchinson House** (1790), built by William Cuttino. The

State Champion live oak, on Prince Street in Georgetown PATRICIA PIERCE

Federal-style **Charlotte Ann Alston House** (1815) is on your right at 422 Prince Street.

The **Savage Smith House** (1790), also built by William Cuttino and used by Union soldiers as a hospital during the Civil War, is at 421 Prince Street.

Cross Cannon Street and on your left at 509 Prince Street is the **Winyah Indigo Society Hall** (1853) that served as a school for children. During the Civil War Federal troops used the building as a hospital.

The **Charlotte J. Atkinson House** (1825) is to your right at 502 Prince Street, and at 513 Prince is the **Frances Withers Colonial House** (1760) on your left. Look for the state champion live oak near the back of 515 Prince Street. The tree, estimated to be around 600 years old, measures 23 feet in circumference and 120 feet in height and has a crown spread of 125 feet.

Cross Queen Street. On your right at 614 Prince Street is the **Samuel and Joseph Sampson House** (1760). Across from **Alexander's Inn Bed and Breakfast** at 620 Prince Street is the **Baptist Church Cemetery** where William Screven, first pastor of the earliest Baptist Church in the South, is buried. Screven brought a northern congregation to Charleston, South Carolina, in 1698. Later he came to Georgetown, where he continued to pastor until his death in 1713. Park and walk the stone path to the left of the historical marker beside the white 2-story house at 619 Prince Street to visit the small plot decorated with four rounded boxwoods and enclosed within an iron and brick fence.

At 632 Prince Street on your right is the old **Colonial Banking House** (ca. 1735).

On the north corner of Screven and Prince Streets at 702 Prince Street is the **Jeremiah Cuttino House** (1740). Cuttino is said to have been a gunsmith. Catty-corner to the museum on the western corner of Prince and Screven Streets is the **Georgetown County Courthouse** (129 Screven St.), built around 1824 and designed by famed South Carolina architect Robert Mills.

Turn left (southwest) on Screven Street. Directly ahead is the **Old Market Building** (1842), also known as the **Town Clock**, at the intersection of Front and Screven Streets. Inside is the **Rice Museum** (633 Front St.), dedicated to the history of the cultivation of rice, the crop on which Georgetown's great wealth was based in the 18th and 19th centuries, and indigo, one of the first commercial crops grown in Georgetown. The museum's highlight is the Brown's Ferry Vessel, a merchant ship that sank in the 1700s and was pulled from the Black River in 1976. At that time, a scholar called the boat the "most important single nautical discovery in the United States to date."

Tiny **LaFayette Park** is adjacent to the museum, and behind it is the 1,000-foot Harbor Walk along the Sampit River docks. The Francis Marion Park is farther west down the **Harbor Walk**, adjacent to the River Room restaurant (801 Front St.).

Be sure to park in the Front Street area and stroll down the Harbor Walk to enjoy views of shrimp, fishing, and pleasure boats, and the bend in the Sampit River.

Public restrooms are available at the corner of Screven and Front Streets near the fountain. You can also visit the Georgetown County Museum which is home to artifacts and stories about Georgetown County's 300 years of American History at 120 Broad, just off Front Street. For brochures about walking tours and other historic structures in Georgetown, stop by the Visitor Center at 531 Front Street.

A couple of blocks down on the banks of the Sampit River is the **Dr. Charles Fyffe House** (1765), now serving as the Harbor House Bed and Breakfast (15 Cannon St.). Across the street is the **Red Store Warehouse**, built around 1765 and considered the oldest commercial structure in Georgetown County. To the right of the warehouse is the **Independent Seafood Market** (1 Cannon St.), a great place to shop for local seafood. This is also the spot where Theodosia Burr Alston, daughter of American Founding Father Aaron Burr, boarded *The Patriot* on December 30, 1812. The ship was lost at sea, and her ghost is said to haunt the coastal area.

Boardwalk alongside Sampit River in downtown Georgetown JOHN CLARK

Continue northwest on Front Street to enjoy Georgetown's thriving downtown, where you will pass unique antique and coffee shops, and craft and book stores, along with sandwich and fine-dining restaurants worth a try.

The **South Carolina Maritime Museum** is at 729 Front Street. Heading northwest again on Front Street for several blocks, just after you pass King Street (The **Gullah Museum** is a half block away at 123 King Street), look to your left to see the **Kaminski House Museum**, at 1003 Front Street. Built around 1769, it is filled with antiques, including a Spanish wedding chest dating back to the 15th century. Guided tours are available for a small donation.

The **Stewart-Parker House** (1019 Front St.) to the right of the Kaminski House was built in the 1740s by Robert Stewart. This house is the only extant brick residence in Georgetown built before the American Revolution. When President George Washington arrived in Georgetown on April 30, 1791, during his southern tour, he spent the night here as the guest of a local merchant.

Georgetown to McClellanville

As you approach the end of Front Street where it intersects with US 17, you pass Georgetown Steel Mill. Its future at time of publication was uncertain. Turn left onto Fraser Street (US 17 South) and cross the bridge over the **Sampit River**.

One mile from the Sampit River, turn left onto S-22-18/South Island Road toward Belle Isle into the Winyah Community. Travel 3.2 miles southward through a residential community. Where the road forks, go left to continue on South Island Road.

South Island Road meanders through quiet, woodsy Winyah Community. Go 5 miles to the end of South Island Road where you'll see the South Island Boat Landing at the Estherville Minim Creek Canal and a parking lot on the water's edge. The canal that separates the mainland from **Cat Island** is only about 20 feet across. Marshland teeming with egrets and other waterfowl borders the parking area.

To visit Cat Island and the **Tom Yawkey Wildlife Center Heritage Preserve**, sometimes called the most valuable gift in public conservation's history, you'll need to make a reservation (843-546-6814). A gift from Yawkey to the state of South Carolina, the wildlife center is operated by the South Carolina Department of Natural Resources. Lying on either side of the mouth of Winyah Bay, the center's 17,700 acres are split among North, South, and Cat Islands.

Ecosystems range from ponds and barrier island beaches to maritime forest and pine flat woods. Huge numbers of waterfowl and shorebirds visit, especially during spring migrations, and endangered loggerhead sea turtles nest on the 13 miles of undeveloped beach. Turkey, deer, and quail are permanent residents at the center. Access to the center is severely limited. Bus tours of the center are often booked months in advance.

Turn around in the parking lot and head north on South Island Road. After only a half mile, turn left on S-22-30/South Estherville Road. Continue (west) down this curving, dark road. At 2.8 miles from your turn onto Estherville Road, make a sharp right turn at a stop sign. The road remains S-22-30, but it is now North Santee River Road.

Although all of the plantations on S-22-30 are private, a drive down this canopied passage of enormous oaks dripping with Spanish moss allows slight glimpses of old homes, slave quarters, and farm buildings, and is well worth the quiet drive. Estherville, Pine Grove, Annandale, Millbrook, Wicklow Hall, Kinloch, Newland, Woodland, and Rice Hope are among the private plantations you will pass. The **Retreat Rice Plantation** is perhaps one of the most well-known of these old home sites. Oak trees leading up to and around the house give one the sense of the old-style plantation. Wild turkeys and deer can sometimes be glimpsed darting across the road and through the woods.

You will reach US 17 after 4.8 miles.

Turn left (south) onto US 17 and enjoy wildlife and historic treasures on both sides of the highway.

Santee River Road in Georgetown County JOHN CLARK

A half mile down US 17 on your right is **Hopsewee Plantation** (494 Hopsewee Rd., Georgetown). Built around 1740, it is the birthplace of Thomas Lynch Jr., a signer of the Declaration of Independence and a member of the committee that drafted the South Carolina Constitution in 1776. This plantation is privately owned but open to the public. There is a moderate admission fee.

Directly across the highway from Hopsewee Plantation is the **Poleyard Public Boat Landing**, affording access to the North Santee River. The landing is the southern terminus of the Santee River Canoe Trail, which flows 65 miles from Lake Marion to its estuary south of Georgetown.

Continue south on US 17 across the **North Santee River**, a beautiful, wide, smooth-flowing brown river that is a key part of the **Santee Delta Recreation Area**. The main dike of the wildlife management area runs south from the bridge over the North Santee. Its parking lot is on the left (east) side of the highway, and it can be walked as a trail.

The Santee Delta, formed by silt deposits that divide the Santee River, is the largest river delta on the Atlantic Coast. Extensive rice plantations were established around the Santee Delta in the pre–Civil War era. These wetlands have been developed as vital wildlife habitats since the demise of rice culture. This wildlife area offers scenic vistas, good bird viewing, and plenty of alligators. Rare bird species include American swallow-tailed kits, bald eagles, and sandhill cranes. Access roads to the eastern and western portions of the Santee Delta Recreation Area are easily visible and accessible on both sides of US 17.

Less than a mile south of the North Santee Bridge, the Santee Swamp, a great area for wildlife viewing, envelops both sides of the highway. White egrets, hawks, and ducks are plentiful in the marsh and easily visible on a clear day.

As you cross the bridge over the **South Santee River**, 2 miles after the North Santee River Bridge, you leave Georgetown County and enter Charleston County and **Francis Marion National Forest**. Go one more mile to the intersection of US 17 and S-10-857, and turn right (northwest) onto Rutledge Road. (S-10-857 is South Santee Road on the southeastern side of US 17.)

*You may want to detour to the **Santee Coastal Reserve** (220 Santee Gun Club Rd., McClellanville). Managed by the South Carolina Department of Natural Resources, it is one of the most pristine places on the East Coast. To visit the reserve, proceed 1.5 miles on South Santee Road/S-10-857 and turn left just before the South Santee Community Center onto unpaved Santee Gun Club Road, which is the entrance to the reserve open daily during daylight hours.*

The reserve is among the most important breeding grounds for wading birds in the eastern United States. The Nature Conservancy maintains possession of a 1,040-acre cypress and tupelo swamp, Washo Reserve, within the boundaries of the Santee Coastal Reserve. Totaling 23,024 acres, the Santee Coastal Reserve is primarily marsh, but the property also has 14 Carolina bays. It is said that every Atlantic spe-cies of shorebird is found in the reserve. Moreover, 12 species of orchids and 5 types of lilies are present here.

Drive 2 miles (northwest) on Rutledge Road to visit **Hampton Plantation State Historic Site** (1950 Rutledge Rd., McClellanville) on the banks of Wam-baw Creek. Turn right (north) into the park. A bumpy dirt road amid thick pines opens up to the majestic plantation house surrounded by lush vegetation and slightly hidden behind the famous **Washington Oak**.

Hampton Plantation, a National Historic Landmark, is an example of 18th- and 19th-century working rice plantations. The Lowcountry rice culture and plan-tation system shaped the lives of the residents of this area. The mansion, open for tours, is built in the Georgian style, circa 1750, and is an architectural monument to the skills of enslaved African Americans.

Hampton Plantation State Historic Site's 322 acres are centered on the plan-tation mansion that has been home to much history and to longtime former state poet laureate Archibald Rutledge, who donated the property to the state. The grounds feature huge live oaks draped with Spanish moss. One of these, the Washington Oak, was left standing on the advice of President Washington during his visit in 1791.

Giant camellias abound, and sundew, pitcher plants, rare orchids, and unusual spider lilies and irises may be found. The park also encompasses cypress swamps, abandoned rice fields, and pine and hardwood forests. Wild turkeys, towhees, deer, hawks, woodcocks, whippoorwills, eagles, ospreys, squirrels, owls, warblers, pile-ated woodpeckers, and Mississippi and swallow-tailed kites can be encountered here, as well as the endangered Rafinesque's big-eared bat. Alligators, otters, snakes, and tortoises roam the dark waters of Witch's Pond and Wambaw Creek.

Picnic tables, restrooms, and vending machines are available, making this a perfect spot to stop for a snack or lunch under the ancient trees and feel the his-tory of the quiet land. You can explore the mansion and walk the grounds, where a 3-mile nature trail is easily accessible. The plantation is a noted wildlife viewing area.

Backtrack out to Rutledge Road, turn left (southeast) and drive a half mile, looking for Old Georgetown Road on your right. Turn right (southwest) onto this heavily packed dirt road and continue 2.3 miles to **Saint James Santee Parish Church** (1787), a National Historic Landmark that was the center of one of the earliest settlements in South Carolina, Saint James Santee Parish, founded in 1706 at the request of French Huguenot settlers. The parish was a major agricultural area, containing a number of large rice plantations. In 1787, at nearby Peachtree Plantation, Jonathan Lucas introduced a watermill for beating rice, which gave impetus to the rice culture in this area.

Continue 3.7 more miles southeast on Old Georgetown Road, through mixed pine and hardwood forestland, until you reach the intersection with SC 45, a paved two-lane road. Turn left (southeast) onto SC 45 and travel on a mostly lush, tree-lined road toward McClellanville. After 2.2 miles, you reach the intersection of SC 45 and US 17.

McClellanville

Cross US 17 onto South Pinckney Street to explore the sleepy fishing village of McClellanville, on the banks of Jeremy Creek.

McClellanville was established in the late 1850s and early 1860s when local plantation owners A. J. McClellan and R. T. Morrison sold lots to planters of the Santee Delta seeking relief from summer fever. The first store opened soon after the Civil War, and the village became the social and economic center for a wide area that produced timber, rice, cotton, naval stores, and seafood. Encircled by the Francis Marion National Forest and Cape Romain National Wildlife Refuge, McClellanville is best known for its shrimp fleet and seafood industry. Beautiful churches and old homes hide behind ancient oaks, including the summer home and birthplace of Archibald Rutledge.

You reach downtown McClellanville a little more than a mile down South Pinckney Street after passing quaint old cottages and some new homes. Artists' studios and small shops filled with unique, handcrafted items are found along the way.

Ramble on down Pinckney past the old McClellanville Public School to the corner of Scotia Street, where you'll see the lovely **New Wappetaw Presbyterian Church** (635 Pinckney St.), a white wooden structure with a columned facade. The "new" building was completed in 1875.

At the next block, turn right on Oak Street. On your left is an open space and the namesake of the street. An enormous oak tree hangs over the road and a public park. The park has a picnic table, in case you want to stop and take a rest.

Continue on Oak Street. **Saint James Santee Episcopal Chapel of Ease** (1890) is on your left at 205 Oak Street at the corner of Oak and Church Streets. Constructed of wood that has weathered through the years, the church is adorned with attractive gingerbread filigree. Chapels of ease were usually built for parishioners who were unable to attend their main church services regularly.

Continue on Oak Street just 0.2 mile past neat bungalows and stately homes to the docks at the end of the street. Here you are afforded a great view of the fleet of local shrimp and fishing boats on **Jeremy Creek**.

Live oak tree on Oak Street in fishing village of McClellanville JOHN CLARK

Backtrack northeast on Oak Street to turn right (south) on Pinckney Street. McClellanville United Methodist Church is on your immediate left, at 568 Pinckney Street.

Little Hampton, the Rutledge summer home and Archibald's birthplace, is 0.2 mile down Pinckney Street on your right beside Rutledge Court. The first Little Hampton was built by Henry Rutledge, the father of the late Archibald Rutledge, poet laureate of South Carolina during the middle of the 20th century. The original log structure was destroyed by Hurricane Hugo in 1989, but the house was rebuilt with unpainted wood and a tin roof, and a screened-in porch facing Jeremy Creek. Rutledge (1883–1973) is best known for *Home by the River* (1941), describing the people, wildlife, and landscape of this area.

Continue on South Pinckney Road for another block to the **Village Museum** next to the McClellanville Town Hall at 405 Pinckney Street. The museum provides a history of the village, a gift shop, and a family history room. The adjacent public park and boat landing are a great place to end your journey, with an expansive view of the mouth of Jeremy Creek, where it flows into the **Intracoastal Waterway**.

Nearby Attractions

Black River Preserve, Black River State Park, Cape Romain National Wildlife Refuge, Ramsey Grove State Park, Sewee Shell Ring, Sewee Visitor and Environmental Education Center, Waccamaw National Wildlife Refuge.

Lake Moultrie Loop

Moncks Corner to Diversion Canal

General Description: A 45-mile trip around the edges of Lake Moultrie, full of canals, history, and natural beauty.

Special Attractions: Old Santee Canal Park, Berkeley County Museum and Heritage Center, Fort Fair Lawn, Tail Race Canal, Francis Marion National Forest, Bonneau Beach, Lake Moultrie, Saint Stephen Episcopal Church, Rediversion Canal, Pineville Chapel, General Francis Marion Burial Site, Diversion Canal.

Location: Lower Coastal Plain, northeast of Charleston.

Travel Season: All year. Fall, winter, and spring are great for waterfowl and other wildlife.

Services: Charleston and Summerville have numerous restaurants and full accommodations and other services. Moncks Corner has accommodations and most services. Saint Stephen has limited services.

The Drive

This semicircular drive around Lake Moultrie is a trip full of canals, natural beauty, and man-made wonders. You begin in Moncks Corner's languidly beautiful Old Santee Canal Park, a landmark of South Carolina's natural and commercial heritage.

Next, you proceed across the Tail Race Canal to the shores of Lake Moultrie, before heading through farmlands and forests to the little town of Saint Stephen and its colonial-era parish church. After returning to Lake Moultrie, cross the Rediversion Canal and ride through countryside to two-centuries-old Pineville Chapel and the idyllic General Francis Marion Burial Site. You complete your trip by crossing the Diversion Canal connecting Lakes Marion and Moultrie, and visiting a fish camp on the backwaters of Lake Moultrie.

Old Santee Canal Park to Saint Stephen

Begin your drive in Moncks Corner at **Old Santee Canal Park**, 900 Stony Landing Road. A small entrance fee is required to enter the parking area, flush with Spanish moss-hung live oaks, sprawling green space, picnic and restroom facilities, the **Stony Landing House** constructed around 1943, a dock extending into the Cooper River, and a reproduction of the "Little David" semisubmersible torpedo attach boat secretly built at Stony Landing for use by Confederates during the Civil War.

Lake Moultrie Loop: Moncks Corner to Diversion Canal

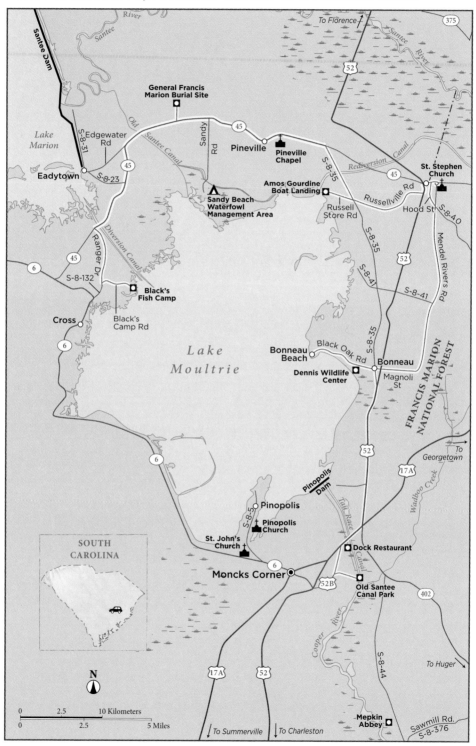

Santee Dam

Santee River

To Florence

375

52

General Francis
Marion Burial Site

Lake
Marion

Edgewater
Rd

S-8-31

Old Santee Canal

Sandy Rd

45

Pineville

Pineville
Chapel

Rediversion Canal

Santee River

St. Stephen
Church

45

Eadytown

45

S-8-23

S-8-35

Amos Gourdine
Boat Landing

Russellville Rd

Hood St

S-8-40

Sandy Beach
Waterfowl
Management Area

Russell
Store Rd

S-8-35

Mendel Rivers Rd

52

Diversion Canal

Ranger Dr

45

6

S-8-132

S-8-41

S-8-41

Black's
Fish Camp

Cross

Black's
Camp Rd

6

Lake
Moultrie

Bonneau
Beach

Black Oak Rd

52-S-5

Bonneau

Dennis Wildlife
Center

Magnoli
St

FRANCIS MARION NATIONAL FOREST

6

52

To
Georgetown

17A

Pinopolis
Dam

Wadboo Creek

Pinopolis

S-8-5

Pinopolis
Church

Tail Race

Tail Race Canal

Dock Restaurant

St. John's
Church

6

Moncks Corner

52B

Old Santee
Canal Park

402

17A

52

Cooper River

S-8-44

To Huger

SOUTH
CAROLINA

N

0   2.5   10 Kilometers
0   2.5   5 Miles

To Summerville

To Charleston

Mepkin
Abbey

Sawmill Rd.

S-8-376

Old Santee Canal Park preserves remnants of the defunct canal's southern terminus, where it brought the waters of the Santee River into Biggin Creek, which flows into the Cooper River.

The Santee River, a giant watershed for much of the state, empties into the Atlantic at a relatively unpopulated area between Charleston and Georgetown. The canal brought the commercial activity of this watershed to the much shorter Cooper River and the Port of Charleston. Under construction for 7 years, the canal was completed in 1800, and for 50 years it carried goods between Charleston and the South Carolina Midlands, including Columbia.

At the time of its completion, it was America's first commercial canal and considered one of the foremost engineering achievements and economic development projects of its day. The canal's economic usefulness withered away in the 1840s when railway lines to Columbia and Camden were completed.

An exceptional historical and natural interpretive center stands at the entrance to the park, operated by Santee Cooper, the state-owned electric utility. The natural beauty of the Santee Canal's location is shown through displays of wildlife and a 30-foot replica of a live oak tree towering to the ceiling of the center. The center is styled after the locks of the original old canal, and it tells the story of the project in diorama.

Outside, 4 miles of trails wind and crisscross along Biggin Creek, Old Santee Canal, and the currently active Tail Race Canal, which carries water and boats from Lake Moultrie and the Santee Cooper hydroelectric facility to the Cooper River.

Trees in the park typify Lowcountry swampland. Giant bald cypress is king, but it is attended by quite a court, including sweet gum, laurel oak, live oak, red maple, dogwood, magnolia, red bay, slippery elm, basswood, sugar maple, redbud, mulberry, and black willow, many of which are draped with ever present gray Spanish moss.

An unusual feature is a steep bluff composed of limestone rock known as Cooper marl, formed from tiny ocean organisms left behind millions of years ago. High levels of calcium in the marl make the soils of the bluff alkaline, allowing plants that require high levels of calcium to flourish here.

The stars of the bird set are ospreys perched high in their nests, but they have plenty of company, including red-winged blackbirds, red-shouldered hawks, wood ducks, little and great blue herons, prothonotary warblers, pileated woodpeckers, vireos, Carolina wrens, and cardinals. Alligators lazily police the waterways, in the company of a variety of frogs and turtles, and white-tailed deer and wild turkeys roam the woodlands.

A variety of piers, boardwalks, and camouflaged observation posts make this a great place for wildlife viewing. Canoes can be rented in order to explore the backwaters.

Within the park boundaries is the **Berkeley County Museum and Heritage Center** (950 Stony Landing Rd.), which tells the 12,000-year story of the region. Exhibits and artifacts focus on Brig. Gen. Francis Marion (the Swamp Fox), Native Americans, Colonial life, the Civil War, early medicine, rural electrification, early education, and the Francis Marion National Forest.

Additionally, the park provides an entrance to **Fort Fair Lawn**, the most pristine, intact, original Revolutionary War fortification in South Carolina.

Exit the park on Stony Landing Road and head right (north) back onto Rembert C. Dennis Boulevard. The tall buildings rising above the trees to your right a half mile up the road are the headquarters of **Santee Cooper** (1 Riverwood Dr.), the state-owned utility established in the 1930s to manage the new hydroelectric project. Today it delivers wholesale and retail electricity to more than a third of South Carolina's citizens, making it one of the largest public power companies in the United States.

After another half mile, merge onto US 52/US 17 Alternate and head northeast.

Just a few yards after you start on US 52/US 17 Alternate, before you cross the bridge over the Tailrace Canal, Dock Road, to your right (east), runs downhill to **Gilligan's at the Dock Restaurant** (582 Dock Rd.) and its boat landing. This is a great place to enjoy views of the Tailrace Canal and the abundant boats traversing the waterway.

The Dennis C. Bishop Bridge over the Tailrace Canal is 0.6 mile from your exit from Rembert C. Dennis Boulevard onto US 52/US 17. Lake Moultrie sends water through generators and a huge lock at the Pinopolis Dam into the 4-mile Tailrace Canal, which connects with the Cooper River to carry water and vessels 48 more miles to Charleston.

US 17 Alternate forks right after 0.6 mile past the bridge. Keep to the left (north) to remain on US 52, passing through the Santee Circle and MacBeth communities into a portion of the vast Francis Marion National Forest.

Continue northward 5.3 miles on US 52 to the town of **Bonneau** (locally pronounced *BUN-oh*), bearing left (northwest) onto S-8-35/Murray's Ferry Road. Drive 0.7 mile, and turn left (west) onto S-8-42/Black Oak Road. Cross over the railroad tracks and head toward Bonneau Beach.

After a half mile, note the **Dennis Wildlife Fish Hatchery Center** on your left (305 Black Oak Rd., Bonneau). Operated by the South Carolina Department of Natural Resources as a research and development center for wildlife and fisheries, the 37.5-acre facility is the largest producer of striped bass larvae in the

US 52 bridge over Tailrace Canal, as seen from Dock Restaurant, Moncks Corner JOHN CLARK

world, shipping to 30 states and as far away as Russia, South Africa, and New Zealand.

Continue westward 2 miles on Black Oak Road and watch the lake's dike emerge on your left as you approach the fishing village of **Bonneau Beach** and the end of the road. On your ride into town, look for hikers and bikers exiting the downward slope of the dike on your left. Palmetto Trail followers navigate the streets of Bonneau Beach before rejoining the dike on the north side of the settlement.

Black Oak Road/S-8-42 ends 0.1 mile farther at the Mac Flood Landing on **Lake Moultrie**, offering a great panoramic vista.

Lake Moultrie was constructed between 1939 and 1941 as part of the Santee Cooper Hydroelectric and Navigation Project, a massive federal effort to provide electricity to rural South Carolina. The lake and dam system diverts water from the Santee River into the Cooper River, the major river feeding into Charleston Harbor.

The 60,000-acre bowl-like lake was carved out of swampland interspersed with farms and a few plantations. Along with Lake Marion to the north, Lake Moultrie is famous for catfish and striped bass fishing.

Saint Stephen Episcopal Church, built in 1769 John Clark

Turn around and backtrack to the town of Bonneau on Black Oak Road/S-8-42 to the intersection with Main Street/US 52. Cross over US 52 as Black Oak Road becomes Magnolia Street and then Mendel Rivers Road after one mile. Cruise 6 more miles on Mendel Rivers Road, passing through parts of Francis Marion National Forest and countryside full of farmhouses, hay and corn fields, pasturelands, and woodlands.

Continue on Mendel Rivers Road until you reach the intersection with S-8-40/Hood Street. **Allen African Methodist Episcopal Church** and **Saint Stephen Cemetery** are on your left at 280 Hood Street.

Turn left (northwest) onto Hood Street/S-8-40, and head into the little town of **Saint Stephen**. About 0.7 mile along the way, you arrive at Elm Street. Cross Elm and pass by the white brick **First Baptist Church** at 126 Hood Street on your left, fronted by a bell tower. This congregation was organized in 1849, and the current structure dates from 1912. Continue north 2 blocks and turn right (east) on SC 45/Church Street.

Travel 0.2 mile and turn right (south) onto Brick Church Circle. This U-shaped one-way street provides excellent perspectives on your left of venerable, colonial era **Saint Stephen Episcopal Church** (196 Brick Church Circle) and its well-worn cemetery. The congregation of the parish church began worship on this spot in 1754, and the present Georgian-style brick edifice was completed in 1769. If you have time, get out and walk the grounds of this impressive reminder of South Carolina's rural colonial past.

Exit Church Circle Road and turn left (west) on SC 45/Church Street, toward downtown. About 0.4 mile along the way, you come to Main Street, paralleling railroad tracks and Depot Street, on the opposite side of the tracks. The old train depot and storefronts of this now decrepit little downtown area take you back to the early decades of the 20th century.

Turn left (south) on South Main Street and drive past old storefronts and homes 4 blocks back to Elm Street/S-8-40. Turn right (west) on Elm, cross the train tracks, and take a left (south) on US 52. Go 2 blocks and turn right (west) on S-8-18/Russellville Road.

Saint Stephen to the Diversion Canal

Drive 3 miles through fairly densely populated rural lands to the crossroads community of Russellville. Turn right (north) on S-8-35 and then take an immediate left (northwest) to continue on Russell Store Road/S-8-204 1.2 miles for another look at Lake Moultrie.

On your way to the waterfront, cross 2 railroad tracks and travel through thick forest before the Lake Moultrie dike emerges into view on your left as you arrive at the Amos Gourdine Public Boat Landing.

This is a great scenic spot, where Lake Moultrie flows into the **Rediversion Canal**. The Palmetto Trail is to the south along the top of the dike, with lovely views of the lagoons and backwaters of the lake. The large main body of Lake Moultrie stretches to the west, and the grassy shores of the Rediversion Canal are on the north side, offering attractive opportunities for sunbathing and fishing. There is a swimming area just south of the boat trailer parking space.

The Rediversion Canal was built in the 1980s when federal officials decided that waters rushing from Lake Moultrie through the Pinopolis hydro facility were responsible for carrying excessive amounts of silt down the Cooper River into Charleston Harbor, exacerbating the continual need for dredging in order to provide adequate clearance for large ships. Their solution was the Rediversion Canal, which reduces water flow into the Cooper River by channeling much of Lake Moultrie's water into the Santee River, about 8 miles downstream. A small hydro project south of here helps compensate for the reduction of hydroelectric output at the Pinopolis Dam.

Turn around here and head back along Russellville Store Road/S-8-204 to the Russellville intersection with S-8-35. Turn left (northwest) on S-8-35 and ride about a mile to cross the Dr. Joseph H. Jefferson Sr. Bridge over the Rediversion Canal. The bridge offers neat views of the canal. For an up-close view, turn left (west) just past the bridge and follow a short dirt frontage road to a parking area beside the canal.

Ride one mile farther past little homes, vegetable fields, and Singapore and Mystic Lanes to **J. K. Gourdin Elementary School** (1649 SC 45, Pineville), at the intersection with SC 45. Turn left (west) and ride into the isolated **Pineville** community, squeezed between Lake Moultrie to the south and the sprawling Santee River swamps and wetlands to the north. Pineville was once a high-ground haven for plantation inhabitants in the lowlands below.

After 2.4 miles, turn left (south) on Matilda Circle. Tiny, quaintly beautiful, antebellum **Pineville Chapel**, an Episcopalian place of worship constructed around 1810, is a few yards along, on your left.

Pineville was established in 1794 as a summer retreat for nearby wealthy families desiring to escape the heat and mosquitos of their lower-lying rice plantations. The community never recovered from destruction by Union forces near the end of the Civil War.

Return to SC 45 and turn left (west).

After 2.2 miles you reach an unpaved left (south) turn for Sandy Beach Road. If you have time and inclination for an adventure, head down Sandy Beach Road,

Pineville Chapel, built in 1810 John Clark

hemmed in on both sides by thick forest. After 2.3 miles bear right at the fork. Cross over the dike and continue until you arrive at a parking area beside the dike. Here you may want to stroll westward along the trail on top of the dike. The dike, decorated with fleabane, dandelion, and deep purple bull thistles, continues for 1.1 miles before ending in a quiet spot at the northern remnant of the Old Santee Canal. You can cross the canal on the railroad trestle, which offers a pleasing view of the dark waters below, and walk a short distance alongside the stream. In spots where the water is most calm, fragrant water lilies and white-water buttercups are abundant, while bald cypress trees rise grandly from the dark surface.

Follow the dirt road south across the dike and continue to another parking area 0.6 mile along. From here, you may walk into the **Sandy Beach Waterfowl Management Area**, *except during winter closure periods.*

The trail passes through wetlands and past a broad, shallow pond where deer enjoy grazing. The best time to appreciate this field of fragrant water lilies is before noon, when the flowers are in full bloom. After midday, the large white flowers close and sink, allowing just the tips to be seen above the water.

Sandy Beach lies about a mile from the parking area. It is a bald cypress–framed area with primitive camping facilities, a sandy lake floor ideal for frolicking, and a panoramic view of Lake Moultrie looking south.

On SC 45, 3.5 miles west of Pineville Chapel, turn right (north) on General Francis Marion Avenue into the entrance for the **General Francis Marion Burial**

Statue of American Revolution hero General William Moultrie, at Black's Fish Camp on Lake Moultrie JOHN CLARK

Site. The secluded wood-lined drive takes you one mile to a pretty little cemetery holding the long-interred remains of Marion, aka the "Swamp Fox," and a number of family members. A lovely array of trees and shrubs decorates the area, and the tombstone inscriptions are fascinating.

Drive southward back to SC 45 and take a right to continue west. After 2.2 miles Edgewater Road/S-8-31 forks to the right.

For a pleasant side trip, take this fork and ride 4.1 miles through the Eadytown community and along the edge of the Diversion Canal to reach Santee Dam. Here, the Diversion Canal sends some of Lake Marion's water to Lake Moultrie. Another portion is released through a series of floodgates into the meandering Santee River, which snakes through wetlands all the way to the Atlantic Ocean, at a spot between Georgetown and Charleston.

Continue on SC 45 for an additional 3.2 miles, where you reach the Amos Nathaniel Rogers Bridge over the **Diversion Canal**.

The Diversion Canal connects Lakes Marion and Moultrie, South Carolina's two great fishing lakes, especially famed for striped bass and record-size catfish. It is a key component of the original hydroelectric project that enabled water to be diverted from the Santee River through power generators near Moncks Corner and into the Cooper River. The Diversion Canal also allows boats to travel all the way from Charleston to Columbia.

As you top the bridge over the canal, you will likely see a profusion of fishing and pleasure boats, along with an eclectic string of commercial fish camps on the west bank of the busy water thoroughfare.

Complete your tour by visiting **Black's Fish Camp** (1370 Black's Camp Rd., Cross) a few miles south. Cross the bridge and turn left (south) immediately after you cross the bridge onto Ranger Drive/S-8-132, the first road just past the bridge. Ride 2.2 miles and turn left (east) on Black's Camp Road/S-8-1141. Then drive 1.2 miles to a back-water lagoon of Lake Moultrie. Here, beside green duckweed, marsh grasses, and water-swollen, moss-hung bald-cypress trees, you will find a boat landing, grassy campgrounds, a modest motel, an excellent seafood restaurant, and a rather peculiar statue of Revolutionary War General William Moultrie, who faces away from the water.

Nearby Attractions

Biggin Church Ruins, Biggin Creek Trail, Cypress Gardens, Eutawville, Lake Marion, Mepkin Abbey, Pinopolis, Santee River, Strawberry Chapel.

16

Wateree Basin

Wateree River to Santee National Wildlife Refuge

General Description: This 85-mile drive through rural Coastal Plain South Carolina is a delightful blend of nature, history, agriculture, and southern culture in its most basic sense.

Special Attractions: Boykin Mill and Pond, Swift Creek Baptist Church, Episcopal Church of the Ascension, Oakland/Dixie Hall Plantation, High Hills Baptist Church, General Thomas Sumter Memorial Park, Stateburg, Episcopal Church of the Holy Cross, Wedgefield Presbyterian Church, Manchester State Forest, Poinsett State Park, Rimini, Saint Mark's Episcopal Church, Sparkleberry Swamp, Elliott's Pond, Richardson Cemetery, Liberty Hill AME Church, Lake Marion, Santee National Wildlife Refuge, Fort Watson/Santee Indian Mound.

Location: Middle of the state, east of Columbia.

Travel Season: All year.

Services: Columbia, Camden, and Sumter have full services. Santee, on I-95, offers motels and restaurants. Summerton has eateries and limited services.

The Drive

This drive takes you through rural countryside on the east side of the Wateree River Basin and the old bed of the Santee River, mostly following the route of the former King's Highway, which connected Camden with Charleston in the 1700s. This area was saturated with antebellum plantations. Today, most of the former plantation lands are small farms or hunting preserves. Change has come slowly, and a large portion of the people who currently live here are descended from the area's inhabitants prior to the Civil War.

The tour is rich in history, including Revolutionary War, Civil War, and civil rights. You pass numerous churches, many of which are historically significant. Social institutions are strong, including appreciation for family, land, church, and nature.

Your journey starts in the quaint, historic Boykin settlement. From there, pass farmland and historic structures before visiting the tomb of General Thomas Sumter and Stateburg, the village the American Revolution hero had hoped to establish as South Carolina's capital. Continue to Wedgefield, Manchester State Forest and Poinsett State Park, Sparkleberry Swamp, and Santee National Wildlife Refuge.

Wateree Basin: Wateree River to Santee National Wildlife Refuge

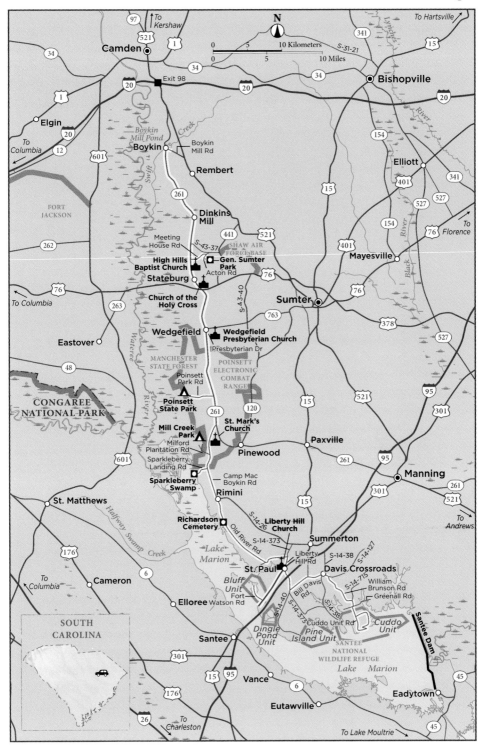

Boykin to Stateburg

Begin your drive in the tiny community of **Boykin**, at the intersection of SC 261/Boykin Road and State Road 2-28-2/Boykin Mill Road, 6.5 miles south of the intersection of I-20 and US 521, near Camden.

Although this drive provides few glimpses of the Wateree River, its beautiful vistas are entirely encompassed within the vast watershed of the Wateree and connecting rivers.

The **Wateree River** is the easternmost major artery of the **Santee-Cooper River Basin**, the biggest river drainage system in South Carolina. The Wateree River begins in the mountains of North Carolina as the Catawba River. The Catawba flows through unimpounded stretches and through lakes, such as Norman and Wylie, for more than 200 miles. It courses past Charlotte and Rock Hill, and joins with Big Wateree Creek on the Fairfield/Kershaw County line to form Lake Wateree and the Wateree River. The Wateree River empties through Lake Wateree Dam and returns to its normal riverbed about 10 miles north of the I-20 Bridge over the river.

South of the bridge, the Wateree snakes through the massive Wateree Swamp all the way to its convergence with the Congaree River, where the two waterways form the Santee River just north of Lake Marion. The Santee River exits Lake Marion at the lake's southern end and flows through more wetlands to the Atlantic Ocean at a point south of Georgetown. However, much of the water in Lake Marion is diverted through a canal into Lake Moultrie and then into the Cooper River, the biggest stream that empties into Charleston Harbor.

The Wateree, Upper Santee, and Congaree River systems run through the **COWASEE Basin**, a 215,000-acre area stretching from I-20 in Kershaw County south to Lake Marion between Rimini and Lone Star, and up the Congaree River as far north as I-77. The area is filled with bottomland hardwood forests, river bluffs, and high hills and uplands in parts of Kershaw, Sumter, Richland, Calhoun, and Lexington Counties.

Private landowners, nonprofit organizations, and state and federal entities have partnered to promote habitat protection, waterfowl restoration, research, and management within the COWASEE Basin. About two thirds of the protected land within the focus area is owned by private landowners. The other one third is made up of state and federal lands, including Manchester State Forest, Poinsett State Park, Sparkleberry Swamp, Congaree Bluffs Heritage Preserve, and Congaree National Park.

The community of Boykin is packed with well-preserved buildings from the 19th and early 20 centuries. Both the Boykin community and its millpond are National Historic Sites. For your GPS, use 84 State Road 2-28-2, Rembert.

Swift Creek Baptist Church, built in Boykin in 1827 PATRICIA PIERCE

The area was settled in 1755 by William Boykin II and his sons. It became a regional focal point as the family, over time, built a water-powered flour and grist-mill, a cotton gin, a sawmill, a church, and a tavern. Most of the property around here is still owned by sixth-generation descendants of William Boykin II.

At the intersection of SC 261 and S-28-2/Boykin Mill Road, a historical marker tells the story of South Carolina's last Civil War engagement, the Battle of Boykin Mill. Here, on April 18, 1865, Confederate regulars and home guards-men fought a delaying action against Union troops from Georgetown who had marched north to destroy a railroad track connecting Camden and Sumter. Among those killed was the last Federal officer to die in a Civil War battle, as well as 15-year-old Burwell Boykin, son of Confederate Colonel Alexander Hamilton Boykin.

On your right as you proceed east on Boykin Mill Road from the intersection are the **Boykin Company Store** and the **Boykin Company Grille**, housed in late-1800s wood-frame buildings. On your left is 200-year old **Boykin Mill,** which for centuries continued to grind out freshly milled whole-grain grits and meal on well-worn millstones. Next on your left is **The Broom Place**, a shop in a restored 1740s home that sells brooms made with century-old equipment.

The **Mill Pond Steakhouse** (84 Boykin Mill Rd., Rembert) is a fine-dining restaurant housed in a series of old buildings where a pre–Civil War post office used to stand. The kitchen building was the community's second post office, built here in 1874. The dining area is housed in an old store dating back to the 1800s. Fine regional cuisine, including steak and seafood, is served here.

The restaurant overlooks Boykin Mill Pond, which is spectacular in the evening.

To see the refurbished **Swift Creek Baptist Church**, a gray and white two-story Greek Revival building constructed in 1827, drive 0.2 mile (east) on Boykin Mill Road. The building, also on the edge of the expansive mill pond now functions as a wedding venue.

Return to the intersection of Boykin Mill Road/S-28-2 and SC 261/Boykin Road and turn left to continue southward along the eastern edge of the Wateree Swamp as you cross from Kershaw into Sumter County. Drive through pastoral settings of old farm homesteads, pecan groves, live oaks adorned with Spanish moss, barns, goats, horse pastures and pens, country stores and churches, woodlands, and fields of corn, cotton, soybeans, and hay.

After passing Wateree Correctional Institute, a minimum-security prison farm, look on your right for the **Episcopal Church of the Ascension** (5190 SC 261, Rembert), about 3.7 miles from Boykin Mill Road. This delicate white Gothic-style building, constructed in 1895, sits beside a charming cemetery dating back to 1807.

Drive southward 1.2 miles farther to **Oakland/Dixie Hall Plantation** on your right. This 3-story clapboard home was built in 1735. It was occupied at different times by both Confederate and Union forces in April 1865 during what has come to be known as Potter's Raid (April 8-21) named for Union Brigadier General Edward Potter's march on Sumter that destroyed cotton, warehouses, barns, trains and other structures.

Continue south on SC 261 for 2 miles and pass the Rafting Creek community. The remains of the old **Dinkins Mills**, site of a skirmish between Confederate and British troops on April 19 near the end of "Potter's Raid" on Sumter, are on your left (east), at the corner of Dinkins Mill Road/S-43-76.

Cruise south 4 more miles on SC 261 past farmland, country stores, and the Sanders Corner community before turning left (east) on S-43-488/Meeting House Road to see the **General Thomas Sumter Tomb**. A brown sign noting a left-turn to visit the tomb is just before Fish Road, but you should continue to Meeting House Road.

On your right after 0.4 mile is **High Hills Baptist Church** (6750 Meeting House Rd., Dalzell), a white Greek Revival structure. This building was erected in 1803, and the congregation, which began in 1770, is the second oldest Baptist

Gravesite of daughter-in-law of American Revolution hero General Thomas Sumter, in park near Stateburg PATRICIA PIERCE

congregation in South Carolina. At the beginning of the 19th century, the Reverend John Roberts opened Roberts Academy, the state's first Baptist educational institution, at this location, and he went on to establish Furman University in Greenville in 1826.

Ride east 1.2 miles farther on Meeting House Road to visit General Thomas Sumter Memorial Park. Pass by High Hills African-Methodist-Episcopal Church (6780 Meeting House Rd., Dalzell) and Pine Hills Baptist Church, to enter a residential neighborhood. Follow the brown signs directing you to the park.

Turn right (northeast) on S-43-400/Acton Road and go 0.2 mile farther to arrive at the charming little cemetery known as **General Thomas Sumter Memorial Park**.

General Sumter, nicknamed "The Gamecock" for his ferocious, tenacious fighting tactics in the South Carolina midlands during the American Revolution, lived in this area and led Patriot forces in a number of engagements against British and Loyalist troops. On the enclosed grounds are a memorial to Sumter, graves of the general and many members of his family, and a chapel surrounding the grave site of Sumter's French-born daughter-in-law, Nathalie Marie Louise Stephanie Beatrix de DeLage de Volude Sumter. This quiet, restful spot is a great place to relax, offering stone benches, magnolias, and shady hardwood trees. The park is open daily.

Return westward 1.8 miles and turn left (south) onto SC 261 to resume your journey toward Stateburg, 2 miles south. **Stateburg** was laid out by General Sumter in 1783 and given its name in the hope that it would become the state capital when lawmakers moved their seat of government inland from Charleston. Alas, lawmakers chose a plot of land on the banks of the Congaree River and named it Columbia, leaving Stateburg an unincorporated village sleepier today than it was more than 200 years ago. Therein lies its charm.

Stateburg was the birthplace of Mary Boykin Chestnut (1823–1886), the renowned author of *A Diary from Dixie*, a personal account of life during the Civil War and southern society at that time in South Carolina.

As you enter the settlement, take note of several private mansions on your right, marked by white fences, shady yards, and private signs. Among them is the **Miller/Ellison House**, built around 1816 for Governor Stephen Decatur Miller. It was purchased in 1836 by William Ellison, a wealthy Black freedman who owned a plantation and 50 slaves.

On your left is the lovely **Episcopal Church of the Holy Cross** (335 N. Kings Hwy. 261), begun as a chapel of ease in 1770. The driveway is one-way, and you need to enter at the second turn into the parking area.

The current Gothic Revival *pisé de terre* (rammed earth) structure, designed by architect Edward C. Jones of Charleston, was built between 1850 and 1852. The

Episcopal Church of the Holy Cross, completed in 1852 in Stateburg PATRICIA PIERCE

east and west stained-glass windows were made in Bavaria, and the 19th century organ inside was built by Henry Erben, the renowned organ maker from Newark. It was installed in 1851 and is one of the few Erben organs still in use.

The charming cemetery holds the remains of a number of local notables, including war veterans, several Sumter family members, and Joel Poinsett, the noted botanist and statesman who brought the poinsettia plant to this country from Mexico, where he served as US Ambassador.

On the right, across the street from the church, is the **Borough House**, where Poinsett died. It was built as a wood-frame house in the 1750s and remodeled in 1821. During the American Revolution it served as headquarters for both British General Cornwallis and American General Nathaniel Greene.

Stateburg to Poinsett State Park

From the churchyard, turn left and drive south on SC 261 for 0.7 mile to the intersection with US 76/US 378.

You may choose to take a short detour here to enjoy the best available highway view of the Wateree River and Swamp. To do so, turn right (west) toward Columbia

"Church of the Pines" Presbyterian Church in Wedgefield, built in 1882 Patricia Pierce

and drive 5 miles over swamp-surrounded causeways to the bridge over the river. Cross the river and drive 1.2 miles up the bluff, turn left at the intersection with SC 263, and return 6.2 miles on the eastbound lane of US 76/US 378.

Cross US 76/US 378 and continue southward toward Pinewood on SC 261/ Charles L. Griffin Memorial Highway. Travel 3.8 miles past modest homes to the crossroads community of **Wedgefield**.

In town, after crossing the railroad tracks and SC 763/Wedgefield Highway, turn left on S-43-420/Presbyterian Drive to see pretty **Wedgefield Presbyterian Church**, a wooden structure with forest green shutters and trim, built in 1882 and sometimes called the "Church of the Pines."

Return to SC 261/Kings Highway and resume your southward journey to visit Poinsett State Park. After about 2 miles, SC 261 begins a long stretch as the border between a US Air Force bombing range on the left (east) and **Manchester State Forest** on the right. On your left 3.6 miles from Wedgefield, at a fork in the road, is a historical marker noting that the town of Manchester once stood in this area.

Manchester was a stagecoach relay station and a shipping center for cotton. A busy point on the Wilmington and Manchester Railroad, it also served as an entertainment center, with taverns, horse racing, ball games, and other contests. In 1840, it was listed as one of the ten largest towns in the state. The inhabitants were wealthy planters who owned plantations along the Wateree River. Manchester was burned by Union troops in 1865 and never rebuilt.

The state forest contains 23,500 acres of pines and hardwoods. This public property was once the site of three former estates: Bellefield, Melrose, and Milford.

Ridges, sand hills, hardwood bottoms, bays, ponds, and swampland are scattered throughout the property, and you will find pockets of mountain laurel, red cedars draped with Spanish moss, dogwoods, and live oaks, composing a rather unique plant mix for the state. Deer are plentiful, and birds include red-cockaded woodpeckers, songbirds, wading birds, and birds of prey. Separate trails are available for horses, mountain bikes, motorcycles, and hikers, and you are free to drive the dozens of dirt roads that crisscross throughout the forest.

Bear left (southeast) to stay on SC 261 for an additional 2.5 miles before turning right (west) onto S-43-63/Poinsett Park Road. Follow this road 1.7 miles to the entrance gate of **Poinsett State Park** (6600 Poinsett Park Rd., Wedgefield), in the midst of the state forest. The parking area is 0.3 mile farther. Poinsett, constructed by the Civilian Conservation Corps in the 1930s, offers 5 miles of hiking along three connecting trails through hilly and wonderfully diverse terrain, presenting an interesting juxtaposition of mountain and coastal plain flora.

The park is a unique and exciting place, a taste of mountains in the coastal plain. The park features 1,000 acres of hilly terrain adjacent to Wateree Swamp, and it incorporates a small part of the swamp. These undulations are called the High Hills of Santee, an area famous for producing political and military leaders. The elevation changes create a fascinating environment and marvelous hiking, as well as a variety of natural habitats. The park is a great place to picnic, fish, hike, bike, or horseback ride.

Surveys have identified 337 flowering plants in the park. Wildflowers put on an impressive show in the early spring. Naturalists have also identified 65 trees and shrubs here. Wildlife includes snakes, alligators, eastern fence lizards, bullfrogs, southern leopard frogs, squirrels, white-tailed deer, rabbits, raccoons, opossums, and bobcats, along with more than fifty bird species.

Old Levi Mill Pond, bordered by moss-draped bald cypresses and tupelo gums, is beside the park headquarters and is the trailhead for the interpretive Coquina Trail circling the pond. Coquina, a naturally cemented rock formation laced with seashells, is abundant in the park, reflecting the fact that this area was underneath the sea in prehistoric times. The lake was built as a freshwater reserve for flooding rice fields in the 18th century, and only later used as a millpond.

The Hilltop Trail forks away from the Coquina Trail, and then descends to intersect with Laurel Group Trail. Both require a fair amount of climbing and have a nice winding character over pleasantly rolling terrain. The mountains-to-the-sea Palmetto Trail also passes through here, running concurrently with park trails for a distance.

Poinsett State Park to Santee National Wildlife Refuge

Head back out on S-43-63/Poinsett Park Road and turn right (south) on SC 261. Drive 2.5 miles through forest, and then veer right (southwest) onto S-43-51/Camp Mac Boykin Road toward Rimini. About 1.5 miles farther, turn left into the grounds of **Saint Mark's Episcopal Church** (6205 Camp Mac Boykin Rd., Pinewood), founded in 1757.

The current structure was erected in 1855, made of brick baked from local clay. The church is coated with white stucco that contrasts nicely with the pretty red tile roof. The church is built on property donated by Richard Richardson, a plantation owner from this area. He was a magistrate and delegate to the First and Second Provincial Congresses. Six governors who were his descendants and a number of other notables attended Saint Mark's. A pleasant, tree-shaded cemetery adjoins the church.

Turn left out of the churchyard and continue south on S-43-51/Camp Mac Boykin Road.

If you have time, you may want to detour by taking a right (northwest) on S-43-808, 1.4 miles from the church. Drive 0.8 mile, to where the pavement ends, and turn right (east) into **Mill Creek County Park** *(7975 Milford Plantation Rd., Pinewood.*

Bear left after you enter the park and ride past the western side of dark Mill Creek Pond, filled with lily pads. You pass a lodge building and then enter a sprawling, shaded picnic area with campsites, restrooms, and showers. The clean ground cover is grass and pine straw. This is the southern trailhead for the High Hills of the Santee Passage of the Palmetto Trail, leading to Poinsett State Park, plus a horse trail.

At 2.7 miles from Saint Mark's Episcopal Church, turn right (west) off S-43-51/Camp Mac Boykin Road and onto unpaved Sparkleberry Landing Road. A brown sign noting Lake Marion access marks the turn. Drive downhill for 1.5 miles past fields and mixed forest to reach the boat landing for **Sparkleberry Swamp** (3198 Sparkleberry Landing Rd., Pinewood).

This is a great place to view the bald cypresses, tupelos, and huge amounts of aquatic plant life that populate the upper swampland reaches of Lake Marion. Fishing boats, canoes, and kayaks put in at this point to explore the far reaches of Sparkleberry Swamp. Grassy knolls and green trees make this an enjoyable picnic spot.

Backtrack to S-43-51/Camp Mac Boykin Road and turn right (south) to continue toward **Rimini**, 2.7 miles away, passing a massive hazardous waste landfill site on your right. Just as you cross from Sumter County into Clarendon County,

Sparkleberry Swamp, on the eastern edge of Lake Marion PATRICIA PIERCE

slow down as you enter the Rimini community. The intriguing, isolated village, has a few small stores and churches and an assortment of modest homes.

Bear right onto S-14-76/Old River Road and head southeast. About a mile south of Rimini, pass the site of the Battle of Halfway Swamp, where, in 1780, Patriot forces and smallpox combined to defeat British forces heading north from Charleston.

Immediately after passing the South Carolina Waterfowl Association's Head-quarters (9833 Old River Rd., Pinewood) on your right, slow down to take in **Elliott's Pond**, a hauntingly beautiful cypress lagoon on your left. The road that leads you to Elliott's Landing and Campground is to the right of the pond.

A mile farther, you come to the **Richardson Cemetery**. Turn right (west) and drive about 300 yards to a remote fenced-in graveyard surrounded by crop fields. Among the notables buried in this bleak setting are Revolutionary War brigadier general Richard Richardson (the same Richardson who donated the property for Saint Mark's Episcopal Church), James Burtrell Richardson (governor of South Carolina from 1802 to 1804), and John Peters Richardson, who founded The Citadel to train militia to defend against slave revolts, and served as governor of South Carolina from 1840 to 1842.

Continue 7.5 miles southeast on S-14-76/Old River Road, passing through an impoverished, somewhat densely populated area of farm fields and forestland punctuated with modest homes and a country church. Cross the wetlands of Big Branch before arriving at a stop sign at the intersection with S-14-373/Liberty Hill Road. Turn right (southwest) and turn right again after a few yards, into the parking lot of **Liberty Hill African Methodist Episcopal Church** (2310 Liberty Hill Rd., Summerton), with its adjacent old cemetery.

Liberty Hill Church was established in 1867; the present redbrick building was completed in 1905. Meetings held here in the 1940s and 1950s led to local court cases, centered on *Briggs vs. Elliott*, that culminated in the landmark US Supreme Court ruling of 1954 that segregated public schools are inherently unequal and thus unconstitutional.

The cases originated when local African American parents were unable to persuade the all-white local school board to provide bus transportation for their children to attend school. Their courage paved the way for a series of legislative, executive, and judicial decisions that ultimately resulted in victory for the civil rights movement.

From Liberty Hill Church, continue southwest on S-14-373/Liberty Hill Road for a mile, past Saint Paul Holiness Church and Saint Paul Primary School, to the intersection with US 301/US 15.

Turn right (southwest) on US 301/US 15 and drive through farmland and forest 3.3 miles to the causeway over Cantey Bay, a backwater of **Lake Marion**.

Travel a half mile farther and turn right (northwest) on S-14-803/Fort Watson Road to enter the **Bluff Unit of Santee National Wildlife Refuge** (2125 Fort Watson Rd., Summerton).

Santee National Wildlife Refuge is a 12,400-acre tract on the northern side of Lake Marion, consisting of mixed hardwoods, mixed pine-hardwoods, pine plantations, marsh, croplands, old fields, ponds, impoundments, and open water. It was created in 1941 as a way station for migrating waterfowl and is a winter stopover point for about 50,000 ducks and 8,000 geese and swans. There are thousands more year-round residents, including red-cockaded woodpeckers, bald eagles, hawks, killdeer, ospreys, alligators, white-tailed deer, raccoons, squirrels, and bobcats throughout the four separate units of the refuge.

Ride past moss-hung oaks and other hardwoods 0.3 mile to the visitor center on your left. This is a good place to view interpretive exhibits, obtain information about the refuge, and enjoy great views of **Lake Marion** from the center's wraparound porch. Look north across the cove to get your first glimpse of Santee Indian Mound.

Lake Marion's 110,000 acres were carved out of the swampy Santee River Basin in the late 1930s and early 1940s for a massive hydroelectric project to provide power to rural South Carolina and to provide jobs during the Great Depression. Because of the sudden wartime power needs of World War II, the basin was flooded in 1941, earlier than planned; one result was numerous trees left both standing and fallen in the water. Those trees produce great fish habitat, and Lake Marion is one of the nation's premier freshwater fishing locales. More than 120 fish species flourish in Lake Marion, including ten varieties of catfish, longnose gar, Atlantic and shortnose sturgeon, striped mullet, and striped, white, and largemouth bass.

Proceed northward from the visitor center a half mile to **Fort Watson/ Santee Indian Mound**. This spot was used as an Indian ceremonial mound around AD 1200–1400. During the Revolutionary War, the British established Fort Watson on top of the mound to command a strategic position on the Santee River, and its fall to General Francis Marion's Patriot forces in 1781 was an early part of a string of setbacks for the British that led to their final defeat two years later. In fact, Fort Watson was the first post in South Carolina to be taken from the British by Patriot forces. This is another good spot for viewing Lake Marion.

A little farther north is a parking area for hiking trails and bike paths. Turn around here and head back to the entrance to the Bluff Unit of Santee National Wildlife Refuge.

From the refuge entrance, turn left (northeast) on US 301/US 15/Saint Paul Road, drive 3.8 miles back to the intersection with S-14-373/Liberty Hill Road, and turn right (southeast).

Travel 2.1 miles, crossing I-95, and turn left (northeast) onto S-14-127/Bill Davis Road. Drive 4 miles past forest and fields through Davis Crossroads. A brown sign notes the turn to the John C. Land III Boat Landing.

Turn right (southeast) on S-14-559/William Brunson Road toward Potato Creek. After 3.5 miles, you come to a stop sign. Turn right (south) on Rogers Road to stay on S-14-559 for almost a half mile.

At the next stop sign, turn right (west) onto Greenall Road/S-14-260 and immediately left (south) onto Wildlife Drive, an unpaved road, for a 7.5-mile interpretive drive through the **Cuddo Unit of the Santee National Wildlife Refuge**. The Cuddo Unit is one of the best inland birding areas east of the Mississippi during the winter months. Pick up information at the kiosk at the entrance.

Drive a mile past open fields, shrub wetlands, and forest. Continue straight south through dark hardwood forest with a sprinkling of dogwoods and then past more shrubs and wetlands. After another mile, you pass the exit for a second one-way road, on your left. Proceed straight ahead 0.3 mile more through fields and wildflowers. At a gate where the road goes left (east), you can park and walk westward along a pathway toward Black Bottom, a good place to find alligators.

Continue east on what has just become a one-way loop road through more fields. After a half mile, bald cypress and tupelo trees rise to your right, with Lake Marion on the other side. Clearer views of Lake Marion appear as you round a curve after another half mile and head back west. A half mile farther, you leave the fields on your left altogether and curve north and then back east through forests and beautiful, soggy marshland. You pass lovely lily ponds that are home to alligators, frogs, turtles, and snakes. After 0.8 mile, you reach the entrance to 1.4-mile Foot Trail One.

Turn left and drive north about 0.1 mile. Here you can walk to your right (east) to reach the beginning of Foot Trail Two, also 1.4 miles. Take a left (west), and you reach a fork after another 0.1 mile. The road straight ahead goes back to the main entrance road; turn right (north) and head 1.1 delightful miles past open fields, dark hardwood forest, and shrub wetlands. When you reach the next junction, turn left (straight ahead is a dead end), and proceed westward for a winding 1.2 miles through forest and fields.

Turn right (north) on the tree-canopied main entrance road to head north for one mile and complete your scenic drive by exiting the Cuddo Unit of Santee National Wildlife Refuge.

Nearby Attractions

Goodale State Park, Kensington Mansion, Lake Marion 301 Pedestrian Bridge, Shaw Air Force Base, Sumter Opera House, Sumter County Museum, Swan Lake and Iris Gardens, towns of Manning, Santee, and Summerton.

17

Congaree Basin and Lake Marion

Congaree National Park to Santee State Park

General Description: This is a pretty 65-mile countryside ride to scenic natural areas and remote villages in South Carolina's upper coastal plain.

Special Attractions: COWASEE Basin natural area, Congaree National Park, Congaree River, Fort Motte, Lone Star, Low Falls Landing and Upper Santee Swamp, Halfway Swamp Creek, Elloree and Elloree Heritage Museum and Cultural Center, Santee State Park, and Lake Marion.

Location: Middle of the state, south of Columbia.

Travel Season: All year. Fall, winter, and spring are best for watching wildlife in Congaree Swamp National Park, but summer is a great time to enjoy Santee State Park and the rich crops and pasturelands along the way. Autumn is the best time to savor lush cottonfields along the way.

Services: Columbia has full accommodations and services. Santee, on Interstate 95, offers motels and restaurants. St. Matthews and Elloree have eateries and limited services.

The Drive

This drive takes travelers through the COWASEE Basin natural area, dominated by attractive countryside, forests, and wetlands typical of South Carolina's rich agrarian and natural heritage. You visit the fabulous Congaree National Park, ride through densely populated rural areas in Richland County, enjoy scenic cotton fields of Calhoun County, wander through the almost ghost towns of Fort Motte and Lone Star, gaze at the Upper Santee Swamp from Low Falls Landing, amble into quaint little Elloree, and conclude at nature-filled Santee State Park, on the shores of huge Lake Marion. As is often the case when riding through rural South Carolina, you pass many little churches along the way, and homes whose occupants descend from local families that have been in these specific locales since the 1800s or before.

Congaree National Park to Fort Motte

This drive takes you through the **COWASEE Basin Focus Area**, 215,000 acres along the Congaree-Wateree-Upper Santee River system protected for the purpose of promoting habitat protection, waterfowl restoration, research and management in the bottomland hardwood forests, river bluffs, and uplands within the basin.

Congaree Basin and Lake Marion:
Congaree National Park to Santee State Park

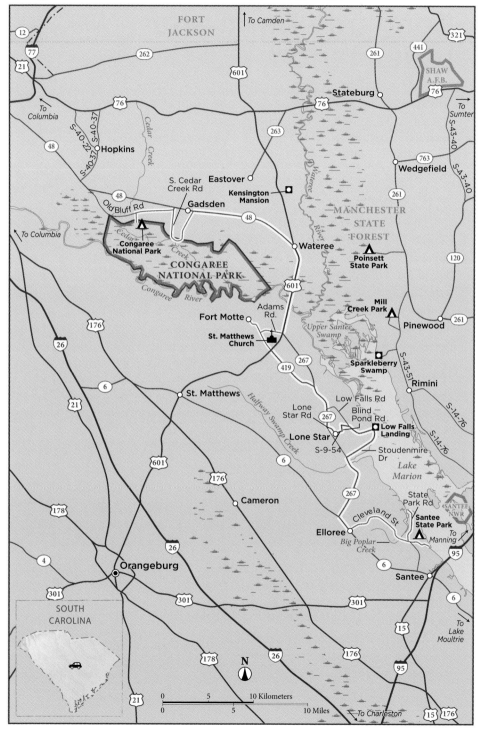

Approximately one-third of the protected land is made up of state and federal properties, including Manchester State Forest, Poinsett State Park, Upper Santee Swamp, Congaree Bluffs Heritage Preserve, and Congaree National Park. The remaining protected property is privately owned.

Begin at the Congaree National Park's **Harry Hampton Visitor Center** (100 National Park Rd., Hopkins), which offers excellent interpretive displays, a free film about the swamp, brochures, maps, and guidance from park staff and volunteers. Restrooms, water fountains, and vending machines are available.

Congaree National Park, nearly 27,000 acres in the heart of the Congaree River floodplain, represents the largest stand of old-growth river bottom hardwood forest in the United States. In 1983 it was designated as an International Biosphere Reserve.

Hit hard by Hurricane Hugo and other powerful windstorms in recent years, Congaree Park has lost many of its national record trees, but a host of huge, impressive specimens still remain, including three that are still the largest of their type in the country: a 42-foot possum haw, a 132-foot persimmon, and a 148-foot water hickory.

Congaree Park offers more than 30 miles of interlocking hiking trails, including a 2-mile boardwalk loop from the visitor center. This short loop carries you past towering loblolly pines, water-soaked floodplain, enchanting Weston Lake, fascinating bald cypress trees and knees, immensely diverse vegetation, and one of the highest forest canopies in the world. Other walkways include Weston Lake Trail, River Trail, Oak Ridge Trail, Kingsnake Trail, and Bluff Trail. Cedar Creek offers superb canoeing and kayaking options, and, along with Weston and Wise Lakes, good fishing.

In addition to those named above, the area's more than 80 tree and shrub species include beech, hornbeam, sycamore, pawpaw, red maple, red mulberry, sassafras, cottonwood, sweet gum, water tupelo, dwarf palmetto, tulip tree, 5 hickory varieties, mountain laurel, holly, black walnut, magnolia, dogwood, wax myrtle, 3 types of elm, and 14 varieties of oak. Wild azaleas bloom around the Bluff Trail.

The plentiful wildlife-viewing opportunities include 170 bird species. Among them are herons, ducks, egrets, white ibis, ospreys, vultures, bald eagles, bobwhites, wild turkeys, doves, cuckoos, hummingbirds, wrens, flycatchers, bluebirds, robins, mockingbirds, red-winged blackbirds, orioles, blue jays, 4 owl species, 4 swallow species, 5 varieties of vireos, red-cockaded and 6 other types of woodpeckers, 8 hawk varieties, 10 swallow species, and 26 types of warblers.

Additionally, the park offers a native plant butterfly garden with 45 varieties of butterflies, skippers, and moths. There are 8 types of bats that inhabit the forest, but none are of the Transylvanian variety.

Congaree National Park boardwalk, near Columbia John Clark

Furthermore, the site hosts 5 lizard species, 7 types of turtles, 11 kinds of salamanders, 18 snake varieties, and 19 species of frogs and toads, in addition to white-tailed deer, feral hogs, bobcats, raccoons, opossums, gray foxes, river otters, marsh and cottontail rabbits, and gray, fox, and flying squirrels. The park is truly an ecological wonderland.

Head 1.2 miles out on National Park Road through coastal plain forest to S-40-734/Old Bluff Road and turn right (east). Drive 2.6 miles past homes and fields to a stop sign. Take a right on S-40-1288/South Cedar Creek Road and drive 1.8 miles to the Cedar Creek parking area for Congaree National Park. Stop here and walk a few yards downhill to the eastern trailhead for Kingsnake Trail and a footbridge over mystical, meandering **Cedar Creek**. The lush vegetation and slow, foreboding stream provide a great locale for pictures, meditation, and relaxation.

From the Cedar Creek parking area, turn right, head east on S-40-1288/ South Cedar Creek Road, and then curve northeastward past more fields, forest, and modest dwellings for 3 miles. Just after crossing a railroad track, South Cedar Creek Road intersects with SC 48/Bluff Road in **Gadsden**, an old railroad village. Turn right and drive 7.6 miles on SC 48/Bluff Road through more densely populated countryside.

At the intersection with US 601 in the **Wateree** settlement, look to your left (northeast) to see the tall structures of Dominion Energy's Wateree coal-fired power plant rising above the forest.

Turn right and head south on US 601/McCords Ferry Road. This road provides a great perspective of the Congaree River and its wetlands. After a half mile, you come to the first of a series of causeways and bridges across vast river wetlands, with excellent views east and west of the dense bottomland forest and waters. About 3.5 miles along the elevated wetland roadway, you reach Bates Bridge Landing on your right, just before crossing the John M. Bates Bridge over the **Congaree River**. Turn right (southwest) and drive a few feet down into the landing area. Here you can get an up-close view of the mighty Congaree.

Go back up to US 601, turn right, and continue south, passing over the Congaree River with nice views on both sides of the winding central South Carolina water artery. On the south side of the river, you ascend quickly up a bluff to emerge into the farmlands of Calhoun County, named after antebellum firebrand statesman John C. Calhoun.

At 2.3 miles past the beginning of the bridge, turn right (west) on S-9-80/Adams Road, toward Fort Motte. (McCords Ferry Road on your left heads east.) Drive past kudzu, cotton fields, and scattered farmhouses for 1.5 miles to a stop sign; turn right (northwest) onto SC 419/Fort Motte Road. This is prime hunting country, especially for pheasant, quail, and deer.

Ease downhill for a mile to enter **Fort Motte**. As you cross Buck Head Creek and a railroad track, turn right (northeast) on S-9-150/Old Town Square. You may feel as though you have entered a town deserted for a hundred years. Abandoned storefronts facing the train tracks are now tangled in vines and canopied with moss-hung trees.

The town is named for Revolutionary War heroine Rebecca Motte, who lived nearby and drove a British garrison from her home by setting it ablaze with fire-tipped arrows. Fort Motte was once a bustling cotton and timber shipment center, but 20th-century highways passed the town by long ago. Now it is a small neighborhood of homes and forsaken buildings overgrown with kudzu.

Ride 2 blocks down S-9-150/Town Square Street and follow the road as it turns left (northwest) away from the tracks. Turn left again to remain on Town Square Street, this time southwest. Tin-roofed cottages with comfortable porches are tucked into the undergrowth here and there as you follow a 1-mile loop around the little village. Turn left (southeast) one more time to stay on S-9-150/Town Square Street and pass another forgotten commercial building before arriving back at the railroad tracks after completing your loop.

Fort Motte to Santee State Park

Turn right (southwest), drive a few yards, and turn left (southeast) to exit Fort Motte the way you came in, passing over the railroad tracks and Buck Head Creek. This time, however, stay on SC 419 past S-9-80/Adams Road and continue another mile to **Saint Matthews Parish Episcopal Church** (1164 Fort Motte Rd., Saint Matthews), on your left, established in 1765. The current Gothic-style structure was built in 1882, and the old church cemetery contains the remains of a number of local notables, including South Carolina writer and Pulitzer Prize winner Julia Peterkin.

Continue southeast another 0.4 mile to Wiles Crossroads. Cross US 601 to pass through countryside full of cotton fields, red barns, farmhouses, and churches until you reach SC 267/McCords Ferry after 4 miles.

Yield right (southeast) and drive 3 more pretty miles. At the intersection with SC 33, turn left onto S-9-11/Lone Star Road (southeast) toward Lone Star. Follow

Cotton field in full autumn bloom MARIE GOFF

S-9-11/Lone Star Road for 0.7 mile into **Lone Star**, another farm/railroad town that time and highways passed by long ago. The train still comes through, but it has been decades since it stopped here. The old railroad depot is on your left as you enter town, having been moved from its original location.

As you turn left (northeast) on S-9-54/Lone Star Road, dilapidated old stores line up on your left, facing the tracks. On the opposite side of the tracks, a rustic convenience store on a dirt road still does neighborly business with families nestled in cottages amid the trees.

Go a half mile beside the tracks and turn left (north) on S-9-402/Blind Pond Road. Follow this road for a mile north, and then another half mile as it turns east. At the stop sign, bear right (southeast) on S-9-129/Low Falls Road to ride through vast plant nursery fields toward **Low Falls Landing**, 2 miles away.

Low Falls Landing Bait House sits atop the hill as you turn into the landing's parking lot. Here you can pick up live bait, tackle, and snacks. On the porch

Low Falls Landing on west side of Lake Marion, near Lone Star JOHN CLARK

and inside the tiny store are stuffed beavers, snakes, fish, and other interesting creatures.

Low Falls Landing is a beautiful spot to view the **Upper Santee Swamp of Lake Marion**, where Lake Marion pushes northward to blur the dividing line between the bottom end of the northern section of the Santee River and the beginning of the lake.

Swollen-based, moss-hung bald cypresses and water tupelos dot the waters. Floating mats of vegetation provide excellent habitat for numerous types of fish, including bass, catfish, and bream, plus waterfowl in winter and migrating songbirds in spring and fall. This swamp also hosts a huge nesting colony of blue herons, as well as other wading birds, alligators, and numerous snakes, frogs, and

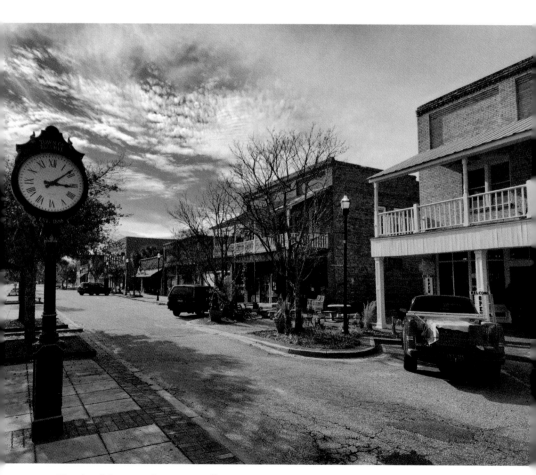

Cleveland Street in downtown Elloree John Clark

turtles. A pier provides good opportunity for fishing, wildlife viewing, and photography. Kayaks, canoes, and all manner of boats can put in here.

Backtrack on S-9-129/Low Falls Road for 0.1 mile up a hill; then turn left (south) on S-9-286/ Stoudenmire Drive. This winding road carries you a pleasant 3 miles past lake cottages to your left and cotton fields, forestland, wetlands, and horse pastures on your right. When you reach SC 267/McCords Ferry, turn left (southeast) and cross a double bridge over **Halfway Swamp Creek**. Continue 4.5 miles to the intersection with SC 6, where you bear left and head into Elloree, a half mile southeast. Here, SC 267 and SC 6 run concurrently.

Elloree is a pretty little community with an attractively maintained downtown area. Comfortable old homes line the road as you enter town on Old Number 6 Highway.

At the stoplight, turn right (southwest) on Cleveland Street to tour the quaint 1-block downtown area, lined with antique shops, gift boutiques, an art gallery, restaurants, and the **Elloree Heritage Museum and Cultural Center** (2714 Cleveland St.), offering a fascinating view of South Carolina rural life. The 100-foot-wide street has brick crosswalks and is lined with flowering and hardwood trees. Horse breeding and training are big in this area, and much of the artwork reflects equestrian themes. This is a great place to stop and linger.

Turn left (southeast) on Railroad Avenue, left (northeast) on Barkley Street, and left again on Old Number 6 Highway to return to the intersection with Cleveland. This time, turn right and head east (right) on S-38-105/Cleveland Street toward Santee State Park, 5 miles away. Horse pastures, hay fields, and forestland line the way.

Santee State Park (251 State Park Rd., Santee) is the only major public park on 110,000-acre **Lake Marion**. Its 2,500 acres offer fishing, boating, swimming, birding and ten miles of biking and hiking trails. Special features are rare limestone sinkholes and caverns, which can be viewed from the trails. The park has a fact-filled interpretive center and offers great views of Lake Marion from the fishing pier area on the west side and the swimming area on the east side.

When you arrive at the intersection of S-38-82/State Park Road and S-38-105/ Cleveland Road at the park entrance, continue on Cleveland Road through the park's East Entrance 1.5 miles to the swimming and boat launch area, where you can enjoy expansive views of Lake Marion. Retrace your route back to the intersection and turn right on State Park Road to pass through the West Entrance. To conclude your scenic drive, travel 2.3 forested miles to the fishing pier, park store, interpretive center, and rental cabins, ten of which are on piers over the lake, along with 20 bordering the shoreline.

Birds frequently seen in the park include quail, eastern wood pewees, wild turkeys, brown thrashers, ospreys, bald eagles, mourning doves, owls (great

Santee State Park, on southwest side of Lake Marion JOHN CLARK

horned, eastern screech, and barred), Carolina wrens, and all South Carolina woodpeckers, including the rare red-cockaded. Anoles scamper on the ground, while metalmark butterflies flit overhead. Deer, raccoons, opossums, and gray and fox squirrels are among the park's other wildlife. Rare southeastern myotis bats inhabit the limestone regions.

Trees in the park include loblolly and longleaf pines, swamp and turkey oaks, dogwoods, bald cypresses, sweet gums, red maples, and red bays. Dog-hobble, yucca, wax myrtle, wild ginger, pawpaw, trumpet creeper, and partridge pea are among the wildflower varieties at Santee.

Nearby Attractions

Columbia's Main Street and the Vista, Columbia Museum of Art, Congaree Bluffs Heritage Preserve, Congaree Creek Heritage Preserve, Edisto Memorial Gardens, Historic Columbia House Museums, Kensington Mansion, Lake Marion 301 Pedestrian Bridge, Riverbanks Zoo and Garden, South Carolina State House, South Carolina State Museum, University of South Carolina, Three Rivers Greenway.

18

Historic Charleston

Daniel Island to Ashley River

General Description: This 45-mile drive in metropolitan Charleston takes visitors across major waterways, through stunning saltwater marshlands, along inviting beaches, and past numerous beautiful homes, gardens, and historic sites.

Special Attractions: Daniel Island, Palmetto Islands County Park, Boone Hall Plantation and Gardens, Charles Pinckney National Historic Site, Intracoastal Waterway, Isle of Palms and Isle of Palms County Park, Breach Inlet, Atlantic Ocean, Intracoastal Waterway, Sullivan's Island, Fort Moultrie, Pitt Street Bridge Park, Mount Pleasant Old Village, Shem Creek Park, Arthur Ravenel Jr. Bridge, Historic Charleston and its homes and gardens, spectacular views of the Cooper, Wando, and Ashley Rivers.

Location: Central coast.

Travel Season: All year. Flowers and weather peak in March and April.

Services: There is a plethora of hotels, restaurants, and all services in Charleston, North Charleston, Mount Pleasant, and Summerville.

The Drive

Beginning on I-526 in North Charleston, this drive takes sightseers over the bridges of the Mark Clark Highway with views of the Cooper and Wando Rivers, past Daniel Island, and across a high-rise span over the Intracoastal Waterway, providing a stunning overlook of the waterway, adjacent salt marshes, and the barrier Isle of Palms. Next, visitors travel past Atlantic Ocean beaches to historic Sullivan's Island and on to the Old Village neighborhood of Mount Pleasant before crossing the Arthur Ravenel Jr. Bridge spanning the Cooper River. In Charleston you'll see numerous gardens and significant structures in the historic district and along the waterfront Battery, before heading south to panoramic views atop a bridge over the Ashley River.

Daniel Island to Isle of Palms

Begin by traveling east on the **Don N. Holt Bridge**, on I-526 E/Mark Clark Highway, taking you from North Charleston to Daniel Island.

At the crest high above the **Cooper River**, look south, to your right, and enjoy captivating distant views of the magnificent Arthur Ravenel Jr. Bridge over the Cooper River, connecting Mount Pleasant and the elegant, beautiful Charleston city center. Straight ahead to the east, flocks of gulls and pelicans hover over

Historic Charleston: Daniel Island to Ashley River

ATLANTIC OCEAN

CAPE ROMAIN NATIONAL WILDLIFE REFUGE

Capers Island

To Georgetown

Copahee Sound

Isle of Palms

Isle of Palms County Park

703

Waterway

Intracoastal Wtrwy.

Sullivan's Island

Fort Moultrie

Fort Sumter

Charleston Harbor

May Forest State Park

JAMES ISLAND

Charleston Inlet

Folly Beach

Boone Hall Plantation and Gardens

517

41

Palmetto Islands County Park

Needlerush Parkway

Charles Pinckney National Historic Site

Mount Pleasant

703

703

703

Center St.

Middle St.

Long Point Rd. S-10-97

17

Memorial Waterfront Park

Patriots Point

17

Daniel Island

Cooper River

Wando River

S-8-33

Mark Clark Highway

Don Holt Bridge

North Charleston

526

52

26

642

Ashley River

171

Charles Towne Landing State Historic Site

Charleston

61

17

30

171

Stono River

700

To Rockville

To Johns Island

61F

61

526

642

26

Charleston International Airport

To Columbia

SOUTH CAROLINA

N

0   2.5   5 Kilometers
0   2.5   5 Miles

Charleston inset

Charleston Harbor

Concord St.

East Bay St.

SC Aquarium

Intl. African American Museum

Waterfront Park

The Battery and White Point Gardens

East Bay St.

Charleston Visitor Center

Meeting St.

King St.

N. Market St.

S. Market St.

Anson

Church

Meeting

King St.

S. Battery St.

Murray Blvd.

Logan

East

S

Broad

Tradd

College of Charleston

King St.

St. Philip St.

Coming St.

Saint Philip St.

Smith St.

Pitt

Rutledge Ave.

Ashley Ave.

Gadsden St.

Barre

Gadsden Blvd.

Lockwood Blvd.

Halsey

Calhoun St.

Bee St.

Doughty St.

Calhoun

Line St.

Ashley Ave.

Hagood Ave.

Fishburne St.

17

The Medical University of South Carolina

Ashley River

Albemarle Point

James Island

30

marshlands that form Clouter Island, a small piece of land between the Cooper River and Clouter Creek, formed mostly by sediment from river dredging operations. Looking north, you see the North Charleston Terminal of the State Ports Authority, riverside industrial facilities, marshland, and forest.

As you head down the east slope of the bridge and onto **Daniel Island** in Berkeley County, you view a scattering of docks extending like long, skinny fingers from unseen, tree-shrouded homes, past spartina grass and palmetto trees to meandering, dark marshland tidal streams.

The first exit you reach is for Clements Ferry Road/S-10-33 (exit 23), 2 miles from the crest of the Holt Bridge. It is located on a peninsula connected to the mainland. South of here are remnants of a rustic, rural African American community that was quite isolated prior to the construction of the bridges on the Mark Clark Highway about three decades ago.

Continuing on I-526/Mark Clark Highway, cross the winding, tidal Berefords Creek, and enter Daniel Island.

At 1.2 miles from Clements Ferry Road, you reach the exit for the island's residential and commercial complex, a tastefully planned mixed-use community that is part of the City of Charleston, although it is in a different county from the rest of the city and contiguously connected only by river.

For a taste of this interesting development, turn here on exit 24 for the "Town Center" and adjoining residential area built in the "new urbanism" architecture. Homes here are built in the style of the 1930s and '40s and provide a real sense of community, with sidewalks, parks, and porches encouraging neighbors to visit in their front yards.

Look to your right to see Credit One Stadium and tennis center (161 Seven Farms Dr., Charleston), on Daniel Island, home of an annual high profile women's professional tennis tournament accented by an impressive 10,000-seat center court stadium. The stadium is also a major, frequently used entertainment venue.

Cross a bridge that leads you off Daniel Island and over the Wando River, where you have a terrific view to your right (south) of the tennis complex and Daniel Island Town Center on the west side of the river, and the Wando State Ports Authority Terminal on the east side. As you continue your crossing of the wide Wando River, and enter the city limits of Mount Pleasant, take in another, closer perspective of the Arthur Ravenel Jr. Bridge and the Charleston skyline to your right, looking southwest.

On the far (west) side of the Wando, 1.5 miles past the river, take exit 28 onto Long Point Road/S-10-97. Turn left and ride east 1.9 miles, and then turn left (north) for Needlerush Parkway, which takes you 1.3 miles to **Palmetto Islands County Park** (444 Needlerush Pkwy., Mount Pleasant). The park, which charges a nominal entrance fee, offers playgrounds, a water park, boating, bicycling, viewing

Boardwalk in Palmetto Islands County Park, Mount Pleasant JOHN CLARK

towers, and walks through a wonderland of tidal marsh, maritime forest, and a multitude of palmetto trees.

Backtrack to Long Point Road and turn left (east). Ride a half mile past marshland and overhanging oaks to the entrance to **Boone Hall Plantation and Gardens** (1235 Long Point Rd., Mount Pleasant).

There is a substantial admission fee for Boone Hall. If you choose to visit, turn left on Oak Avenue to enter the plantation. The estate dates from 1681 on land granted by the lords proprietor to Major Hon Boone, a member of Charles Town's first fleet of settlers. Today its ancient live oaks decorate a 0.75-mile-long avenue to Boone Hall, a Georgian mansion constructed in 1935 on the site of the previous house. The original cotton gin house and slave row are standing, and visitors can tour the plantation, gardens, and Butterfly Pavilion.

The **Charles Pinckney National Historic Site**, 0.2 mile farther east, on the right (south) side of the road (1254 Long Point Rd., Mount Pleasant), touts archaeological remains of brick foundations and an unfurnished 1820s tidewater cottage. These are the last protected remnants of **Snee Farm**, the country estate of Charles Pinckney, a drafter and signer of the Constitution. The national park site offers interpretive exhibits free of charge and you can walk the grounds at your leisure. Picnic tables are shaded by huge oak and magnolia trees. Restrooms are just off of the gravel parking lot. Admission is free.

Continue eastward on Long Point Road another 0.6 mile to the intersection with US 17/Sweetgrass Basket Makers Highway.

Sweetgrass baskets, made of coiled native sweetgrass and pine needles sewn together with strips of palmetto leaves, are unique to the Lowcountry, and represent one of the oldest West African art forms in America. Basket design and craftsmanship that originated from the rice culture in West Africa were brought to America by enslaved people who made the cultivation of rice a financial success in South Carolina. These unique baskets were originally used on plantations in the production of rice, and the art of weaving the baskets has been handed down through African American families since the 1700s and the earliest days of the colony. Unfortunately, development has erased most of the roadside vendor stands on this section of the highway.

Turn right (south) on US 17 and ride one mile to a stoplight and left-hand turn to SC 517/Isle of Palms Connector/Clyde Moultrie Dangerfield Highway, leading to the Isle of Palms. Turn left (southeast). A little over a mile down the road, palmetto trees, spartina grass, and marshlands line the Intracoastal Waterway. Ospreys fly overhead, and huge nests sit atop poles in wetlands and forests tucked close to the highway.

Crossing the bridge over the **Intracoastal Waterway**, you have an expansive view of the waters surrounding the entire island dotted with vacation and year-round homes, the inland waterway and its boat traffic below you, and the majestic **Atlantic Ocean** on the far side of the Isle of Palms.

When you reach the end of the bridge, 4 miles from US 17, you are on the **Isle of Palms**, an incorporated city; the road becomes 14th Avenue on the last 0.2 mile of the bridge.

For many years visitors to the Isle of Palms arrived by water or via a single railroad bridge from Sullivan's Island. Today this resort island is accessible by two highway bridges. The island includes the gated golf course/beach/yachting community of Wild Dunes at its north end, as well as numerous residential and vacation homes and family beach areas where dolphins romp offshore. Although many people have made the Isle of Palms their permanent home, it remains a quiet, family-oriented vacation spot.

At the intersection at the base of the bridge, cross over Palm Boulevard/SC 703. The **Isle of Palms County Park** (1 14th Ave.) is on your left 0.1 mile ahead, and for a small fee you can enjoy the public beach here.

Follow 14th Avenue as it curves to the right and becomes **Ocean Boulevard**, leading you to the heart of the island's commercial and public beach areas. Cross Pavilion Drive. To the right (west) of Ocean Boulevard is a large public parking area and an ice-cream parlor, along with sandwich shops, bike rentals, and boutiques selling swim gear.

On your left (east), facing the ocean, are restaurants, bars, and even beach volleyball.

Travel a mile down Ocean Boulevard to experience the residential area of the island. Newly built modern homes stand on the beachfront to your left (east) and right. A few older, more traditional beach homes remain.

Isle of Palms to Ravenel Bridge

Turn right (west) on Third Avenue. Cross over Charleston and Carolina Boulevards. At the third stop sign, turn left (southwest) onto Palm Boulevard/SC 703 to head south 0.7 mile to Sullivan's Island. Hamlin and Swinton Creeks and the Intracoastal Waterway are to your right. Pass by a marina and restaurant and drive on H. L. Hunley Bridge across the tidal waters of **Breach Inlet** to enter aged, serene **Sullivan's Island**. Palm Boulevard/SC 703 becomes Jasper Boulevard once you enter Sullivan's Island.

Charleston residents built summer homes here in the early 19th century. Edgar Allan Poe was a resident at one time, and based his tale *The Gold Bug* on pirate treasure believed to be buried on the island. (Street names here include Poe and Goldbug Avenues, as well as Raven Drive.) Between 1700 and 1775 the island was a holding site where tens of thousands of kidnapped Africans were brought to North America to be sold into enslavement.

After you cross the bridge, bear left (southwest) off Jasper Boulevard onto Middle Street. Go 0.1 mile and turn left (southeast) onto Station 32. Travel over I'on Avenue alongside Breach Inlet and then turn right (southwest) onto Marshall Avenue, lined with beachfront homes.

These impressive new structures on highly valuable property were built after their predecessors were destroyed during 1989's Hurricane Hugo. Many older homes, however, serve as restful reminders of the island's longtime role as summer quarters for Charleston's elite. Ride past villas protected by whitewashed picket fences covered with blue and purple dappled morning glories, and sandy yards dotted with palmettos and oleanders.

Travel 5 blocks on Marshall and turn right (north) onto Station 28. Drive one block, and turn left (southwest) on Atlantic Boulevard. Go 6 blocks to Station 23 Street, turn right (north), travel 2 blocks, and turn left (southwest) onto Middle Street.

You are now in the heart of tiny downtown Sullivan's Island, featuring a substantial variety of excellent food and drink establishments.

Continue west past quaint cottages for 1.4 miles to **Fort Moultrie National Historic Park** (1214 Middle St.), on your left (southeast). A unit of Fort Sumter and Fort Moultrie National Historic Park, Fort Moultrie overlooks the Atlantic

Ocean and the city of Charleston to the south, guarding the entrance to Charleston Harbor along with Fort Sumter across the water.

Originally constructed of palmetto logs during the Revolutionary War (thus the origin of the palmetto tree symbol on the South Carolina state flag), the fortification has since been rebuilt many times and testifies to the development of coastal defenses. This fort protected Charleston in every major war from the War of 1812 to World War II. It is most famous for its role in April 1861 when cannons from this location and others touched off the Civil War by bombarding Fort Sumter, to which Union garrison forces from Fort Moultrie had fled.

Walk or drive to the northwest side of Fort Moultrie, at the end of Station 12 Street, for a great view of **Fort Sumter**, on an island in the middle of the entrance to Charleston Harbor and accessible only by tour boats.

From Station 12 Street, backtrack east on Middle Street for 0.6 mile, then turn right (south) on Station 17 Street. Drive 2 blocks and then turn left (northeast) on I'on Avenue to see some of the largest and oldest homes on Sullivan's Island, decorated with huge wraparound porches and stately colonial and Victorian facades. Sprawling live oaks, palmettos, and other lush greenery surround these beautiful structures.

On your right (east) you will see the **Sullivan's Island Lighthouse** rising 161 feet above sea level, and pass the **Edgar Allan Poe County Library** (1921 I'on Ave.) and **Sullivan's Island Elementary School**, which were built in bunkers that served as military batteries during the first half of the 20th century.

Go 0.8 miles on I'on Avenue and then turn left (northwest) on Station 22. Drive one block, turn right (northeast) on Middle Street, and then left on Station 22½ Street/SC 703 to head northeast toward Mount Pleasant.

Travel northwest 2 miles on the causeway through aromatic tidal salt marsh bordering Charleston Harbor and the Intracoastal Waterway, lined with delightful oleanders and palmettos. Often you can see locals fishing and crabbing in the ponds and creeks. Midway along, cross the **Ben Sawyer Bridge**, a swing span bridge over the Intracoastal Waterway that opens for boat traffic. It was constructed in 1945, and until 1993, when the Isle of Palms Connector was completed, was the only means to reach not only Sullivan's Island, but also the Isle of Palms.

On the north side of the marsh, you enter the city of **Mount Pleasant** on SC 703/Ben Sawyer Boulevard, now a sprawling suburb but once a sleepy harborside village across the water from Charleston. To reach the heart of the old village, turn left (southwest) on Center Street, at a traffic light 1.3 miles from the Ben Sawyer Bridge. Travel 1.2 miles on Center Street to the southern tip of Mount Pleasant, past new residential developments overlooking the marsh and older ranch-style homes on your right.

Pitt Street Bridge Park, Mount Pleasant JOHN CLARK

One block before Center Street ends, turn left (southwest) onto Pitt Street and drive 0.2 mile past neat old cottages and some newer homes under moss-hung oaks to reach a causeway leading into the marsh. The old causeway roadbed, once part of a trolley passage and auto highway to Sullivan's Island, is now a lovely greenway called **Pitt Street Bridge Park**. Stretching almost a half mile through marshland to Cove Inlet of the Intracoastal Waterway, this is a great place to stop for a stroll and enjoy terrific views of the water, the salt air, fishermen, and crabbers, along with gulls and herons playing amid the spartina grass.

Backtrack to Center Street, turn left (west), go one block, and then turn right (northwest) on Middle Street to enter Mount Pleasant's Old Village. Cozy bungalows fortified by short picket fences and ivy-covered 2-story brick and wooden homes line the streets of this tranquil neighborhood. After one very long block, you cross McCormick Street. A children's park lies to the east side of Middle Street, and picturesque **Alhambra Hall**, a public facility at 131 Middle St., is on the west side of the road, surrounded by green space.

This a good spot to walk to water's edge and view Charleston's Battery waterfront across the way, as well as Fort Sumter to the south. Middle Street, like others in the neighborhood, stretches past and around old oaks, adding a special touch to the community.

After one more long block on Middle Street, turn right (northeast) on McCants Drive, go 2 short blocks, and take the second left (northwest) onto Pitt Street. The old sanctuary of **Saint Paul's Lutheran Church**, constructed in 1884, is 2 blocks along, at 604 Pitt Street on your right (east).

Patjens Post Office, constructed by Postmaster Henry Patjens in 1899, is on the right another 2 blocks along, at the corner of Pitt and Banks Streets. It was built beside the Patjens family business at a more central location, but moved to the present location at the edge of a town park in 1971.

Another block along the way, at 302 Pitt Street, is the tan **Darby Building** (1884), originally the Berkeley County Courthouse. Mount Pleasant served as the Berkeley County seat from 1883 to 1895. This structure has also served as a Baptist Church, a school, a seminary, a town hall, and a newspaper office. Today it serves as the Mount Pleasant Recreation Department and Fine Arts Center.

Continue 2 more blocks to arrive at the Old Village's tiny, quaint downtown area. At the corner of Venning and Pitt Street on your left (101 Pitt St.) is the **Post House Inn and Restaurant**, built in 1896.

Take a right (northeast) on Venning Street, go a few feet, and then turn left (northwest) on Church Street. Drive one block on Church Street past more lovely old dwellings. At the intersection with Hibben Street after 2 blocks, the **Mount Pleasant Presbyterian Church** is directly in front of you at 302 Hibben Street. This white, wooden, 2-story structure, erected around 1854 and originally

Fishing boats and restaurants on Shem Creek, Mount Pleasant JOHN CLARK

a Congregational Church, served as a Confederate hospital during the Civil War and then briefly housed a school for freedmen during Reconstruction.

Go right (northeast) one block on Hibben and turn left (northwest) on Whilden Street. Travel one block and then bear left (northwest) at the traffic light to merge into Coleman Boulevard/SC 703/US 17/US 701.

Cross over **Shem Creek**, where a number of fishing and shrimping boats are sure to be docked and bobbing in the waters bordering the numerous local seafood restaurants, on both sides of the creek. Just past Shem Creek, on your left, is the parking area for **Shem Creek Park**, full of boardwalks and trails with marsh and creek views. Public restrooms are at the entrance.

Continue northwest on Coleman Boulevard for 2 miles past Shem Creek to access the **Arthur Ravenel Jr. Bridge** over the **Cooper River**. Often simply called the Cooper River Bridge, it opened in 2005, replacing two much older spans. At the time of its completion, it was the longest cable-stayed bridge in North America and the tallest structure in South Carolina.

Patriots Point Naval and Maritime Museum *(40 Patriots Point Rd., Mount Pleasant) can be reached by turning left at the Coleman Boulevard Intersection with Patriot Point Road (west) 1.5 miles from Shem Creek, a half mile prior to accessing the bridge.*

The museum's centerpiece is the retired aircraft carrier USS Yorktown. Its 41,000 tons and 888 feet of steel are permanently moored in the mud. Originally

Ravenel Bridge over the Cooper River MARIE GOFF

named Bon Homme Richard, *the ship was renamed in 1942 to honor the previous Yorktown aircraft carrier that was lost at the World War II Battle of Midway. The present ship was the 10th aircraft carrier to be commissioned by the US Navy. It saw extensive action in the Pacific during World War II and played a key role in the Vietnam War. The walking tour of the gigantic ship allows you to see fascinating maritime equipment and other historical material that tells the story of the importance of sea power.*

Other ships at Patriots Point include the USS Laffey *Destroyer and the submarine* **Clamagore***.*

Nearby, at 71 Harry Hallman Boulevard, is **Memorial Waterfront Park***, where you will find a spacious park, the Mount Pleasant Pier, the* **Mount Pleasant Visitor Center***, and the* **Sweetgrass Cultural Arts Pavilion***, all tucked underneath the on-ramps of the Arthur Ravenel Jr. Bridge.*

Ravenel Bridge to Historic Downtown Charleston and Ashley River

Cross the **Ravenel Bridge** over the **Cooper River** into the heart of old Charleston. From the bridge, you'll see ship terminals of the State Ports Authority to your left (south), and Daniel Island and the Mark Clark Highway in the distance to your right (north). Travel 2.5 miles and take the Meeting Street exit to your right. Turn left (south) at the traffic light onto Meeting Street. Follow signs to the Charleston Visitor Center 1.1 miles ahead on your right.

Charleston was settled in 1670, and by the mid-1700s it had become the richest and fourth largest city in colonial America. Plantation owners flocked here during the summer to escape the malarial backcountry and to experience the theater, ballrooms, and other cultural and social events of the times. The city maintains its aristocratic, southern gentility established during the plantation era, and remains an eclectic and inviting locale to this day.

Traditionally based architecture rules here, but homes are set apart with colorful paints, one-of-a-kind wrought-iron gates, and banisters and balconies. Enormous columned homes on the waterfront Battery and densely packed shanty homes make Charleston unlike any other city you will ever visit.

Although this is a driving tour, Charleston is best seen on foot. This drive will only whet your appetite for the narrow avenues and gardens tucked behind stately homes that you can only truly appreciate on foot. Walk on the cobblestone streets, speak with the Gullah basket weavers in the Market, and step into the numerous ice-cream parlors, sandwich shops, and fine-dining restaurants. You'll never have enough time to enjoy all there is to do in this stimulating, historic city.

The **Charleston Visitor Center** (375 Meeting St.) is at the intersection of Meeting and Mary Streets. Turn right here and find a wealth of information on places to stay and eat and things to do. The facility offers maps with a variety of walking tour options. For a nominal fee, you can watch the excellent, 21-projector, multi-image slide show *Forever Charleston*. You can also buy a day pass to ride on the DASH, a shuttle bus that circles around and through the historic area.

Exit the visitor center and turn right (south) onto Meeting Street. On your left at 360 Meeting Street, across the street from the Visitor Center, is the **Charleston Museum**, collecting and preserving artifacts relating to the Lowcountry.

Although the present building is modern, the Charleston Museum dates from 1773 and is considered America's first museum.

Cross over John Street. On your left at 350 Meeting Street is the **Joseph Manigault House** (1803), a National Historic Landmark. The home is open to visitors.

Continue south on **Meeting Street** and take in the pink Embassy Suites Hotel on your right (west) at 337 Meeting St., located in the original building (ca. 1822) of the South Carolina Military College, The Citadel. The hotel looks like a fortressed castle at the top of **Marion Square Park**, a pedestrian green space decorated with azaleas, magnolias, crepe myrtles, and palmettos that offers a peaceful refuge in the midst of bustling downtown Charleston. It is named for a Revolutionary War hero, General Francis Marion, the "Swamp Fox." Note the

Holocaust Memorial on the south side of the square. As you pass Marion Square, you reach the intersection of Meeting and Calhoun Streets.

If you wish to detour to visit the **South Carolina Aquarium** *(100 Aquarium Wharf), and the* **International African American Museum** *(14 Wharfside Street) turn left (east) on Calhoun Street, drive 4 blocks to East Bay Street, and continue a couple of blocks farther to the two magnificent venues. The departure docks for boat tours to* **Fort Sumter**, *as well as harbor tours, are also at the wharf.*

On your way, you'll pass "Mother" Emmanuel African Methodist Episcopal Church, on your left at 110 Calhoun Street, founded in 1817. The present structure dates from 1891 and was the scene of an infamous mass shooting by a white supremist that took the life of Senator and Reverend Clementa C. Pinckney and eight of his fellow parishioners who had invited the gunman to their Bible study one evening in June 2015. Senator Pinckney was a highly respected friend of both authors of this book.

From Marion Square continue driving south on Meeting Street. At the intersection with Market Street, about 6 blocks past Calhoun, is **Market Hall**, at 188 Meeting Street. This is the site of the first public market established after the Revolutionary War. The Greek Revival structure dates back to 1841. Look for the frieze of the sheep and bull's head, which indicated that meat was sold here. Today the market sells an array of handmade crafts and interesting items, including sweetgrass baskets woven by Gullah women. The Market is worth a walk-through even if you are not looking to buy.

Continue southward on Meeting Street. Pass Cumberland Street on your left and Horelbeck Alley on your right. The **Circular Congregational Church** (1891), organized around 1681 as the Independent Church of Charles Town, is on your left at 150 Meeting Street. The first building for this church, made of white brick, was called the "The White Meeting House" and is believed to be the namesake of Meeting Street. The church's cemetery is the oldest in the city, with graves dating as far back as 1695.

Next, to your right at 135 Meeting Street, is the **Gibbes Museum of Art**, established in 1858. The present building was constructed in 1905. Noted for its outstanding collection of South Carolina portraits and miniatures, the museum offers the Robert Marks collection of photography, a 20th-century African American art collection, a Japanese woodblock gallery, a miniature portrait gallery, and the Charleston Renaissance Gallery. It includes works of well-known Charleston artists who brought national attention to Charleston in the 1920s, such as Anna Heyward Taylor, Elizabeth O'Neil Verner, and Alice Ravenel Huger Smith.

The **Mills House Hotel** is on your right at 115 Meeting Street. The current Italian style building stands on the site of the original Mills House Hotel (ca.

1853). It has incorporated the original iron balcony where, in 1861, General Robert E. Lee watched a great fire sweep through Charleston.

Next to the Mills House Hotel is historic **Hibernian Hall** at 105 Meeting Street. Built in 1840 by one of the oldest Irish fraternal societies in America, this enormous Greek Revival structure plays host to elegant wedding parties and the annual Hibernian Society's Saint Patrick's Day party. The porch is decorated with stone brought from Ireland in 1851.

To your left at 100 Meeting Street, at the corner of Chalmers Street, is the **South Carolina Historical Society**, housed in the "Fireproof Building." Designed by renowned South Carolina architect Robert Mills and constructed of brick (ca. 1822–27), this stone and iron building is the first fireproof structure built in the United States.

Next on your left is **Washington Park**. The monument in the center was erected by the Washington Light Infantry to honor its members who died

Four Corners of Law, at intersection of Broad and Meeting Streets Marie Goff

in the Civil War. This small urban jewel is, surprisingly, a great setting for bird-watching.

The famous **Four Corners of Law** is at the intersection of Broad and Meeting Streets, so named because each corner represents a different branch of the law: city, county, federal, and religious.

To your immediate left (east), just past Washington Park at 80 Broad Street, is **Charleston's City Hall**, designed by Gabriel Manigault and built in 1801. Several historic portraits hang here, including Trumbull's painting of George Washington in 1791.

To your right is the **Charleston County Courthouse**, site of the original State House of South Carolina, built in 1752. The present building was completed in 1792, two years after Columbia became the state capital. It was refurbished and reopened in 2002.

Across Broad Street on your right is the **US Courthouse and Post Office**, constructed in 1898. A post office museum is inside and open to visitors during regular post office hours. Sweetgrass baskets and cut flowers are sold by local women on the sidewalk here, an old Charleston tradition.

On the far left corner of Meeting and Broad Streets at 71 Broad Street is **Saint Michael's Episcopal Church**, the oldest church building in the city, constructed in 1752–61. The clock bells were imported from England in 1764. The church's steeple served as the city's lookout and alarm tower for many years and was used by pilots at sea to find their bearings.

During the Civil War, however, the steeple was painted black so the enemy could not spot the city so easily. The church welcomes visitors, and you might also wish to visit Saint Michael's churchyard, where two signers of the US Constitution are buried, as well as James L. Petigru, a noted (and rare) South Carolina anti-secessionist. (Petigru is famous for saying, "South Carolina is too small for a Republic and too large for an insane asylum.")

Cross Broad Street and continue southward on Meeting Street. Just past **Saint Michael Alley** at 72 Meeting Street, on your left is the **South Carolina Society Hall** constructed in 1804. The society was founded by French Huguenots in 1737 to help support a local tavern that was doing poorly. Today, the Society remains charitable by donating scholarships to the College of Charleston.

On your left at 64 Meeting Street is the **Andrew Hasell House**. Built in 1789, this house represents typical Charleston design with its deep, narrow lot. Charleston's piazzas are built to protect from the hot afternoon sun and to provide cross-ventilation from the southwesterly breezes when the homes' windows and doors are open.

Across the street at 59 Meeting Street on your right is the **Branford-Horry House**. Built in 1751, this structure is called a "double house" because it is two rooms wide and two rooms deep on each floor. A center hallway and stairwell divide the house. The parlor is located on the second floor.

Cross Tradd Street. On your right at 57 Meeting Street is the **First (Scots) Presbyterian Church**, established when twelve Scottish families withdrew from the Independent Church in 1731 and formed the "Scots Kirk," or Scotch Meeting House. The building was completed in 1814. Note that the church bell is missing. Its metal was given to the Confederacy in 1863, and it has never been replaced.

Beside the church is the **Nathaniel Russell House** at 51 Meeting Street. Built between 1808 and 1811 by Nathaniel Russell, who made his fortune as a Charleston merchant, this home is decorated with a free-flying staircase that remains unsupported for three floors. The brick adorning the exterior of the home was made on local plantations. Look closely for Russell's initials in the wrought-iron balcony. The home is open to visitors for a small fee.

Continue southward on Meeting Street, past Prices Alley and Water, Ladson, and Atlantic Streets, all the way to South Battery. You'll pass a number of interesting homes, including the **Otis Mills House**, the **Bull-Huger House**, the **Colonel Isaac Mottee House**, the **Major James Ladson House**, the **Thomas Heyward House**, the **John Edwards House**, the **Calhoun Mansion**, and the **Tucker-Ladson House**. Each home has a unique design and a quaint garden worth a peek.

Meeting Street ends at South Battery Street, with White Point Gardens across the way. **Two Meeting Street Inn** is to your left (east), on the corner of South Battery and Meeting Streets. This mansion (ca. 1892) has Tiffany windows, crafted and installed by Louis Tiffany himself.

Turn left onto South Battery Street. At 8 South Battery, on your left (north), is the **Colonel William Washington House**, built in 1768 and purchased by Colonel William Washington, cousin of George, in 1785.

At 4 South Battery Street is **Villa Marguerita** (ca. 1892). This home was built as a gift by a Charleston businessman for his bride. In 1905 the home was made into a luxury hotel that played host to Henry Ford, Alexander Graham Bell, and Teddy Roosevelt.

On your right (south) is **White Point Gardens**, named for the large mounds of white oyster shells that once blanketed the southern tip of the city and were used to cover the streets in earlier days. This southern portion of the city, known as the **Battery**, is the meeting place of the Ashley and Cooper Rivers, where Charlestonians claim the Atlantic Ocean begins. The Battery is so named because of fortifications that were placed along the seafront.

At the next corner, turn right (southeast) onto East Battery Street. On your left, paved walkways line the harbor's concrete seawalls. As East Battery curves around and heads northeast, look southward across the water to the island fortress of **Fort Sumter** in the distance. To the left of Fort Sumter is Fort Moultrie on Sullivan's Island. To its west is Fort Johnson on James Island.

Follow East Battery past White Point Gardens until the road becomes Murray Boulevard; continue northwest on Murray Boulevard for another 0.8 mile past magnificent old homes that face the **Ashley River**.

Near the end of Murray, turn right (north) onto Ashley Avenue to enjoy a glimpse of an early-20th-century residential section. Cross over Tradd and Broad Streets and view lovely **Colonial Lake**, a saltwater pond on your right surrounded by blooming oleanders and lined with stately 3-story homes.

Follow Ashley Avenue 0.8 mile past Colonial Lake and turn right (east) on Calhoun Street. Pass through a portion of the Medical University of South Carolina (MUSC) campus on the north (left) side of Calhoun and continue to the delightful, historic College of Charleston campus, beginning 4 blocks ahead.

The **College of Charleston** was chartered in 1770, and today it is renowned as one of the premier public liberal arts institutions in America. After passing the **Addlestone Library** at 205 Calhoun Street and Coming Street, on your right, are the fences and buildings encircling the college's pedestrian mall. Drive one more block and turn right (south) on Saint Philip Street. Drive slowly to get a peek to your right (west) at the live oaks dripping with moss that decorate the oldest portion of the college's campus, the **Cistern** green space in front of **Randolph Hall** (66 George St.) where students loll about. The location has been used for scenes in several movie and television productions.

Follow Saint Philip Street past George Street to Wentworth Street and turn right (west). Travel one block on Wentworth and turn right (north) on Glebe Street, just before the lovely **Grace Episcopal Church** (98 Wentworth St.) on your left. At 6 Glebe Street on your right (east) is the **College of Charleston President's House**, built in 1770 as a church rectory. Drive Glebe Street's one short block past historic houses incorporated into the college campus. At the intersection of Glebe and George Streets, look ahead to your right to see the **Porter's Lodge**, with its elegant arched gateways, the Cistern courtyard, and the front facade of Randolph Hall and other new and old college buildings.

Turn left (west) on George Street and drive one block past administrative buildings. Turn right (north) on Coming Street and drive another block. Then take a right (east) on Calhoun past a variety of C of C buildings on both sides of the street. Drive 2 blocks to King Street, where the early-20th-century **Francis Marion Hotel** towers on your left, across King Street from Marion Square.

Turn right (south) onto King Street to experience the hustle and bustle of the historic district's retail shopping area, where antiques, unique gifts, clothes, and shoes abound, as well as some popular college eating and drinking spots tucked along the way.

Follow King Street 0.7 mile and then turn left (east) on Broad Street. Travel 2 blocks to Church Street, and turn right (south). Cross Saint Michael's Alley. On your left at 94 Church Street is the **Thomas Bee House** (ca. 1730), where Theodosia Alston, daughter of Aaron Burr, resided and where John C. Calhoun and his supporters drafted nullification papers in 1832.

The homes of **"Cabbage Row"** extend from 89 to 91 Church Street. These post-Revolutionary double tenements are called Cabbage Row because African American tenants displayed cabbages and other vegetables for sale on their windowsills here. DuBose Heyward, who lived at 76 Church Street, used this area as a model for his novel *Porgy*, on which George Gershwin's opera *Porgy and Bess* was based. Heyward called the neighborhood "Catfish Row" and based the character Porgy on an actual resident, Goatcart Sammy.

On your right at 87 Church Street is the **Heyward-Washington House**, built in 1770 for Thomas Heyward, a signer of the Declaration of Independence. President George Washington rented the house during his visit to Charleston in 1791. The home is furnished with Charleston-crafted furniture pieces, which are considered to be the finest examples of American-made furniture in existence today. A formal garden is found here too. Now owned and operated by the Charleston Museum, the home is open to visitors for a small fee.

Continue south on Church Street past a number of famous homes and structures, such as the **Colonel Robert Brewton House** at 71 Church, the **First Baptist Church** at 61 Church, the **Thomas Rose House** at 59 Church, the **A. W. Todd House** at 41 Church, the **George Eveleigh House** at 39 Church, the **George Matthews House** at 37 Church, and the **Thomas Young House** at 35 Church. Also on Church Street are a number of art galleries and rare-book stores.

Once you cross over Water Street, be sure to veer right and then swing left to remain on Church Street, which becomes a very bumpy brick road that takes you past elegant private residences. Where Church Street ends at South Battery 2 very long blocks from Water Street, turn left (east), and then take an immediate left (north) onto East Battery Street to see more historic waterfront homes on your left (west).

Dr. Saint Julien Ravenel, inventor of the "Little David," a semisubmersible vessel used by the Confederate navy, once lived in the **John Ravenel House** (ca. 1847–49), at 5 East Battery.

The **William Roper House** at 9 East Battery is a Greek Revival mansion built in 1838. A fragment of a Civil War cannon shell is embedded in the home's roof rafter.

At 13 East Battery is the **William Ravenel House** (ca. 1845), and at 21 East Battery is the **Edmonston-Alston House**. The latter home was built from 1817

East Battery Street in Charleston John Clark

to 1828 by Charles Edmonston, a merchant and wharf owner. It was purchased and remodeled by Charles Alston, a wealthy rice planter, into the home you see today. Visitors are welcome for a moderate fee.

Continue northward on East Battery as it becomes East Bay Street. From 79 to 107 East Bay Street, on your left (west), pass a stretch of joined houses known as **Rainbow Row**. The colorful buildings constructed between 1740 and 1787 were originally merchants' homes, with shops on the first floors and living quarters on the second floors. During the colonial period, these homes were directly on the water, providing easy access to nearby ships.

If you would like to stroll on the **Waterfront Park** *pier or along its walkways beside the Cooper River, turn right (east) on Adger's Wharf, Boyce's Wharf, or Exchange Street and drive one block.*

Resume northward on East Bay until it intersects with Broad Street, about 4 blocks ahead. You'll see the **Old Exchange and Provost Dungeon** (ca. 1767–71), on your right, at 122 East Bay Street. The pirate Stede Bonnet was imprisoned at a facility in this location in 1718, and three signers of the Declaration of Independence were incarcerated here when the British occupied the city in 1780. The building is open for a small fee.

In the 19th century, enslaved men, women, and children were sold beside the Old Exchange Building, until a city ordinance was approved in 1856 forbidding such outdoor sales. The open-air market has been called the "Ellis Island of Black

America" because more than a third of all enslaved people in the American colonies arrived here. This was once the commercial center of Charleston.

Turn left (west) on Broad Street. To your left at 1 Broad Street is the Carolina First Bank Building (ca. 1853), built with Connecticut brownstone. Turn immediately right (north) on State Street, and then take a quick left (west) onto cobblestoned **Chalmers Street**. These cobblestones are from partially empty European ships that traveled to Charleston and needed the extra weight to keep the vessels upright. When the ships arrived from Europe, the stones were removed from their ballasts and used to cover the streets of Charleston. The ships were reloaded with such South Carolina goods as rice, cotton, and indigo before heading back to Europe.

At 6 Chalmers Street is the **Old Slave Mart Museum**, located in a building that came into use in 1859. It tells the story of Charleston's role in the domestic inter-state slave trade from 1856 to 1863.

If you are in the market for some unique art, antique furniture, and paintings, you're in the right area to find it. Charleston's **French Quarter Galleries** are found tucked on Church, East Bay, Queen, and Meeting Streets. The Charleston Visitor Center has a complete list of the member shops.

Turn right (north) onto Church Street at the next intersection. At 135 Church Street, on your left, is the historic **Dock Street Theater**, built on the site of one of America's first playhouses, first constructed in 1735. The present structure was built in 1809, and it is used extensively to this day.

To your right is the **French Huguenot Church** at 136 Church Street, organized by French Protestant refugees in 1681. Services were held according to the tides because Huguenot planters would come to town via water. The current structure dates from 1845. The adjoining cemetery hosts the remains of a number of notables, some long past and some more recent.

Cross over Queen Street and notice the **"Pirate House"** (ca. 1740) at 145 Church Street, built of Bermuda stone, by a Huguenot merchant. Pirates traded here until they began pillaging the merchant ships of Charles Town and were no longer welcome.

Directly ahead is **Saint Philip's Episcopal Church** (142 Church St.), organized in 1680 and home of the oldest congregation in Charleston. This building is the third church built for the congregation at this site, constructed around 1838; the other two were destroyed by fire. The steeple at this church was used as a guide for ships entering the port, and its bells were donated to the Confederacy for cannon material. The church is open to visitors daily.

Saint Philip's churchyard is divided into eastern and western segments. Across from the church is the western graveyard, which was set aside in 1768 for burial of "strangers and other transient whites." Some of the men buried here are

John C. Calhoun, fiery defender of southern rights, US senator and vice president of the United States; Edward Rutledge, signer of the Declaration of Independence; and DuBose Heyward, author of *Porgy*.

Continue northward across Cumberland Street. Worth noting on your left, at 79 Cumberland, is the **Old Powder Magazine**, the oldest public building in Charleston. Built in 1712, just inside the northern wall of the city, the structure's 32-inch brick walls and vaulted ceiling were designed to contain any potential explosion of its contents. The magazine is open daily to visitors for a small fee.

Follow Church Street 3 blocks ahead, passing by several popular restaurants before turning right (east) on South Market Street to enjoy the congested marketplace on your left. Travel another block north and turn left (north) on State Street, and then immediately left (west) on North Market Street. After one block, take a right (north) on Anson Street to enter **Ansonborough**, where you'll find a number of beautiful brick homes built after the Great Fire of 1838 that devastated much of this neighborhood.

Continue 2 blocks on Anson, crossing Pinckney Street before you turn left (west) on charming Hasell Street. Look to your right at **Saint Johannes Evangelical Lutheran Church** (48 Hasell St.), a circa 1841 church designed by E. B. White. At 50 Hasell Street is the **Saint Johannes Rectory**, built around 1846 by planter Joel Smith. Take in the **Colonel William Rhett House** at 54 Hasell Street, a gem built around 1713 and thought to be the oldest dwelling in the city. It was once the main house of a 30-acre plantation owned by Colonel Rhett, who was responsible for the capture of Stede Bonnet and his pirate crew in 1718.

At 60 Hasell Street is the **George Reynolds House** (ca. 1847). At 64 Hasell Street is a mansion built in 1843 by Charleston merchant Benjamin F. Smith.

Continue west on Hasell across Meeting Street. On your right at 90 Hasell Street is the **Kahoal Kadosh Beth Elohim Synagogue**, built in 1840–41 to replace the first synagogue, which was built in 1792. This Classic Revival structure is the country's second oldest synagogue and the oldest synagogue in continuous use in the United States.

On your left is the **Saint Mary's Roman Catholic Church** at 89 Hasell Street. The present structure was completed in 1839. This is believed to be the first Roman Catholic parish in South Carolina, established in 1789.

Turn left (south) on bustling King Street, go one block, and turn right (west) on Beaufain Street. Go 2 blocks on Beaufain and take a right (north) on Coming Street. After one block, turn left (west) on Wentworth Street. Follow Wentworth through a pleasant turn-of-the-20th-century residential area for about a half mile.

At the end of Wentworth Street, take a right (northwest) on Lockwood Drive and go a half mile to SC 30 West. The Ashley River and a large yacht marina at 33 Lockwood Drive, will be on your left. Follow signs directing you to James Island

and Folly Beach. Bear right to ascend the **James Island Expressway**, a high, 2-mile-long bridge that takes SC 30 westward from the Charleston peninsula to James Island.

At the crest of the span, you will have an expansive view of the **Ashley River**. Sailboats dot the waters to your left and right, and sunlight dances on the flashing dark water. The historic district of Charleston and its lovely, steepled skyline fall behind as you approach the ever-thickening marshlands on the western side of the Ashley.

Ahead lie James Island, and beyond, rustic, eclectic Folly Beach.

Nearby Attractions

Angel Oak, Bull Island, Cape Romain National Wildlife Refuge, Capers Island Heritage Preserve, Charleston Tea Garden, Cypress Gardens, Dewees Island, Folly Beach County Park, Hampton Park, James Island County Park, Johns Island County Park, Francis Marion National Forest, Kiawah Beachwalker Park, Laurel Hill County Park, May Forest State Park, Meggett County Park, Morris Island Lighthouse, North Charleston Wannamaker County Park, Rockville and Wadmalaw Island, Sewee Visitor and Education Center, Stono River County Park, The Citadel.

19

Edisto Island and Environs

Hollywood to Edisto Beach

General Description: This 50-mile trip across South Carolina's rural Sea Islands environs begins in the town of Hollywood and ends at Edisto Beach on the Atlantic Ocean, crossing through the Toogoodoo River watershed, the ACE Basin National Wildlife Refuge, Edisto Island, and Edisto Beach with views of the Edisto River, sandy beachfront, the Intracoastal Waterway, and beautiful tidal marshlands.

Special Attractions: Toogoodoo River, ACE Basin National Wildlife Refuge and the Grove Plantation, Edisto River and Willtown Bluffs, Atlantic Intracoastal Waterway, Edisto Island, Edisto Island Museum, Botany Bay Heritage Preserve, Indian Mound Trail, and Edisto Beach and Edisto Beach State Park.

Location: Midcoast, just below Charleston.

Travel Season: All year.

Services: All services are plentiful in Charleston. Edisto Island, Edisto Beach, and Hollywood offer limited services.

The Drive

This tour of the eastern edge of the great river watershed known as the ACE Basin (Ashepoo, Combahee, and Edisto Rivers) takes travelers through delightful marshland, maritime forest, and other coastal area scenery. You begin in the town of Hollywood, near the Toogoodoo River. You follow the Toogoodoo, visit the enchanting ACE Basin National Wildlife Refuge headquarters at the Grove Plantation, Willtown Bluff on the Edisto River, Botany Bay Heritage Preserve, and an ancient Indian shell mound, before ending your drive in the peaceful oceanfront community of Edisto Beach. It should be noted that several miles of this drive involve dirt roads. Those parts are identified in the text and can be omitted if so desired although they lead to some quite scenic spots.

Toogoodoo River Basin to ACE Basin National Wildlife Refuge

Begin your drive at the intersection SC 162 and SC 165/Toogoodoo Road, a block west of a Piggly Wiggly grocery store (6251 SC 162, Hollywood) in the middle of the town of **Hollywood**, a sprawling exurb 20 miles southwest of Charleston, but still in Charleston County.

Edisto Island and Environs: Hollywood to Edisto Beach

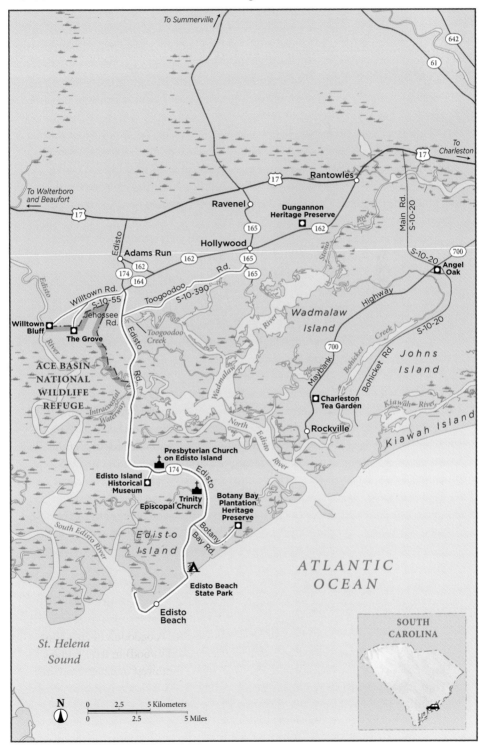

With a population approaching 6,000, South Carolina's Hollywood embraces 25 square miles, more than six times the land area of "the other Hollywood" out west. Also, unlike the other Hollywood, which is about 5 percent Black, our Hollywood is almost two-thirds African American, a significant portion of whom are descendants of people who were enslaved in this general vicinity prior to the Civil War.

This area, once plantation country, has a rich history. A historic marker here tells of Colonel William A. Washington's grave nearby. Colonel Washington, a native Virginian, made his home in this area and led Patriot cavalry during the American Revolution. In 1791, Colonel Washington entertained his kinsman, President George Washington, during the president's tour of the South.

From your starting point, drive south on SC 165/Toogoodoo Road toward Meggett. After one mile, SC 165 turns sharply left, but you should continue straight on S-10-390/Toogoodoo Road.

For a short and pleasant detour, turn left and follow SC 165 southwest a half mile to the town center of Meggett, a sylvan oasis of old homes and quiet, quaint beauty. Chartered in 1905, Meggett rose to prominence as a major Lowcountry freight hub in the 1920s, connecting the waterway freight system and truck farmers. The town also served as a major distribution point for the second largest oyster and fish cannery in the state.

The source of this prosperity was the rich soil on which the town is situated, coupled with a spur of the Atlantic Coast Line Railroad and a large wharf on Yonges Island. The primary crops were cabbage and potatoes. To better market their crops, a group of farmers banded together to form the South Carolina Produce Association. Shortly after World War I, the group built a brick office building to accommodate the office staff, which brokered deals nationwide using ticker tape and telephone lines. A bank and a library were also located in the 1921 structure, which has been beautifully preserved to this day. A few yards south of the Produce Association building is Calvary Baptist Church, also built in 1921.

Today, Meggett is a peaceful community boasting awe-inspiring views and charming homes.

Enjoy 7 pleasant winding miles though beautiful horse pastures, hay fields, and plentiful marshlands on both sides of the road fed by the **Toogoodoo River**, off to your left. Three miles past the Meggett turnoff, you cross Swinton Creek. If you traverse the roadway at high tide, you will feel almost engulfed.

Continue on Toogoodoo Road until where it ends at SC 174/Edisto Road. Turn right (north) onto SC 174 and drive 1.2 miles. Turn left (west) onto S-10-55/Willtown Road. A brown sign notes the turn into the **ACE Basin National Wildlife Refuge** (8675 Willtown Rd., Hollywood).

Travel 2 miles to the refuge's entrance road, S-10-346/Jehossee Island Road, and turn left (south). The surrounding woods are dark and dense, full of short palms and tall pines. This is a terrific place for wildlife viewing.

Two miles down this dirt road, you will see the entrance to the **Grove Plantation Manor**, constructed in 1828. Bird-watching pamphlets are available in a kiosk. The plantation house, headquarters to the ACE Basin National Wildlife Refuge, and its parking lot are a half mile directly ahead. The entrance gate is usually, but not always, open during weekday daylight hours.

The 2-story white, antebellum mansion is one of only three homes in the ACE Basin that survived the Civil War. The Grove was formerly a rice plantation home. It now serves as the office for the Edisto Unit of the refuge. Park to the left of the house, near the whitewashed former slave quarters that have been transformed into maintenance buildings.

Behind the home are ancient oak trees strewn with Spanish moss. The lawn is a green terrain that stretches deep into the marshlands. Egrets glide over the tall grasses, and other small birds flit around the yard. The grass trails that wind throughout the property provide ideal bird-watching. The quiet and frequent breeze in this awesome yard is delightful. A picnic table sitting under the oaks is perfect for snacking before exploring the area.

Happily, the grounds contain both walking trails, picnic tables, and restrooms.

This site is only a small portion of the 350,000 acres of marsh, swamp, and uplands that make up the **ACE Basin**, stretching across Beaufort, Colleton, Hampton, and Charleston Counties. Although much of the land in the ACE Basin is privately owned, most of it is under permanent protection from development, due to conservation arrangements between landowners and state and federal government agencies. Private and public conservation agencies own and manage the public properties, which include the Donnelly Wildlife Management Area (WMA), Bear Island WMA, Botany Bay Plantation Heritage Preserve and WMA, ACE Basin National Estuarine Research Reserve, and ACE Basin National Wildlife Refuge.

Protection of wildlife habitats in the ACE Basin, the watershed of the Ashepoo, Combahee, and Edisto Rivers that flow into Saint Helena Sound, is the primary goal of the ACE Basin management areas. These areas contain upland habitats, freshwater and brackish impoundments, mixed pine/hardwoods, bottomland hardwoods, longleaf pine forests, shortleaf/loblolly pine forests, maritime forests, and saltwater marsh. Wildlife viewing is plentiful here. You'll encounter a wide variety of birds—waterfowl, birds of prey, wading birds, songbirds, shorebirds, including the white ibis, snowy egret, blue heron, wood stork, and Swainson's warbler—and other wildlife, such as alligators, deer, and wild turkeys. The

Road to Willtown Bluff JOHN CLARK

ACE Basin is also home to the largest nesting population of bald eagles in the state.

This portion of the ACE Basin refuge adjacent to the Edisto River lies along the Atlantic Flyway, often referred to as the "highway in the sky." Here, numerous waterfowl, shorebirds, neotropical songbirds, and birds of prey migrate from their nesting grounds to find wintering areas throughout eastern North America.

Exit the refuge on the same dirt road, S-10-346/Jehossee Island Road. Backtrack north 2 miles and turn left (west) on S-10-55/Willtown Road.

The pavement ends a mile from Jehossee Island Road. The site of old Willtown, or New London, established in 1685 alongside the South Edisto River, is 1.5 dirt-road miles farther.

Entrances to antebellum plantations dot the roadway to your right. The charming **Willtown Bluff** community lies at the end of the road. Here, take in the splendid view of the **South Edisto River** and its adjacent alligator-infested rice field marshlands.

ACE Basin National Wildlife Refuge to Edisto Beach

Turn around and drive 4.4 miles back (east) on S-10-55/Willtown Road to the intersection with SC 174/Edisto Road in the Adams Run community. Turn right (south) toward Edisto Island and Edisto Beach to ride through maritime forest lands and across somnolent saltwater marshes.

Pass over the majestic **McKinley Washington Jr. Bridge** after 5 miles to enter Edisto Island. Elevated for boat passage below, the bridge provides a panoramic view of the **Atlantic Intracoastal Waterway** and the surrounding marsh. The tufts of grass, wading egrets, and perched pelicans are breathtaking. Drive slowly and take in the Lowcountry's salty air and visual wonders.

Edisto Island, one of South Carolina's largest barrier islands, is a treasure. The North and South Edisto Rivers border two edges of the island, connected by the Atlantic Ocean and the Intracoastal Waterway. This island is home to unspoiled saltwater marshes, rich agricultural lands, and some of the tallest palmetto trees in the state. The beaches are among the state's best shelling beaches and havens for prehistoric fossils such as sharks' teeth.

The Edisto Indians first inhabited Edisto Island 4,000 years ago. Spanish explorers arrived here during the 1500s but didn't settle; the English who arrived in the 1600s stayed. It is believed that the Earl of Shaftsbury, one of the original lords proprietors, purchased Edisto Island in 1674 from the Edisto Indians. Settlers tried their hand at rice and indigo crops, and then cotton. The cultivation of the popular Sea Island cotton in the 1790s established the prosperity of the island, as evidenced by some of the plantation homes that were built during the late 18th century. Some stand today and are listed on the National Register of Historic Places.

Early Union occupation of the island during the Civil War made the area a home base for Union troops and a haven for emancipated enslaved people, and thus helped prevent destruction by Sherman's army near the war's end.

The early prosperity of the island did not last. The Civil War and the boll weevil wiped out the cotton industry by the early 1900s, so islanders focused on Lowcountry seafood as a means of income. The area might have lost its wealth, but it never lost its charm. In the early 20th century, Edisto Beach Island, a sandy barrier island, became a popular summer beach resort, and it remains so today. On the northwest side of the barrier island beach community, Edisto Island is a quiet, largely unspoiled haven of land, marsh, and water, with secluded beaches here and there.

The road on the south side of the bridge passes through a wonderful variety of forests, fields, marshlands, tiny communities, and diverse homes. Roadside establishments offer vegetables, fruits, jellies, breads, homemade desserts, and casseroles and flowers.

The tiny, eclectic, delightful **Edisto Island Museum and Gift Shop** is a little over 5 miles past the bridge over the **Intracoastal Waterway**. If you wish to visit the museum, turn right (southwest) on Chisolm Plantation Road. The museum

Presbyterian Church of Edisto Island, built in 1830 PATRICIA PIERCE

is on your left, just 0.1 mile off the highway (8123 Chisolm Plantation Rd.). The Edisto Island Historic Preservation Society manages the museum and a multitude of related activities.

Exit the museum on Chisolm Plantation Road and continue southeast on SC 174/Edisto Road. After 0.7 mile pass the **Presbyterian Church on Edisto Island** (1890 SC 174), founded in 1685, on your left. The current church structure was built in 1830. The enchanting, adjoining cemetery dates from 1787.

A mile farther southeast on your left, is **Edisto Presbyterian Church**, same denomination. Why two churches? After the Civil War, white landowners returned to claim their property. Former enslaved people were not welcome in the local, long-established Presbyterian Church and thus were forced to form their own, separate congregation.

On your left 0.8 mile farther at the corner of Oak Island Road/S-10-768 is the white, wooden **New First Missionary Baptist Church** (1644 SC 174, Edisto Island), constructed in 1818 with funds donated by Hephzibah J. Townsend (1780–1847), who founded the Wadmalaw and Edisto Female Mite Society, the first home and foreign mission society of Baptist women in the South.

The white congregation was formed in 1686. Before the Civil War, enslaved people were allowed to worship from a balcony above the main floor of the sanctuary. After the Civil War, white congregants chose not to worship in the same facility as their former Black "property." While changing names, the African American congregation continued to worship here as they had begun to do after Union occupation of Edisto Island in 1861.

Next, travel 0.2 mile to **Trinity Episcopal Church** (1589 SC 174, Edisto Island), on your right, a church with a rich history and strong community ties even today. The congregation was founded in 1774. The present building, completed in 1881, is the third church building constructed here, and it remains in exceptional condition.

The **Old Post Office Restaurant** is 0.7 mile past the Episcopal Church at 1442 SC 174 on your left. Originally constructed as Bailey's Store in 1825, it became a post office building around the turn of the 20th century and remained so for about 50 years. After continuing to serve various commercial functions, it has served off and on, but mainly on, as a fine dining restaurant for the past 40 years, under various owners and chefs.

Cross over Store Creek and 0.2 mile on your left is the **Edisto Island Serpentarium** (1374 SC 174). Stop here to explore reptiles found in the southeastern United States. The Clamp brothers of Edisto Island have created an indoor and outdoor garden house to view reptiles in their native habitat. Alligators and turtles are found outside, and snakes and other reptiles can be viewed in an indoor atrium.

Drive a half mile farther on SC 174/Edisto Road to **Botany Bay Road** on your left (east), the entrance to 4,687-acre **Botany Bay Heritage Preserve and Wildlife Management Area**. Idyllic saltwater marshlands spread to the right (west), where ever-changing "art" installations arise from the waters. An even greater expanse of marshland extends to your left (northeast) as you make the turn.

Turn left on this sandy road to step back into the days of rice and indigo plantations. White-framed Allen African-Methodist-Episcopal Church is 0.2 mile along the way, on your left, with a majestic view of the marshlands upon which it sits astride.

Botany Bay Road is almost completely canopied with huge, gnarled oak tree limbs that interlock above your head. Thick Spanish moss dangles from the trees, which are so closely grown that the sky is hardly visible through the dark canopy overhead.

The entrance to Botany Bay Heritage Preserve and WMA is 1.3 miles southeast past the church.

Botany Bay Beach John Clark

The former plantation property was made available to the public in 2008. The preserve is under conservation easement with the Nature Conservancy, and the South Carolina Department of Natural Resources (DNR) manages it.

This area is important to numerous wildlife species, including federally threatened loggerhead sea turtles, which use the beach for nesting areas, and the least tern, which is state threatened. Neotropical songbirds, including painted buntings and summer tanagers, are also found here. The uplands, tidal marshes, and managed wetlands support habitats for numerous wildlife species. The area also has significant cultural resources, dating as far back as the Late Archaic Period through the 19th century, including the Fig Island Shell Rings and out-buildings from Bleak Hall Plantation.

Maps of the preserve are available at the kiosk located at the entrance gate. The property offers an attractive 6.5-mile dirt road route, beginning with an avenue of oaks interspersed with loblolly pines and cabbage palmettos. Colonies of resurrection ferns adorn the oak limbs.

At the four-way stop, a right turn will take you to the beach access parking area. From there, you can walk across a causeway through marshland to reach a barrier island with 2.8 miles of seashore. Erosion on Botany Bay Beach has left a beguiling "boneyard" of dead trees along the seaside sand. Shell collection is prohibited, resulting in a beach full of a vast array of sand dollars, sea stars, and numerous other sea-life remains, most visible at low tide.

The suggested driving route next takes you past two small outbuildings con-structed in the 1800s. One is a white Gothic Revival structure that once served as the plantation's ice house. Owners would have large ice blocks shipped from the North and stored in the foundation of the tabby walled facility. The other tabby building was a gardener's shed erected beside what was once a Japanese formal garden. Farther along the drive is yet another tabby structure; this one dates from the colonial era and was once used as a barn.

As you continue your drive, you will pass by salt marsh, lovely views of Ocella Creek, and magnificent old live oaks draped in Spanish moss. The road leads you past ponds built as habitats for wood ducks and other waterfowl, as well as remains of an old slave house, a plantation manor, and a brick beehive.

Exit Botany Bay Heritage Preserve and backtrack on Botany Bay Road back to SC 174/Edisto Road. Turn left (southwest).

The **Edisto Island Chamber of Commerce and Visitor Center** is 2.6 miles down the road on your left. Continue a half mile farther to the northern sec-tion of **Edisto Beach State Park** (8377 State Cabin Rd.), on your right.

A rough and bumpy dirt road leads to the Live Oak Camping Area, as well as the trailhead for **Indian Mound Trail**. The trail is an easy 1.8-mile jaunt through maritime forest to an ancient mound of seashells called Spanish Mount, said to

Ice house constructed in the early 1800s on plantation at Botany Bay JOHN CLARK

be more than 4,000 years old. Parts of the trail overlook the salt marsh expanses of Big Bay Creek and its tributaries, and visitors can often catch glimpses of such local denizens as the clapper rail, brown pelican, painted bunting, marsh wren, tern, gull, and heron.

Next, travel 0.7 mile farther south on SC 174/Edisto Road across marshland of Scott Creek to Edisto Beach. The main entrance of Edisto Beach State Park is on your left (east).

Edisto Beach State Park, developed by the Civilian Conservation Corps in the 1930s, covers 1,255 acres. It is home to a dense maritime forest, an expansive salt marsh, and a 1.5-mile stretch of beach bordered by some of the state's tallest palmetto trees. Porpoises are frequently spotted frolicking in the surf.

Picnic areas, ocean fishing and swimming, and summer nature programs are available here. The park offers a number of free entertaining and educational programs at its nature center, including a 45-minute program about the Indian Shell Mound. Park rangers conduct walks on the beach and to the saltwater marsh to discuss plant and animal habitats and threatened species such as the loggerhead turtle. They also teach children how to crab, and about fossils that may be found in the area. A small admission fee is charged for entrance to this southern section of the park.

To complete your drive, continue past the park, turn right, and cruise southeast along the coast for 4.5 miles to the end of SC 174/Palmetto Boulevard. The

Edisto Beach at sunset JOHN CLARK

Town of Edisto Beach is a wonderfully noncommercial coastal vacation and retirement community, composed mainly of single-family dwellings and is great for bikers, joggers, and walkers.

Nearby Attractions

Angel Oak Tree, Charleston Tea Garden, Dungannon Planation Heritage Preserve, Edisto Nature Trail, Johns Island County Park, Meggett County Park, Rockville and Wadmalaw Island, Stono River County Park.

20

Edisto and Ashley Rivers

Charleston Plantations to Francis Beidler Forest

General Description: Beginning on the west side of Charleston, this 70-mile drive takes you to Drayton Hall, Middleton Place, and Magnolia Plantations on the Ashley River, then through isolated rural areas to two state parks on the Edisto River before ending at an old-growth swamp sanctuary, the Francis Beidler Forest.

Special Attractions: Ashley River, Drayton Hall, Magnolia Plantation and Its Gardens, Audubon Swamp Garden, Middleton Place, Edisto River, Givhans Ferry State Park, Colleton State Park, Koger House, Appleby's Methodist Church and Cemetery,

Saint George, Indian Field Methodist Campground, Francis Beidler Forest.

Location: Coastal Plain northwest of Charleston, along the Ashley and Edisto Rivers.

Travel Season: All year. Spring and fall are prime times for wildlife viewing and seeing the plantation gardens in full bloom. The plantations along Ashley River Road host numerous events throughout the year.

Services: Motels, hotels, and all services are plentiful in Charleston, North Charleston, and Summerville.

The Drive

This drive parallels the venerable Ashley River, taking visitors to the antebellum houses and gardens at Drayton Hall, Magnolia Gardens, and Middleton Place. Next, it travels along the Edisto River, through wetlands, forests, farms, and small communities, stopping at the state parks of Givhans Ferry and Colleton, which hug the foreboding, black-water Edisto. After passing through historic Saint George, the tour finishes at the Beidler Forest, a splendidly preserved old-growth wetland forest in the middle of Four Holes Swamp, where bald cypresses and tupelos grow to magnificent sizes amid a plethora of alligators, waterfowl, and other wildlife.

Drayton Hall

Begin at **Drayton Hall** on SC 61/Ashley River Road, a State Scenic Highway, 5 miles north of the intersection of SC 61 and I-526.

Located at 3380 Ashley River Road, Drayton Hall is a National Historic Landmark owned jointly by the State of South Carolina and the National Trust for Historic Preservation. An accredited museum, Drayton Hall remains the oldest preserved plantation house in America open to the public, one of the finest

Edisto and Ashley Rivers: Charleston Plantations to Francis Beidler Forest

Pinopolis

Lake Moultrie

Moncks Corner

6

52

329

Goose Creek

52

26

To Charleston

Charleston International Airport

North Charleston

526

Drayton Hall

Magnolia Plantation

61

642

Middleton Place

Drayton

17A

176

17A

78

Ashley River

165

Summerville

26

78

Ashley River

165

River

27

Ridgeville

Four Holes Swamp

Mims Rd

Francis Beidler Forest

S-18-28 Beidler Forest Rd

Taylor Pond Rd

178

26

To Columbia

27

Givhans Ferry Rd

Givhans Ferry State Park

Givhans

61

Ashley River

Edisto River

10 Kilometers

10 Miles

Dorchester

78

Harleyville

178

Cottageville

Pierce Rd

651

Augusta Highway

Edisto River

Polk Swamp

15

St. George

15

Grover

61

Canadys

61

S-18-73

Indian Field Campground

Quaker Rd

Koger House

Appleby's Church

Wire Rd

Cowtail Rd

Edisto

61

78

Reevesville

95

To Florence

15

Colleton State Park

15

17A

17A

Walterboro

95

64

17A

95

64

To Hampton

63

To Savannah

21

21

N

5   5   10

SOUTH CAROLINA

To Florence

examples of Georgian Palladian architecture in America, and the only surviving colonial plantation house on the **Ashley River**. The mansion was saved from Sherman's troops in 1865 by the Drayton family, unlike nearby plantations that were pillaged and burned to the ground. Today, Drayton Hall shares its beauty and history with visitors year-round.

Royal Judge John Drayton (1713–1779) failed to inherit his family's Magnolia Plantation, so in 1738 he acquired the land on which Drayton Hall sits and made it the center of his extensive indigo and rice planting ventures. In 1744 Drayton acquired next-door Magnolia Plantation from his nephew, William Drayton, who moved out of the state.

Construction on Drayton Hall, a 2-story brick plantation home, was completed in 1742. With the assistance of European and enslaved African American craftsmen, Drayton constructed first- and second-floor front porches centered between the home's extensive brick wings and two staircases, giving the home a commanding presence. Two chimneys over the left and right walls of the home create a balanced, symmetric, and classic design. Indoors, the absence of furniture in the home emphasizes the craftsmen's detailed wooden banisters and ornamented doorways and mantles.

Admission to the grounds and guided tours of Drayton Hall are offered for a moderate admission price. Visitors are encouraged to take a leisurely stroll along the scenic trails through the marshes and along the banks of the Ashley River or enjoy the picnic tables that sit under ancient oak trees. Throughout the year, special events and educational programs are offered here, so be sure to check out Drayton Hall's website since there is more to do than can be accomplished in one day.

Exit Drayton Hall to the right (northwest) onto SC 61 West/Ashley River Road. Drive 0.7 mile, and Magnolia Plantation and Its Gardens will be on your right (east).

Magnolia Plantation & Its Gardens

Magnolia Plantation and Its Gardens (3550 Ashley River Rd.) adjoin Drayton Hall Plantation and have remained in the Drayton family for nine generations, since the arrival of Thomas Drayton from Barbados in 1671. Both the original plantation home and the garden are National Historic Landmarks, and the garden can boast of being America's oldest.

Thomas and Anne Drayton, whose family played an important role in America's colonial revolution and independence history, completed the first residence at Magnolia Plantation in 1676. After this home burned, a second was built on the banks of the Ashley River with bricks salvaged from the first structure. The second

Alligators sunning themselves at Magnolia Gardens JOHN CLARK

dwelling, a 3-story structure built mainly of cypress, burned in 1865 at the hands of Sherman's troops. Only the steps and the ground floor were saved. During the Civil War era, the Reverend John Grimke Drayton, rector of nearby St. Andrews Episcopal Church, inherited Magnolia Plantation. In order to rebuild, he sold his sea island plantation, his town house, and much of the property surrounding Magnolia Plantation. Rev. Drayton owned a pre-Revolutionary summerhouse near Summerville. He disassembled this home, loaded it on barges, and floated it 14 miles on the Ashley River to Magnolia Plantation, where he mounted it on the brick remainders of the second home. It has since been expanded, and the stucco that covers the house was made from the phosphate mined on the plantation and applied after the earthquake of 1886. Tours of the existing home highlight the Drayton family history, life on the plantation for the past three centuries, and the home's extensive collection of Early American furniture.

One of the most notable aspects of Magnolia Plantation is its garden, the oldest in America. The most formal portion of the garden, "Flowerdale," was established the same year the plantation home was built, and it remains mostly unchanged even today. The gardens are planted for year-round blooms, and they include a Barbados tropical garden, an 18th-century herb garden, a Biblical garden, a topiary garden, the Audubon Swamp Garden, and a horticultural maze of camellia and holly bushes. Although spring offers a terrific array of the 250 varieties of azaleas, winter is equally beautiful, with 900 varieties of camellias in bloom.

Audubon Swamp Garden boardwalk JOHN CLARK

For a moderate admission price, the plantation offers a number of ways to enjoy its grounds. A nature train provides 45-minute narrated tram rides through Magnolia Plantation's historic wildlife areas and rice field reserve lakes that border the Ashley River. Guides interpret daily life on the plantation from the colonial period to the present, highlighting the flora and fauna here, such as the plantation's alligators, turtles, herons, egrets, and a variety of birds.

The nature boat offers a 45-minute tour of the old 150-acre flooded rice field, now a wildlife refuge for many water-loving birds and aquatic creatures. Guides describe the role of the Ashley River and the plantation's wildlife.

The **Audubon Swamp Garden,** a 60-acre black-water cypress and tupelo swamp full of boardwalks, bridges, and dikes, lets you experience a variety of wildlife among native and exotic flowering plants.

Since 1975, the entire 500 acres of the plantation have been managed as a wildlife refuge. The diversity of the terrain lends itself to a variety of bird, animal, reptile, and plant life, and is an unusually productive bird-watching area that can be reached by walking and bike trails. Canoe rides offer an especially neat view of the rice fields, which are also open to freshwater fishing. A wildlife observation tower within 50 yards of the garden also provides an excellent view of waterbirds and small land birds. In the Audubon Swamp, blue herons, wood ducks, snowy egrets, and anhingas are commonly spotted among the water oaks, cypress trees and knobs, tupelos, duck weeds, exotic ferns, bulbs, and lilies, along with a variety of bog plants, ornamental grasses, and colorful wildflowers.

Middleton Place

Exit Magnolia Plantation and turn right (northwest) on SC 61/Ashley River Road, a shady, canopied highway of Spanish moss–draped oaks. Even on a sunny day, this road feels dark and cozy. Continue for 3.5 miles, until you see Middleton Place on your right (east).

As you enter **Middleton Place** (4300 Ashley River Rd.), the plantation's dark brick home is seen in the distance behind a green pasture of grazing livestock. This National Historic Landmark, home to America's oldest formal landscaped gardens (1741), was also the home of one of South Carolina's most influential families. Not only did Henry Middleton once have some of the largest

Middleton Place, dating from 1741, is America's oldest landscaped garden. John Clark

landholdings in America, it has also been said that the Middletons "started high society" this side of the Atlantic.

Henry Middleton, builder of the 60-acre landscaped garden and accompanying plantation home, was president of the First Continental Congress. His son, Arthur Middleton, was a signer of the Declaration of Independence. Arthur's son, Henry, was governor of South Carolina and an American minister to Russia, and Williams, Henry's son, signed the Ordinance of Secession.

Built in 1755 on the banks of the Ashley River, Middleton Place continues to thrive today. Most of the gardens and the home were burned in 1865 by Sherman's army; only the gentlemen's guest wing survived. After Union troops departed, this wing was refurbished and became the family residence.

Guided tours of the home interpret the Middleton family's role in South Carolina and American history and highlight the home's furniture, paintings by Benjamin West and Thomas Sully, rare books by Audubon, antique rice beds, the family's original silver and china, and other personal belongings.

Middleton Place's formal gardens are nationally recognized. In 1941 the Garden Club of America awarded Middleton Place the Bulkley Medal "in commemoration of two hundred years of enduring beauty." Fifty years later, in 1991, the International Committee on Monuments and Sites named Middleton Place one of six United States gardens of international importance.

Stroll through the terraced gardens on the banks of the Ashley and wander through the intricate mazes that were influenced by English and French landscape design. A gardener was brought from England to design the terraced gardens above the butterfly lakes. Vast plantings of rare camellias, the first four ever grown in America, were planted here. All of the gardens are interesting in design and use of color. Camellias, azaleas, crepe myrtles, orchids, roses, and magnolias are spectacular.

One unique feature of Middleton Place is its stable yards, featuring a resident blacksmith, potter, carpenter, and weaver who re-create activities of a self-sustaining Lowcountry plantation and sell their wares in the **Middleton Place Museum Shop**. Horses, mules, hogs, milking cows, sheep, goats, and guinea hens are still raised here and represent the life of the rice plantation home and era. A freedman's home, **Eliza's House**, presents the story of the African American community.

The plantation offers kayak trips on the Ashley River and a black-water cypress swamp, horseback riding, biking tours, and guided nature walks around the rice field banks and the Ashley River. Throughout the grounds and tidal estuaries, herons, egrets, bald eagles, otters, alligators, bobcats, and other creatures abound. A number of special events are scheduled throughout the year, highlighting particular gardens, nature walks, and plantation life at Middleton Place.

Separate admissions are charged for the grounds and for the house tour.

Middleton Place to Beidler Forest at Four Holes Swamp

Exit Middleton Place and turn right (northwest) onto SC 61/Ashley River Road. Travel almost 10 miles to the intersection with Alternate US 17. Turn left (west) at the stop sign to travel 0.4 mile on Alternate US 17/SC 61. Then bear right (northwest) to continue on SC 61 North.

Travel 5 miles on SC 61 through forest and swampland and past some modest country dwellings to reach the isolated crossroads outpost of Givhans.

Then continue 3.2 more miles on SC 61 to Givhans Ferry State Park (746 Givhans Ferry Rd., Ridgeville), just before the bridge that spans the Edisto River. A brown sign notes the right-hand turn (north) onto S-18-30/Givhans Ferry Road. Travel 0.1 mile to enter the state park, on your left (west).

Givhans Ferry was originally a ferry crossing in the 18th and 19th centuries, connecting Charleston with inland areas. **Givhans Ferry State Park**, a 988-acre park built on high bluffs along the scenic **Edisto River**, offers terrific views and access to the black-water river. President Roosevelt's Civilian Conservation Corps constructed the park in the 1930s, one of a series of similar work projects across the nation.

When you drive into the rustic but well-maintained park, on a dirt road passing rental cabins and campsites to Overlook Picnic Shelter, you see the beautiful, meandering Edisto River. Picnic tables are scattered throughout the park, which also provides a 1.5-mile River Bluff Nature Trail, fishing opportunities, and a meeting facility. The park is situated along the 56-mile Edisto River Canoe and Kayak Trail, a river course that carries paddlers past scenic natural areas. Wildflowers bloom along the banks in both spring and fall, and giant live oaks, black willows, red swamp maples, cypresses, tupelos, gums, and tall stately pines decorate the edges of the river.

Exit the park by turning right (south) onto S-18-30/Givhans Ferry Road, and turn right (northwest) again on SC 61/Augusta Highway. You cross the Edisto River and enter Colleton County riding through wetlands down a rural road. Old farm houses and mobile homes dot the landscape of this country passage. Hunting and fishing reign here.

Continue 17.5 miles northwest on SC 61/Augusta Highway to the Canadys community, home of Colleton State Park (147 Wayside Lane, Walterboro). Turn right (northeast) on US 15/North Jefferies Road. Drive 0.4 mile and turn left (west) into the park.

Colleton State Park, a 35-acre facility also built by the Civilian Conservation Corps in the 1930s, serves as the headquarters for the Edisto River Canoe and Kayak Trail. The first official canoe and kayak trail in the state, it covers 56 miles of the Edisto River, from Whetstone Crossroads near the intersection of US 21 and SC 61 to an area near Jacksonboro on US 17.

The Edisto forms the northern border of the ACE Basin, an important watershed and natural area in South Carolina. Black water indicates the peaceful rate of flow of the river and accurately describes the coloration of the tannin-rich spring water. It is reported to be the longest free-flowing black-water stream in America.

The Edisto River is an ancient waterway that was important to Native Americans and to commerce in colonial times. Today it is a haven for several wildlife species, such as blue herons, turtles, alligators, egrets, and bald eagles.

Colleton State Park has a well-maintained interpreted foot trail (the Cypress Swamp Nature Trail) along the river bank. Fishing is encouraged, and bream, redbreast, and catfish are plentiful. River access for private boats is a quarter mile from the park. Picnic shelters are also available.

Appleby's Methodist Church, constructed around 1850 with separate entrances for men and women Patricia Pierce

Exit the park by turning left (northeast) onto US 15. Cross the Grady C. Murray Bridge over the Edisto River, enter Dorchester County, and pass through substantial wetlands. **Grover** is 3 miles ahead. If you don't slow down, you won't know that you have missed this quiet town, where horses and cows graze. You might spot rabbits hopping on the sides of the road and hawks overhead. Ranch-style homes line the highway, usually with small gardens or huge row crops of corn or soybeans.

In Grover, just after you see a convenience store (1939 Hwy 15 S) on your right—where you can purchase bait and tackle, hot dogs, burgers, cold drinks and groceries—turn left (northwest) on Wire Road/S-18-19. Travel 3 miles past fields of corn and cotton, open spaces with grazing horses, and small country homes to Sandy Branch Road/S-18-834.

To the left of Wire Road is the **Koger House**, the oldest residence in Dorchester County. Turn left onto Sandy Branch Road to get a closer look of the dark brown wooden structure built about 1800 for Joseph Koger Jr (1779–1866). Koger was a farmer, a state representative from 1806 to 1812, Colleton district sheriff from 1813 to 1818, and then a state senator from 1818 to 1838. His father also served in the state House of Representatives from 1801 to 1812. The Koger home, constructed along the route from Charleston to Augusta, served as a stage-coach inn at one time.

Continue northwest 1 mile on Wire Road/S-18-19, and pass over I-95 to Cowtail Road/S-18-71 to see **Appleby's Methodist Church and Cemetery**. Turn right onto Cowtail Road to park and walk around the church and its cemetery, surrounded by tall oaks draped with Spanish moss. The church was founded in 1797 and built between 1840 and 1850. This small, white wooden structure has two front entrances, one each for white men and white women, and a back door that was used by enslaved people. The church is now used only once annually for reunions.

Backtrack a mile southwest to Quaker Road/S-18-49, directly across from the Koger House, and turn left (north). Continue 5 miles through pretty countryside filled with corn and cotton crops, old country homes and picturesque barns and silos, hay fields, and grazing cows and horses to the town of **Saint George**, county seat of Dorchester County.

As you enter town, turn right (east) on Dukes Street/S-18-40. Go 2 long blocks, and then turn left (north) onto South Parler Avenue.

Drive north into town, and as you cross over the railroad tracks, look for the historical marker on your right that explains the role of South Carolina's Canal and Rail Road Company. This company began the first successful scheduled steam railroad service in America on December 25, 1830. By 1833, its 136 miles from

Charleston through Saint George and on to Hamburg made it the world's longest railroad.

After a half mile the 2-story brick **Lourie Theatre**, built in the 1920s and still in use today, is on your right at 206 North Parler Avenue. The historic **Klauber Building** is on your left a half block north, at 225 North Parler Avenue. It was built by Jude Leopold A. Klauber to serve as a mercantile store and the headquarters for his other business ventures. Today the structure houses the **Saint George Visitor and Information Center**, two chambers of commerce, and the town museum.

Continue northeast on North Parler Avenue/US 15 for 3 miles past old homes and corn and cotton fields to visit the **Indian Field Methodist Campground**. The 99, 2-story rustic wooden "cabins" form a circle around a central tabernacle.

A portion of the 99 cabins at Indian Field Methodist Campground Patricia Pierce

During the last week of September each year, families travel from all corners of the state to gather for a week of fellowship and worship. Even today, three meals a day are cooked on wood-burning stoves as in years past.

Turn left on Indian Field Circle/S-18-73. A green sign on US 15 marks the turn. Travel a half mile to the campground and drive around the old structures to the left of the road and the matching wooden outhouses on the right.

Exit the campground on Indian Field Circle/S-18-73 and turn left (north) onto North Parler Avenue/US 15. Travel 2.5 miles to Rosinville crossroads and the intersection with West Main Street/US 178. Turn right (southeast) and head toward Harleyville, 4.5 miles ahead. Lovely open fields of grazing horses, goats, and cows line the road, along with modest homes on the outskirts of town.

Pass through Harleyville and continue southeast on East Main Street/US 178 to visit the **Francis Beidler Forest**. After 3.8 miles slow down and look for Taylor Pond Road/S-18-139 on your left. Turn left on Taylor Pond Road (northeast) and follow it for 2.6 miles, crossing I-26.

At the intersection with First Bend Road/S-18-28, continue straight. S-18-39 becomes Bishop Road. Go a half mile and turn left on Mims Road. After 0.7 mile you'll see the entrance to the forest on your right.

Turn right onto Francis Beidler Entrance Road/Sanctuary Road to enter the Francis Beidler Forest (336 Sanctuary Rd., Harleyville), home to the largest remaining virgin stand of bald cypress and tupelo trees in the world, some more than 1,000 years old. It encompasses 6,000 acres of riverine sanctuary and 1,800 acres of ancient trees that tower over black-water streams and clear pools. The swamp forest contains groves of giant bald cypress, tupelo gum, laurel oak, and water ash. It is home to 44 species of mammals, 140 species of birds, 39 species of fish, 50 species of reptiles, 40 species of amphibians, and other creatures.

The forest is part of **Four Holes Swamp**, which begins as a narrow swamp-stream system in Calhoun County. The stream is fed by springs and rainfall to widen and flow 62 miles through four Lowcountry counties before its waters eventually join the Edisto River and the Atlantic Ocean. Because the swamp is largely dependent on rainfall, its water levels fluctuate with the seasons. During wet seasons (winter and spring) the swamp is a shallow river flowing through a 1.5-mile-wide floodplain. In the summer and fall, the swamp shrinks to a series of well-defined creeks connecting larger "lakes."

No one is sure of the origin of the Four Holes Swamp name, but it may refer to four lakes once fished by the Yemassee Indians. Patriot Generals Francis "The Swamp Fox" Marion and Nathanael Greene staged guerrilla actions here during the Revolutionary War.

Francis Beidler, a lumberman and conservationist, acquired this part of the Four Holes Swamp in the 1890s. When he was a young man, he had visited

Yellowstone National Park and was amazed by the beauty of the natural geysers and mountains of that area. He left determined to preserve the land that he had inherited in South Carolina. Better appreciating its beauty and unique habitat, he resolved to leave most of the timber standing. Today the Audubon Society manages Francis Beidler Forest as part of its national system of wildlife sanctuaries.

The National Audubon Society's Francis Beidler Forest at Four Holes Swamp is full of rich habitats. Birds are easily spotted during winter and spring. On the elevated and winding boardwalk, you can catch glimpses of turtles and alligators. The loop boardwalk begins at the visitor center and is a little more than 1.5 miles, with nine rest stops and two rain shelters along the way.

The park, which has a small admission fee, offers guided tours, canoe trips, night walks, and special events throughout the year. The visitor center exhibits information to encourage a deeper appreciation of the area. A self-guided tour book describes the animals and plants that you may encounter. A slide show and other pictures are also on display to help you understand and appreciate the swamp and its inhabitants.

Nearby Attractions

Charles Towne Landing State Historic Site, Colonial Dorchester State Historic Site, Cypress Gardens, North Charleston Wannamaker County Park, Eutawville, James Island County Park, Stono River County Park, Summerville, West Ashley Park.

ACE Basin

Walterboro to Old Sheldon Church

General Description: This trip begins in the charming, well-preserved town of Walterboro, and then takes you through the watershed of the enchanting Ashepoo, Combahee, and Edisto Rivers, one of the largest unspoiled wetlands areas in the nation, featuring lush forests and rich saltwater and freshwater coastal marshes.

Special Attractions: Historic Walterboro, South Carolina Artisans Center, Jones-McDaniel-Hiott House, Colleton County Courthouse, Walterboro Wildlife Center, Saint Jude's Episcopal Church, Bedon-Lucas House Museum, Ashepoo and Combahee Rivers, ACE Basin National Wildlife Refuge,

Donnelley and Bear Island Wildlife Management Areas, Bennetts Point, Mosquito Creek, ACE Basin National Estuarine Research Preserve, Combahee Unit of the ACE Basin National Wildlife Refuge, Yemassee, Old Sheldon Church.

Location: Southern coast.

Travel Season: All year, but fall, winter and spring are best. Heat and insects can be a problem in summer.

Services: Hotels, restaurants, and other services are abundant in Walterboro and Beaufort. Limited services are offered in Jacksonboro and Yemassee.

The Drive

This 75-mile drive begins with a tour of old homes and structures in lovely, historic Walterboro. It then winds you through dark, serene roads lined with Spanish moss–strewn oaks and wildlife-filled estuarine wetlands of the ACE Basin, including stops in the Donnelley and Bear Island Wildlife Management Areas, remote Bennetts Point, and the Combahee Unit of the ACE Basin National Wildlife Refuge. You conclude by driving through the environs of quiet Yemassee and arriving at the ruins of Old Sheldon Church.

Walterboro to Bennetts Point

Walterboro is the county seat and most populous town of heavily rural Colleton County. Named for Sir John Colleton, lord proprietor, whose land grant was bestowed by King Charles II in 1663, Colleton County is one of the oldest counties in America, dating back to 1682. Lowcountry plantations produced cotton, indigo, and primarily rice in Colleton County, making it one of the wealthiest areas in the state and one of the leading rice producers in America during the 18th century. Needing a summer retreat from harsh plantation life and the malaria brought on

ACE Basin: Walterboro to Old Sheldon Church

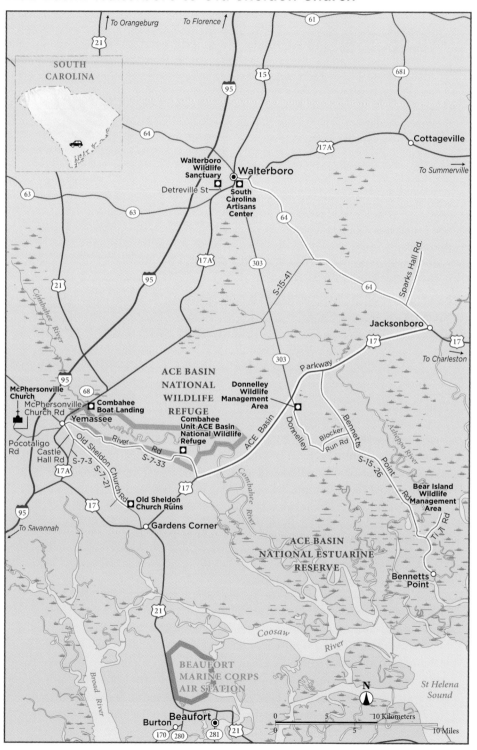

during the summer months, plantation owners Paul and Jacob Walter established Walterboro in 1784. Hickory Valley, Walterboro's historic district, was built between 1821 and 1929. Here you'll find the homes of some of the town's founders and prominent families, offering a glimpse of the wealth and lifestyle of that time.

Begin this drive at the **South Carolina Artisans Center** at 318 Wichman Street/Alternate US 17 in the heart of downtown Walterboro. The center, housed in a historic home with a quaint wraparound porch, showcases and markets the finest handcrafted works of South Carolina's leading artisans.

Handcrafted jewelry, pottery, baskets, furniture, elaborate teapots, gourds, sweetgrass and kudzu vine baskets, handmade paper, and woodcarvings made by South Carolina artists and craftsmen are marketed here. All purchases help support the educational programs, craft demonstrations, year-round special events, and ongoing operation of the center.

Exit the center, by turning right (east) onto Wichman Street. Travel just one block to North Memorial Avenue, and on your right is the **Jones-McDaniel-Hiott House** (418 Wichman St.). The front of this house was built prior to 1838; the back of the house was added in the early 1860s. The second story and piazza were added in 1935. The surrounding gardens are said to have two camellia japonica trees that are estimated to be more than 150 years old. One famous former owner of this home was Mrs. Elizabeth Ann Horry Dent, widow of Captain J. Herbert Dent, commander of the frigate *Constitution* ("Old Ironsides").

Turn right (south) on North Memorial Avenue, travel 2 blocks, crossing Washington Street, to reach Hampton Street and turn right (west). Travel two blocks to see the now famous **Colleton County Courthouse** (101 Hampton St.) on your right. Completed in the fall of 1822, this Greek Revival–style structure has outside walls that are 3 bricks (28 inches) thick. The front portico was designed by noted South Carolina architect Robert Mills.

For almost two centuries the courthouse was most noted for hosting the first nullification meeting in South Carolina, when Robert Barnwell Rhett called for immediate secession in protest of federal tax laws in 1828. Now, however, it is famous as the scene of the 2023 nationally televised trial of once-powerful attorney Alex Murdoch, convicted of killing his wife and son and accused of theft of millions of dollars from clients, law partners, family, and others.

Continue past the courthouse to South Jefferies Boulevard. Directly ahead is the **Walterboro Wildlife Center** at 100 South Jefferies Boulevard.

You may wish to stop here to explore the exhibits that highlight the history, environmental significance and native wildlife of the state's largest city park, the Walterboro Wildlife Sanctuary, located southeast of downtown. Travel 0.8 mile

Colleton County Courthouse in Walterboro, built in 1822 but famous as site of notorious Murdoch murder trial of 2023 Patricia Pierce

(south) on South Jefferies Boulevard and turn right on DeTreville Street. A brown sign marks the turn. The entrance to the park is 0.2 mile farther.

Turn right on South Jefferies Boulevard and travel one block to East Washington Street.

Then turn right on East Washington Street to explore the heart of Walterboro's historic shopping district. Numerous antique and jewelry stores, boutiques, and food and beverage establishments are worth trying.

The old **Farmers and Merchants Bank Building**, built in 1902, is 2 blocks along on your left at 229 East Washington. Close by is Walterboro's City Plaza, a small park adorned with a fountain and benches. Look up to see the old clock that chimes every quarter hour.

Cross over North Lucas Street and go one block past more shops. On your left at 373 East Washington is **Hiott's Pharmacy**, established in 1951, where you can stop in for lunch or an ice-cream float. This pharmacy, housed in an 1890s building decorated with traditional black and white tiles, still fills prescriptions while you pull up to the counter for a snack and an old-fashioned soda.

Bear northeast on East Washington Street for another block. On your right is the **Colleton Museum and Farmer's Market** (514 E. Washington) featuring exhibits of local history and culture and a farmers market a couple of days a week. A cafe and gift shop have local produce and crafts for sale.

Turn right (east) onto Wichman Street/US 17 Alternate. Travel 2 blocks and turn left (north) on Fishburne Street.

After your turn, **Saint Jude's Episcopal Church** (907 Wichman St.), a beautiful, tan wooden church built in 1882, is on your right. It replaced an earlier structure that was destroyed by a cyclone in 1879. The stained-glass windows of the church were made in Munich, Germany.

Directly in front of you at 205 Church Street is the **Bedon-Lucas House Museum** (ca.1820) that serves as the headquarters of the Colleton County Historical and Preservation Society.

The **Little Library Park** on your left is a nice green space to stop for a rest and to enjoy downtown Walterboro. The tiny white wooden structure here is the **Walterboro Library Society Building** (803 Wichman St.), constructed in 1820.

Turn right (northeast) on Church Street to see some of the Historic Hickory Valley homes, where Paul and Jacob Walter built summer homes in 1784 in a hickory grove that formed the nucleus of a summer colony and began the town of Walterboro.

Pass Witsell Street/S-15-240. On your left at 403 Church Street is **Bethel Presbyterian Church**, established in 1728, and originally located near Jacksonboro. The current structure, built in 1969, is the fourth church building at this site.

You can meander through any of these streets and see lovely, historic homes. A suggested route is to turn left (north) on Heyward Street, go 2 blocks, and then turn right (east) on Webb Street. Turn right again (south) on Verdier Street/S-15-23 and then left (east) on Valley Street/S-15-289. Turn right (south) on North Lemacks Street/S-15-152 and travel 2 blocks to Wichman Street.

At Wichman Street, turn left (east) to head out of town. The road forks after 0.1 mile. US 17 Alternate goes left (northeast) to Summerville. SC 64/Padgett Loop Road goes right (southeast) toward Jacksonboro. Bear right and travel a half mile farther on SC 64/Padgett Loop.

At the stop sign, turn left (southeast) to continue 15 miles on SC 64/Hampton Street towards Jacksonboro. As you leave town, SC 64 becomes Charleston Highway. This dark two-lane road lined with thick woods, fields, and pastures with grazing cows and horses takes you past wetlands, over Chessey Creek after 6.5 miles and Horseshoe Creek, 3 miles farther.

Continue another 3 miles to the site of the old **Bethel Church** on your left (east). A marker to the left of the highway shows you where to stop to enjoy a walk through the mossy, overgrown cemetery.

Bethel Presbyterian Church, founded on this site in 1728 by the Reverend Archibald Stobo, served a large Presbyterian congregation here until being replaced by Bethel Presbyterian Church in Walterboro. The cemetery contains the grave of Captain John Herbert Dent, a US naval officer born in Maryland in 1782. Dent served as acting captain of the frigate *Constitution* in 1804 during the war with Tripoli and was senior officer in charge of naval affairs in Charleston during the War of 1812 against the British. He settled in Walterboro and died in 1823.

Almost a mile farther down SC 64 is Sparks Hall Road. Turn left here to visit the **Historic Burial Site of Colonel Isaac Hayne**, *a local planter and iron manufacturer turned Patriot soldier, who was captured and executed by the British in 1781. He is buried in the family cemetery on the site of Hayne Hall, owned by the Hayne family during the colonial and American Revolution era, one mile north. A brown sign notes the turn, so you can't miss it.*

Travel 1.5 miles past Sparks Hall Road on SC 64 to reach the western edge of **Jacksonboro** and the intersection with US 17/ACE Basin Parkway.

If you are interested in visiting the short, excellently interpreted **Edisto Nature Trail**, *an easy 1-mile loop aside the Edisto River, turn left (northeast) and travel one mile through town. The trailhead parking lot will be on your left (north) just before the road reaches the bridge over the Edisto River.*

Turn right (southwest) onto US 17/Ace Basin Parkway and travel 10 miles towards Green Pond. The roadside is lush and green, lined with marsh and woods. About 6 miles along US 17, you'll cross over the **Ashepoo River**, the middle waterway in the heart of the ACE Basin.

Named for the three rivers that drain the watershed—the Ashepoo, the Combahee, and the Edisto—the **ACE Basin** is home to many endangered or threatened species, including shortnose sturgeon, wood storks, loggerhead sea turtles, and southern bald eagles. From the early 1700s to the mid-1800s, the ACE Basin was home to large plantations owned by a small number of individuals who managed their wetlands primarily to grow rice. After the rice culture declined in the late 1800s, wealthy sportsmen purchased many of these plantations as hunting retreats and wildlife refuges. These owners tended this area so wisely that today many of the undeveloped, unpolluted lands provide refuge for a diverse and extremely productive population of wildlife.

The intricate network of marshes, tidal creeks, uplands, and wetlands has supported myriad plants and animals, including waterfowl, songbirds, fish, shellfish, and upland animals. The refuge lies along the Atlantic Flyway, "the highway in the sky." Vast numbers of shorebirds, neotropical songbirds, waterfowl, and birds of prey migrate here from throughout eastern North America. From late fall through early spring, the refuge is a haven for wood ducks, pintails, shovelers, mallards, and widgeons. Songbirds such as painted buntings and ruby-throated humming-birds find haven here.

Endangered wood storks are moving north to places such as the ACE Basin to nest due to loss of habitat in more southern regions. The peregrine falcon, bald eagle, shortnose sturgeon, and alligators all thrive in the area. Wading birds such as egrets, herons, ibis, sandpipers, plovers, yellowlegs, and black-necked stilts populate the vicinity; white-tailed deer, raccoons, bobcats, river otters, gray foxes, rabbits, and squirrels roam the forests and marshlands.

Pass by S-15-26/Bennetts Point Road on your left (south) after a little over a mile past the Ashepoo, and continue 3 more miles to the entrance to **Donnelley Wildlife Management Area** (585 Donnelley Dr., Green Pond), on your left (south). A brown sign to the right of the road marks the left turn.

Proceed 0.6 mile down Donnelley Road to the trailhead for the 1.4-mile Backwater Trail loop on your left (east), and the headquarters and information kiosk just beyond. The kiosk contains excellent maps of the Donnelley tract. It should be noted that most of drive within Donnelly WMA is on unpaved, hard-packed dirt roads.

Donnelley WMA is open for wildlife observation, bird-watching, photography, nature study, and hiking during daylight hours. It is closed on Sundays, and portions are closed from November through January to minimize disturbance to waterfowl.

During times that Donnelley WMA is closed or if travelers do not want to drive on dirt roads, followers of this scenic drive should simply turn southward down S-15-26/Bennetts Point Road, 3 miles northeast of the Donnelley WMA entrance, and head directly to Bear Island Wildlife Management Area.

The 8,000-acre Donnelley WMA, managed by the South Carolina Department of Natural Resources, is a cross section of the Lowcountry. Waterfowl, wildflowers, alligators, wild turkeys, and white-tailed deer are among the natural attractions of this outing through woodlands and along dikes that cross the old rice fields of the former St. Mary's Plantation. It encompasses a diversity of wetland and upland habitats, including managed rice fields, forested wetlands, tidal marshes, and agricultural lands. You'll find a variety of upland forest types here, including a natural stand of longleaf pines.

The area protects and enhances the diverse wetland and upland habitats for resident and migratory species of wildlife, provides quality hunting and other wildlife-related recreation opportunities, maintains and restores representative natural plant communities, and provides an area for natural-resource-related research and education programs.

Swampland in Donnelly Wildlife Management Area JOHN CLARK

Continue 2.2 miles southward past the kiosk and look for a nature trail sign on your right (west). A few hundred yards to the right is the beginning of the **Boynton Nature Trail**, at a parking lot beside an abandoned house.

The trail leads you to a backwater tupelo swamp favored by wood ducks, across rice field dikes with expansive wetland views, and through uplands filled with songbirds and forested with loblolly and spruce pines, live oaks, magnolias, hickories, ferns, red bays, holly, dogwoods, trumpet honeysuckle, yellow jessamine, pink azaleas, switch cane, and dwarf palmettos. The loop trail is 2.2 miles, but you need only to walk a few hundred feet to enjoy fascinating views of the rice fields and the tupelo swamp and often catch views of alligators basking in the sun.

Bald eagles, turkey vultures, ospreys, wood storks, gallinules, coots, cormorants, eastern kingbirds, red-winged blackbirds, anhingas, and varieties of geese, grebes, loons, terns, vireos, ducks, sparrows, wrens, mergansers, warblers, hawks, herons, vultures, and many others make Donnelley WMA a mother lode of birds. Alligators, turtles, otters, and frogs populate the waterways, and the woods teem with deer, raccoons, turkeys, and foxes.

Continue (southeast) on Donnelley Road for 0.3 mile and take a slight left onto Blocker Run Road. Travel another 3 winding miles through forest punctuated by wetlands to reach S-15-26/Bennetts Point Road.

Turn right (south) and head toward Bear Island and the isolated fishing village of **Bennetts Point**, South Carolina's coastal outback a little more than 11 miles south. This winding roadway is lined with thick ancient oaks, forestland, and Ashepoo River wetlands.

After 6.5 miles, cross the Frank E. Baldwin Jr. Bridge over the **Ashepoo River**, where you'll have a terrific panoramic view of the river and its marshlands. A designated nature observation area is on your right once you transit the bridge, offering a closer look at the Ashepoo and its wading birds and other wildlife. Across the street is a parking area that provides one point of access for the hiking trails along the rice field dikes in **Bear Island Wildlife Management Area**.

The main entrance to Bear Island WMA is almost 2 miles farther southeast on Bennetts Point Road. Turn left (northeast) onto unpaved Ti Ti Road. You'll see a kiosk on your left (north) with a map of the area. This is a good spot to park and stroll along the dirt road and rice field dikes. (Depending on seasons and other factors, you may be able here to drive into the WMA for a 2.5-mile ride to the property's eastern boundary.)

Bear Island offers more than 20 miles of walks through mixed pine and hardwood forests, upland pines, and old rice field impoundments. Expansive views across beautiful wetlands are common, and many varieties of wildlife, especially alligators, can be seen. This 12,000-acre wildlife management area features the state's largest expanse of publicly owned and easily accessible marshland. It

Shrimp boat in harbor of Bennetts Point, literally at the end of the road Patricia Pierce

contains about 10,500 acres of tidal marshes and freshwater marsh impoundments, with an additional 1,200 acres of maritime forests and 400 acres of tilled land. This area is excellent year-round for wildlife viewing.

There are a number of dikes, woodland paths, and dirt roads available for hiking. The dike trails are the primary attraction for hikers.

One of the most pleasant outings is the 3-mile walk from Bennetts Point Road near the Ashepoo River Bridge to the dike's intersection with Ti Ti Road between Minkey Island and Upper Hog Impoundments. Giant cordgrass, blackberries, and a variety of wildflowers grow abundantly, and thick stands of cattails inhabit the shallows. Black needle rush and sawgrass can be found in the wetlands, and the island supports small forests of oaks, palmettos, pines, and wax myrtles. Wigeon grass, wild rice, and other avian food plants fill the freshwater impoundments.

Bear Island is managed for waterfowl, other migratory birds, and terrestrial wildlife. Alligators are plentiful and frequently seen, and woodlands teem with white-tailed deer, raccoons, fox squirrels, and wild turkeys.

A variety of ducks visit or live here, including an introduced flock of mottled ducks. Fall and winter visitors include wigeons, teals, pintails, mallards, black ducks, and other puddle ducks. Bald eagles, golden eagles, ospreys, great horned owls, vultures, swallows, wood storks, egrets, herons, cormorants, moorhens, rails, marsh wrens, purple martins, coots, eastern kingbirds, yellowlegs, peregrine falcons, red-tailed and red-shouldered hawks, Cooper's hawks, and great varieties of swallows and shore-birds are in residence year-round or part-time. Tens of thousands of ducks and other seasonal visitors are present in late winter.

Exit Ti Ti Road by turning left (south) back onto S-15-26/Bennetts Point Road. Drive southward for 2.7 miles to reach the remote fishing village of Bennetts Point. A folksy tackle and bait shop, **B&B Seafood** (15823 Bennetts Point Rd.), will be on your left at the end of Bennetts Point Road, beside a boat landing on **Mosquito Creek**. Stop here for a view of the creek as it flows into the Ashepoo River to your right (west). Across Mosquito Creek is part of the **ACE Basin National Estuarine Research Preserve**. This is a good place to watch for brown pelicans, gulls, terns, horned grebes, red-breasted mergansers, and double-breasted cormorants.

You usually see shrimp boats docked here and a variety of other fishermen and boaters enjoying the creek. A variety of homes are scattered across the flat, marshy landscape. Commercial fishing and shrimping boats make their home here, daily following Mosquito Creek and the Ashepoo River a short distance south to Saint Helena Sound and the open sea.

Bennetts Point to Old Sheldon Church

Turn around and head back out on S-15-26/Bennetts Point Road, returning almost 16 miles northward to US 17. The last few miles on Bennetts Point Road are especially shady underneath thick oak canopies.

Turn left (southwest) onto US 17 and proceed 9.5 miles through verdant wetlands and forests to cross the **Combahee River**, the westernmost major stream of the ACE Basin. As you cross the Harriet Tubman Bridge, you leave Colleton County and enter Beaufort County. The bridge provides great north-south views of this river at a vantage point that has unusually high land on both sides. Sugar Hill Landing is after the second causeway, just past the bridge.

Harriet Tubman, namesake of the bridge, was an abolitionist who played a major role in the "Underground Railroad" helping enslaved people flee north to freedom. In 1863, she led 150 African American Union soldiers on a raid up the Combahee River, rescuing more than 700 enslaved people from bondage on surrounding plantations.

Turn right (north) onto S-7-33/River Road, 1.2 miles past the bridge. Drive 1.2 miles north to an entrance to the rice fields and dikes of the **Combahee Unit of the ACE Basin National Wildlife Refuge** on the right (northeast). You are welcome to walk the dikes of these wetlands that border the Combahee River, but heavy boots are probably needed on the overgrown pathways.

Continue northwest on S-7-33/River Road. This dark, wooded road was once dotted with the Combahee River rice plantations of 18th- and 19th-century South Carolina aristocrats. As you traverse this route, glimpses of vegetation let you know that the good life continues behind lush pastures and oak groves.

One site you can't miss is **Auldbrass Plantation**, about 7 miles from your last stop, on the right. The modern, geometric brown fence catches your eye against the natural landscape and creates an interesting pattern as you drive past the plantation. This famous Frank Lloyd Wright home, built in 1939, has no right angles. It is privately owned and open only on special occasions to the public. However, a number of structures, such as the caretaker's quarters, chicken run, two cottages, and the granary, can be seen from the road.

More segments of the Combahee Unit of the ACE Basin NWR are just past Auldbrass. Entrances to these segments begin with the second dirt road on the right (northeast) after Auldbrass. Short walking trails are available at the end of each of these roads, taking visitors to the backwaters of the Combahee River. Bald cypress trees and knees, bobwhites, wild turkeys, deer, and mourning doves are among the sights.

Continue 2 miles farther on River Road northwest into **Yemassee**, a small railroad village. Located astride the boundary between Beaufort and Hampton Counties, Yemassee is the smallest town in South Carolina with an Amtrak station.

The community is steeped in history, reaching far into South Carolina's past. It is named for one of the most powerful and extensive Native American tribes of the late seventeenth century. The Yemassee fought fiercely against European settlers in the early 18th century. The tribe's territory stretched along the coast from southern Georgia to the Edisto River, and its two major centers of power between the Savannah and Combahee Rivers were at Pocataligo and Coosawhatchie, nearby villages that retain those names to this day.

Turn left (southwest) on Railroad Avenue North. Drive 0.3 mile into downtown. Drive southwest past the old Amtrak train station (15 Wall St.), to turn left on SC 3/Yemassee Highway/Castle Hall Road. Cross the railroad tracks and Wall Street.

Travel 0.8 mile (southeast) on Castle Hall Road and bear left onto Old Sheldon Church Road/S-7-21. This road is quite cool because of the dense canopy of trees. Very little light can peek through, but when it does, the sight is one to behold. Well-outlined rays beam through the dark bark overhead.

Travel 6 miles to reach the end of your journey and the beautiful ruins of **Old Sheldon Church**. The ruins are on your left and a parking area is on your right.

Ruins of Old Sheldon Church, destroyed by Sherman's troops PATRICIA PIERCE

The ruins of Old Sheldon Prince William's Parish Church, first built in 1748, stand tall to this day. The church was burned in 1780 by the British, rebuilt in 1826, and burned again in 1865 by Sherman's troops. It was named for the ancestral home of the Bull family in Warwickshire, England. The brick columns and fragile arches of the former church, surrounded by enormous oaks, maintain their grace and beauty in this idyllic grassy clearing amid an enchanting, dark forest. A small, shaded picnic area on the grounds provides a place to contemplate the ruins and the Lowcountry life of the 19th century.

Nearby Attractions

Bluffton, Great Swamp Sanctuary, Lake Warren State Park, McPhersonville Church, Pinckney Island National Wildlife Refuge, Robertville Baptist Church, Savannah National Wildlife Refuge, Tillman Sand Ridge Heritage Preserve, Tuskegee Airmen Monument, Webb Wildlife Center.

22

Historic Beaufort and Sea Islands

Beaufort to Hunting Island State Park

General Description: This 35-mile trip begins in the historic, picturesque waterfront town of Beaufort and carries sightseers across salt marshes, creeks, and the Beaufort River to the quaint town of Port Royal, through farms on Saint Helena Island to wild and beautiful Hunting Island State Park on the shores of the Atlantic Ocean.

Special Attractions: Historic Beaufort, Henry C. Chambers Waterfront Park, Beaufort River, McTeer Memorial Bridge, Port Royal, Sands Boat Landing and Boardwalk, Battery Creek, Saint Helena Island, Frogmore, Penn Center, Brick Baptist Church, Saint Helena Parish Chapel of Ease, Saint Helena Sound, Harbor Island, Johnson Creek, Hunting Island State Park and Lighthouse, Paradise Fishing Pier.

Location: Southern coast.

Travel Season: All year.

Services: Beaufort offers plentiful hotels, restaurants, and other services.

The Drive

The setting for *The Big Chill* and many other movies, Beaufort is a charming old waterfront town that provides the beginning point for this trip on South Carolina's southern Sea Islands. After winding through Beaufort and the adjacent port community of Port Royal, visitors ride across salt marshes, pausing on the grounds of historic Penn Center, symbol of African American freedom, before continuing on to the wild beauty of Hunting Island State Park on the Atlantic Ocean, with its enchanting lighthouse.

Historic Beaufort

Beaufort (pronounced "byou-furt," not "bo-furt"), the second oldest town in the state, is a lovely community on Port Royal Island beside the Beaufort River. It is blessed with a spectacular natural beauty and an exciting, turbulent history that make the area one of the most intriguing places in South Carolina. The picturesque landscape of ancient live oaks, saltwater marshes, creeks, rivers, and deep harbor waters enhances the splendor of Beaufort's antebellum homes. Centuries ago, the natural beauty made the area an attractive locale for Spanish, French, and English explorers to "conquer."

Historic Beaufort and Sea Islands: Beaufort to Hunting Island State Park

ATLANTIC OCEAN

Beaufort

Beaufort River

Short St
Laurens St
Bayard St
Hancock St
Pinckney St
Hamilton St
Federal St
East St
New St
Carteret St
Republic St
Scott St
Port St
West St
Bay St
Prince St
Duke St
Chat St
Craven St
King St
North St
Newcastle St
Church St
Harrington St
Washington St
Wilmington St
Monson St
Bay St

Henry C. Chambers Park

MORGAN ISLAND

Coosaw River

Morgan River

COOSAW ISLAND

Wilkins

LADYS ISLAND

802

Beaufort

21

Meridian Rd

802

Ribaut Rd

US Naval Hospital

Old Shell Rd

281

PORT ROYAL ISLAND

Port Royal

Paris Ave

Sands Boat Landing and Boardwalk

802

280

Battery Creek

Shell Point

170

To Hilton Head

SOUTH CAROLINA

To 95
21

BEAUFORT MARINE CORPS AIR STATION

PARRIS ISLAND US MARINE CORPS

Beaufort River

Broad River

Chechessee River

Frogmore

21

M.L. King

Penn Center

St. Helena Chapel of Ease

S-7-45

ST. HELENA ISLAND

Sea Side Rd

S-7-77

Ephram Rd

Lands End Rd

Sea Side Rd

S-7-45

S-7-77

ST. PHILLIPS ISLAND

Harbor River

Hunting Island State Park

21

Hunting Island Dr

Paradise Fishing Pier

Sea Island Dr

S-7-406

FRIPP ISLAND

0   2.5   5 Miles

0   2.5   5 Kilometers

N

Pedro de Salaza, a Spanish explorer, visited Port Royal Island in 1514, the second landing on the North American continent by Europeans. He was soon followed by another Spaniard, Francisco Cordillo, in 1520, and then by Captain Jean Ribaut, a French Huguenot, in 1562. Ribaut attempted to establish a settlement near the present-day town of Port Royal. This was the first Protestant settlement in the United States, but it was soon abandoned. When Ribaut returned to France to replenish supplies, he left some soldiers behind. Frustrated, the soldiers built their own ship and attempted to sail back to France. They made it home, but only after being rescued by an English ship.

In 1566 Spaniards established a fort, San Felip, and a military port, Saint Elena, considered the capital of La Florida Province for 21 years. Native Americans destroyed this fort, but the Spaniards remained; they built a larger fort, San Marcos, in 1587, the same year that England sent Sir Francis Drake to take the land. Drake successfully pushed the Spaniards back to St. Augustine, making room for the English to settle the area. The town of Beaufort was established in 1711 and named for one of the original lords proprietor of Carolina, Henry Somerset, Duke of Beaufort (1684–1714).

During the 18th century, Beaufort thrived as indigo and cotton plantation owners of Saint Helena and Parris Islands began to build homes here in order to visit each other and to enjoy cultural activities during the summer months. In fact, before the Civil War, Beaufort was considered the wealthiest and most aristocratic town of its size in America.

Beaufort was a political hotbed as well. The first Ordinance to Secede from the Union was drafted here at the Milton Maxey House. South Carolina seceded from the Union on December 20, 1860. Almost a year later, in November 1861, a Federal fleet circled Port Royal Sound, and the Confederates abandoned Beaufort. By December 1861, Union general Isaac Stevens occupied Beaufort's abandoned homes, turning them into hospitals and offices for the remainder of the Civil War. This saved Beaufort from being burned by Sherman's troops on his infamous march from Atlanta.

Present day Beaufort's maritime and tourist-based economy is bolstered by the Beaufort Marine Corps Air Station on the town's north side, Parris Island Marine Corps Recruit depot on its south side, and Naval Hospital Beaufort, in Port Royal. Adding to the military presence is Beaufort National Cemetery, just west of downtown.

Begin your 2-mile drive of the historic district of Beaufort on Bay Street at the **Henry C. Chambers Waterfront Park** on the banks of the Beaufort River. Within the park, you will find shady places to rest, a playground, and an amphitheater beneath enormous oak trees.

Along the rear of the park, restaurants in buildings dating back to the 1700s have back porches that allow you to dine and enjoy a scenic view of the Beaufort River. Unique shops are also accessible from the park through brick alleys that lead to Bay Street and the **Carriage Tours Ticket Office** at 1002 Bay Street, where visitors can find information on carriage tours, riverboat tours, self-guided walking tours, and nearby attractions.

Head east on Bay Street, past upscale antique, jewelry, and book shops and art galleries, and cross over Carteret Street. The bridge to Lady's Island is to your right. On your left, at 601 Bay Street, is the **Lewis Reeve Sams House** (ca. 1852). You might recognize the home, since it was featured in the film *Prince of Tides*. Sitting on the corner of Bay and New Streets, this white wooden home, surrounded by a meek picket fence, is most famous for the bucket brigade that saved the home from burning during the 1907 fire that destroyed many of Beaufort's homes.

Across the street from the Lewis Reeve Sams House is a shaded park on the Beaufort River and the **Stephen Elliott, CSA, Memorial**. Old oaks canopy comfortable benches and a cannon recognizing Brigadier General Stephen Elliott for his leadership in the short-lived Confederate defense of Beaufort.

Turn left (north) onto New Street. At 212 New Street is **The Old Point Inn**, built by William Waterhouse in 1898. At the next block, on the corner of New and Port Republic Streets, the **Thomas Hepworth House** at 214 New Street, the oldest home in Beaufort, is on your left. Built in 1717–1722 and then rebuilt in 1760, this 2-story putty-colored wooden house sits atop a stucco base. Like so many of the homes in this area, its yard is enclosed by a brick wall.

Continue north for another block on New Street, and take a right onto Craven Street and then an immediate left (north) onto East Street. On your right, tucked between Craven and Federal Streets, is the **Joseph Johnson House** (ca. 1861) at 411 Craven Street. This natural-colored medieval-style stone and brick structure, known as **"The Castle,"** is hidden behind palmetto trees and an ivy-covered wall. Used as a hospital by Federal troops during the Civil War, the home overlooks the Beaufort River and is surrounded by colorful gardens. This is one of the most photographed homes in America.

At Federal Street, turn right (east). You'll get a good look of the back of The Castle here. After crossing a small creek, the first house on your left is **Cassena**, at 315 Federal Street. Built in the 1800s by John Blythewood, the home's front yard is filled with camellias, magnolias, and old oak trees. Like many of the homes in Beaufort, Cassena was purchased by one of the family's former slaves after the Civil War.

At 303 Federal Street, to your left on the corner of Federal and Pinckney Streets, is the James Rhett House. Construction began on the home in 1884, with

Joseph Johnson House, known as "The Castle," used by Union troops as a hospital during their long Civil War occupation of Beaufort PATRICIA PIERCE

Mr. Rhett intending to build his home two rooms deep. Rhett did not anticipate the actual cost of his original design, however, and he was forced to pare down his initial plan substantially. Today the home is referred to as **"Rhett's Folly."** Encircled by an iron and brick gate, the house has a commanding presence.

On your right, across the street at 302 Federal Street, is the William Fripp House (ca. 1830). Also known as **Tidewater**, this white, 2-story home faces the Beaufort River and was built by William Fripp, owner of 9 plantations.

At 501 Pinckney Street, directly in front of you, is the **James Robert Verdier House** (ca. 1814). Called **Marshlands**, this 2-story home faces the Beaufort River and is decorated with a porch that wraps entirely around the home. Sprawling oaks fill the front and side yards.

Take a left onto Pinckney Street and continue north for one block. Turn right (east) onto King Street, the first paved road on your right, and follow it to Short Street. Here you have the best view of the Paul Hamilton House (ca. 1855), also known as **"The Oaks,"** at 100 Laurens Street. A French Huguenot's ghost is said to haunt the house.

Follow Short Street past The Oaks to Laurens Street. Take a right here. You'll see the back of The Oaks to your right. At the end of Laurens Street is **Tidalholm** (ca. 1853), the summer home of Edgar Fripp, at 1 Laurens Street, on your left. This home on the Beaufort River has been used in several movies, including *The Big Chill* and *The Great Santini*. It is the only house in town with water on three sides and a widow's watch.

Return to Short Street and turn right. Continue north for one more block and then turn left onto Hancock Street. On your right at 207 Hancock Street is the **Elizabeth Hext House** or **"Riverview"** (ca. 1720), the second oldest home in Beaufort. Ghosts of pirates are said to haunt this dwelling.

Continue west on Hancock Street past Pinckney and Hamilton Streets to East Street. Take a left on East Street and then a quick right onto Prince Street. On your right at the corner of Prince and New Streets, at 511 Prince Street, is the **Henry McKee House** (ca. 1834).

After the Civil War, Robert Smalls, a former enslaved man and Civil War naval hero who became the first black United States congressman, purchased this home at a tax sale. The McKee family contested Smalls' ownership, and the case went all the way to the Supreme Court. Smalls prevailed, and he even let a member of the McKee family reside here until her death. The home remained in the Smalls family until 1940. A portrait of Robert Smalls hangs in the South Carolina State House.

Turn left on New Street and view **First African Baptist Church** (601 New St.), built in 1865 by freed slaves. Continue south for 3 blocks and take a right (west) onto Craven Street. After crossing Carteret Street you'll see on your right

Rhett House in Beaufort, built around 1820 John Clark

the **Beaufort Arsenal Museum** at 713 Craven Street. This blond, castle-like structure, built in 1798 and rebuilt in 1852, holds many relics of nature, war, and early industry.

On the next block is the **Tabernacle Baptist Church** on your right at 911 Craven Street, where Robert Smalls is buried; a bronze bust of the leader greets visitors in the church's front yard. Not only was Smalls an escaped slave who served as a US congressman for nine years, but he also served as captain of the *Planter* naval vessel during the Civil War, as a delegate to state constitutional conventions in 1868 and 1895, and as a member of South Carolina's Senate and House of Representatives. Smalls died in 1915 and is honored at this tall, whitewashed church that has been in service since 1840.

Continue on Craven over Charles Street. On your right at 1009 Craven Street. is the **Rhett House Inn** (ca. 1820), a stately white mansion with first- and second-floor front porches where guests may rest in the shade of the oaks that surround the inn.

Next on your right, at the corner of Church and Craven Streets, is the Maxcy-Rhett House (1113 Craven St.), known more commonly as **"Secession House."** Beaufort delegates met here in 1860 before heading off to participate in the state convention that resulted in South Carolina being the first state to secede from the Union. This structure dates from 1743, with major renovations in 1811 and 1861.

Turn right (north) on Church Street and go one block to the corner of Church and North Streets. Catty-corner on your right behind a brick wall at 501 Church Street is **Saint Helena's Episcopal Church** and its enchanting parish grounds and cemetery. The present church building was constructed in 1817 and substantially renovated in 1842. The church was established in 1712, and construction of the original structure on this site was begun in 1724.

Turn left (west) on North Street and proceed 3 blocks to Monson Street. Take a left (south) on Monson and go one block to Bay Street. The Beaufort River is directly in front of you. Turn left (southeast) onto Bay Street to see a string of magnificent, waterfront homes. The **Leverett House**, at 1301 Bay Street, is an early 1800s home enclosed by a beautiful white wooden gate. On the next block are the **Thomas Fuller House** (ca. 1786), called the **Tabby Manse**, at 1211 Bay; the **Robert Means House** (ca. 1800), at 1207 Bay; and the **John A. Cuthbert House** (ca. 1810), at 1203 Bay, which now serves as an inn.

The William Elliott House, also known as **"The Anchorage"** and former home to one of South Carolina's few anti-secessionist politicians in 1860, is on your left at 1103 Bay Street. It has undergone several renovations since its original construction around 1800 and now is rented for social events.

On your left on the next block at 1001 Bay Street is the **George Elliott House** (ca. 1844). Across the street from the George Elliott House, Carriage Tours

View of Beaufort River from Bay Street John Clark

ticket sales and Historic Tours Shops are on your right, at the front of Henry C. Chambers Park.

Park in the public parking area and stroll down Bay Street to experience Beaufort's downtown on foot. You can choose among numerous places to eat, with many restaurants offering relaxing back-porch dining with terrific views of the Beaufort River.

In the midst of Beaufort's shopping area, at 801 Bay Street, is the **John Mark Verdier House Museum**. One of the few homes open to the public, this Federal-style historic home, built in the 1790s, stands out amid the hustle and bustle of Bay Street. It played host to the Marquis de Lafayette in 1825 on his tour of the states, and during the Civil War served as headquarters for Union troops. Today its first floor houses the Historic Beaufort Foundation.

Exit downtown Beaufort by turning right (southeast) off of Bay Street onto Carteret Street/Business US 21 South to cross the drawbridge that affords a terrific view of the **Beaufort River** and its lush marshlands.

Port Royal

Once over the bridge, you'll be on **Lady's Island**. Go 0.4 mile on US Business 21 South/Sea Island Parkway and turn right (south) on Meridian Road/S-7-36, a beautiful residential road lined with oaks draped in Spanish moss. Ride 1.5 miles and then, at a major intersection, take a right (southwest) onto Lady's Island Drive/US 21/SC 802 to visit the charming town of Port Royal, 1.5 miles away.

As you reach the highest point of the **McTeer Memorial Bridge** over the Beaufort River, the river and its marshlands extend as far as you can see along the horizon to your left. Beaufort can be seen to your right near a bend in the waterway. Its church steeples peek above the treetops, and a marina full of fancy yachts and sailboats bounces at the base of the bridge.

After crossing the bridge, you are back on Port Royal Island. Turn left (south) at the first intersection to continue on US 21/SC 281, which becomes Ribaut Road. Travel 0.3 mile down Ribaut Road and fork left (south) onto Old Shell Road. The **United States Naval Hospital**, at 1 Pinckney Boulevard is on your left.

Continue across Pinckney Boulevard on Old Shell Road. After 0.2 mile, the 3-acre **Fort Frederick Heritage Preserve** is on your left. Here you can visit the ruins of Fort Frederick (601 Old Fort Road), named after the eldest son of King George II of England. Built of oyster shell-based tabby around 1753 to replace the older Beaufort Fort (ca. 1706), Fort Frederick fell to ruins 20 years later.

Travel through a shaded residential area past cute old bungalows. Old Shell Road curves to the right (west) and becomes 14th Street. Cross Richmond Avenue and turn left on London Avenue/S-7-124.

Continue on London Street for 6 blocks. Turn left (east) onto Sands Beach Road and follow it 0.3 mile to the **Sands Boat Landing and Boardwalk** at the southern tip of Port Royal Island.

The expansive boardwalk extends into the water where the Beaufort River and Battery Creek intersect. At the tip of the island, you have a fantastic view of Battery Creek and the Beaufort River. Vibrant marshlands reach out into the water. If you happen to visit when others are not around, you can enjoy the serenity of hearing only the lapping of water on the dock. This is a great place for bird viewing.

At the northwest end of the parking lot is beach access. Be sure to drive out here too for a view of the beach, accessible by car from sunrise to sunset.

Backtrack west on Sands Beach Road. Turn right (north) on London Avenue and, after one block, then left (west) on 8th Street. The **Town Hall of Port Royal** is on your immediate left at 700 Paris Avenue, along with the ornate **Memorial Clock** commemorating the 50th anniversary of V-J Day and the end of World War II.

Turn right (north) on Paris Avenue and travel 3 blocks. Turn left (west) on 11th Street.

On your right at 1004 11th Street is the beautiful white, wooden **Union Church**, built in 1878. The church has been used by Presbyterian, Baptist, and

Methodist congregations, and it has served as a playhouse and office for the Historic Port Royal Foundation.

Continue all the way to the road's end past neat old homes to the banks of Battery Creek. Step outside for spectacular views of shrimp boats and shimmering **Battery Creek** and then go inside one of the restaurants for fresh local seafood.

Backtrack on 11th Street to Paris Avenue and turn left (north). Travel about a half mile on Paris Avenue/SC 281, passing inviting antiques stores, unique shops, and restaurants.

Immediately after passing the post office (1625 Paris Ave.) on your left, you will see the **Port Royal Cypress Wetlands** on your right.

This preserve features a half mile trail around the wetlands of Port Royal—a combination of boardwalks, paved trails, and roadside pedestrian and bike trails. The trail is a perfect spot to park and stretch your legs while enjoying the diverse array of native and migratory wildlife and indigenous plants. Bird sightings often include woodpeckers, Carolina wrens, bluebirds, red-tailed and red-shouldered hawks, and moorhens. Below the surface, alligators patrol the waters, protecting the nesting birds, eggs, and hatchlings from raccoons, opossums, rats, otters, and other land-based predators.

Continuing north on Paris Avenue for 0.1 mile, turn right (east) at the intersection of Paris Avenue and Ribaut Road, and travel 0.8 mile on Ribaut Road/US 21 to Lady's Island Drive. Turn right on Lady's Island Drive/US 21 and cross back over the **McTeer Memorial Bridge** to Lady's Island.

*If you wish to visit the US Marine Base on **Parris Island**, turn left (west) at the intersection of Paris Avenue and Ribaut Road. The Russell Bell Bridge connects Port Royal Island with Parris Island and the Shell Point area of Beaufort County. Lights on the bridge provide a scenic drive at night. The base features Parris Island Museum (111 Panama St., Beaufort), open to the public.*

Saint Helena Island

After crossing the McTeer Bridge onto Lady's Island, continue about 2.3 miles on Lady's Island Drive/US 21 to its intersection with Sea Island Parkway/US 21. Turn right (southeast) on US 21/Sea Island Parkway and head 2.3 miles to **Saint Helena Island** and the community of Frogmore on the other side of Cowen Creek.

First called Santa Elena by the Spanish, this small rural island was later named Saint Helena by the English. In the 18th century, plantation owners became wealthy growing Sea Island cotton here. Enslaved people greatly outnumbered white plantation owners and their families. When Union soldiers captured Saint Helena and other Sea Islands, the enslaved people remained, became free, and later were given land of their own.

Today on Saint Helena, you'll find quaint stores and a sense of the old South. Change comes slowly on this agricultural island. The roads are lined with Spanish moss–draped oak trees, old cottages, and sandy soils that support fields of corn and tomatoes.

Fruit stands dapple the highway with Sea Island produce along the drive into the heart of the **Frogmore** community. Go 2.3 miles past Cowen Creek and slow down to take in the curious stores and unique restaurants along both sides of the road. This is a good place to stop and enjoy the area's legendary Frogmore stew.

Turn right (south) on Dr. Martin Luther King Jr. Drive/S-7-45 to visit the **Penn Center** (16 Penn Center Circle West, St. Helena Island), one of the nation's most historically significant African American educational and cultural institutions. The center is a half mile down the road. Turn right (west) onto Penn Center Circle West.

During the Civil War, Union troops occupied the Sea Islands and made concerted efforts not only to free enslaved people, but to educate them as well. Penn Center was established in 1862 by the Quaker Freedman's Society of Pennsylvania in an effort, sometimes called the Port Royal Experiment, to bring formal education to freed slaves. Laura Towne and Ellen Murray, teachers from Pennsylvania, helped found Penn Center and devoted 40 years of their lives to educating the Sea Islands' newly freed people.

Classes were first held in a single room on Oaks Plantation, but the instruction was later relocated to the **Brick Baptist Church** (built in 1855), which is on your left (85 Dr. Martin Luther King, Jr. Dr., St. Helena), directly across from the Penn Center grounds. In 1864 a prefabricated building was sent from Pennsylvania and placed on a 50-acre tract of land across from the church. The building erected on this land became the first Penn School building. Today there are 19 buildings at the Penn School National Historic Landmark.

In the early 1900s the school adopted the Tuskegee Curriculum, which emphasized agricultural and home economics classes. It worked under this curriculum until the center was absorbed into the South Carolina public school system in 1948. The last class graduated in 1953. In spite of the center closing as a school, it continued to play a central role in the Sea Island community. Dr. Martin Luther King Jr. and the Southern Christian Leadership Conference held annual civil rights movement meetings here. Today the school continues to work on community-based projects, such as bringing public water to the islands, helping farmers to buy and market through cooperatives, and advocating better housing and health care for low-income people.

At the center's grounds, you can visit the **York W. Bailey Museum**, dating back to 1862. Penn School students built it in the Lowcountry's unique tabby-like style structure with oyster shells, concrete, and sand. The museum houses artifacts, photographs, personal and institutional papers, and published materials, as well as video- and audiotapes that interpret the history of Penn Center, the Gullah culture, and the African American connection between West Africa and the Sea Islands.

Another interesting building you might want to explore is **Darrah Hall**, the oldest building (ca. 1894) on the Penn Center campus, built as a memorial to Sophia Towne Darrah. Originally located on "the green" at the intersection of US 21 and Lands End Road, Darrah Hall was moved to the center of Penn's campus in 1940. It was first used as a gymnasium and later as a tomato-packing house. It became the site of temperance meetings, farmer fairs, community sings, and plays. The hall's original basketball scoreboard can still be seen.

Also on the Penn Center grounds are the **Laura Towne Library and Archives**; the **Old Burial Ground**; a kitchen; and dorm rooms. More than 20,000 people visit the Penn Center annually to learn about the history of the Gullah and

Ruins of Saint Helena Island Parish Chapel of Ease, built in the 1740s JOHN CLARK

Sea Island culture, participate in community programs, and attend conferences and family reunions.

Exit the Penn Center by turning right (south) on S-7-45/Dr. Martin Luther King Jr. Drive. The road forks after 0.7 mile from the Penn Center, where S-7-45 becomes Lands End Road. Take the right fork. Drive slowly because 0.1 mile past the fork, on your left, are the enchanting ruins of the **Saint Helena Parish Chapel of Ease**, built in the 1740s.

Tuck in the Wood Campground at 22 Tuc In De Wood Lane is on your left less than a mile past the Chapel of Ease. Continue down Lands End Road, which is shaded by oak canopies, before opening up to bright fields full of tomatoes and corn.

Drive 0.6 mile farther and look for the first paved road on your left, Ephraim Road/S-7-195. Turn left and travel a mile to where the road ends at Sea Side Road/S-7-77.

Turn left (northeast) onto S-7-77/Sea Side Road, and travel 6.8 miles to the junction with US 21/Sea Island Parkway South. Agricultural fields, pecan groves lined with whitewashed fences, fields of colorful wildflowers, and forestlands decorate this quiet, rural road. Many of the homes to the right sit alongside the wetlands of the Harbor River, which is largely out of view from the main road.

Hunting Island

When you reach US 21/Sea Island Parkway, turn right (southeast) toward Hunting Island 4 miles ahead.

After a mile you'll see the shrimp boats docked or making their way through the inlet marshlands of the Harbor River. Seagulls dip down, trying to catch stray shrimp on deck. A little over a mile farther you cross the **Harbor River** and experience a terrific view of **Saint Helena Sound** and Harbor Island's residential development. Once you cross Harbor River on a blue drawbridge, you are on **Harbor Island**. Travel 1.3 miles on the island, enjoying beautiful views of the Harbor River and marshlands on your right.

Next you cross over **Johnson Creek** to enter **Hunting Island State Park**, one of the most popular state parks in South Carolina. The 5,000-acre island was so named because the land was once primarily used for hunting deer, raccoon and other small game, and waterfowl.

At Hunting Island State Park (2555 Sea Island Pkwy.), enjoy 5 miles of beach, maritime forest, and saltwater marshes. The park provides over a hundred campsites and a visitor center and park store that provide educational programs and nature walks year-round. Visitors can fish in a lagoon for whiting, spot, trout, bass, and drum, or, at the southern end of the island, dangle lines from the Paradise Fishing Pier.

Nature trails take you throughout this barrier island. A one-mile nature trail leads from the park's lighthouse, and a 4-mile hiking trail guides you throughout the island's pristine habitats, the best-developed slash pine–palmetto forest in the state. White-tailed deer and raccoons find refuge on this barrier island, as well as more than 125 species of birds, including herons, gulls, terns, and egrets.

Hunting Island still appears much as it did to Europeans when they arrived in America. Unfortunately, the beach is quickly eroding. Between 1830 and 1930, erosion took 1.3 miles from the island. The island has eroded at an average annual rate of 25 feet on the northern tip and 10 feet on the central beach. The presence of a mature forest at the edge of the shore is clear evidence that the sea is rapidly reclaiming the land.

Just after you cross the bridge, the park's campgrounds are to your left on Campground Road. This is the first entrance road to the park. Continue south 1.1 miles to visit one of the most famous sites of Hunting Island, its lighthouse. You'll see the PARK GATE sign on your left, noting the turn into the main part of the park leading to the park office, beach access, and lighthouse.

Turn left on S-7-762/Hunting Island Drive. Follow the dark, winding road for a mile through thick woods of palms, palmettos, pines, and oaks; the park's visitor center is on your right. Continue left at North Beach Road to visit the **Hunting Island Lighthouse**.

The first lighthouse on the island was a brick structure built in 1859. That tower was destroyed during the Civil War. A new lighthouse made of cast iron and designed to be moved if necessary, was constructed in 1875. The bottom two-thirds of this conical, 136-foot lighthouse is painted white; its top is black.

In 1889, the lighthouse was relocated 1.25 miles southeast of the first location because of erosion, and by 1890 the keeper's dwelling, oil house, and other buildings were also moved to the new lighthouse site. A dock and tram road were built to transport oil to the lighthouse. Two other original structures, the oil house and the cistern, remain on the site. Both are listed on the National Register of Historic Places.

After you have toured the lighthouse complex and walked on the beach, with its tall palmetto trees bending over the short stretch of sand, head back out on S-7-762/Hunting Island Drive and turn left (south) on S-7-406/Sea Island Parkway. A marsh boardwalk is on your right 1.7 miles from Hunting Island Drive, offering a nice parking area and a boardwalk that extends far into Johnson Creek and its hammock islands. This is a good place for wildlife viewing.

Hunting Island Lighthouse, built in 1875 and moved in 1889 because of beachfront erosion PATRICIA PIERCE

The end of Hunting Island is a half mile past the marsh boardwalk. On your right is Russ Point Road, which leads to Russ Point Boat Landing, offering nice views of Fripp Island and Fripp Inlet.

Turn left to visit the nature center and fishing pier, just before the bridge to **Fripp Island**, a private, gated community.

The nature center features live native snakes and turtles, a small saltwater aquarium, daily programs, and sea turtle exhibits.

The **Paradise Fishing Pier** extends 1,120 feet into Fripp Inlet, providing a terrific place for fishing and unobstructed views of the inlet and the great Atlantic Ocean beyond.

Nearby Attractions

Hilton Head Island, Historic Bluffton, Lake Warren State Park, Lowcountry Estuarium, Pinckney Island National Wildlife Refuge, Robertville Baptist Church, Savannah National Wildlife Refuge.

Helpful Organizations

State Government

South Carolina Department of Parks, Recreation, and Tourism
1205 Pendleton St.
Columbia, SC 29201
(803) 734-1700
DiscoverSouthCarolina.com
SouthCarolinaParks.com

South Carolina National Heritage Corridor
1205 Pendleton St.
Columbia, SC 29201
scnhc.org

South Carolina Aquarium
100 Aquarium Wharf
Charleston, SC 29401
(843) 577-3474
(800) 722-6455
scaquarium.org

South Carolina Department of Agriculture
1200 Senate St.
5th Floor, Wade Hampton Building
Columbia, SC 29201
(803) 734-2210
agriculture.sc.gov

Greenville State Farmers Market
1354 Rutherford Rd.
Greenville, SC 29609

Pee Dee State Farmers Market
2513 West Lucas St.
Florence, SC 29501

South Carolina State Farmers Market
3483 Charleston Hwy.
West Columbia, SC 29172

South Carolina Department of Archives & History
8301 Parklane Rd.
Columbia, SC 29223
(803) 896-6196
scdah.sc.gov

South Carolina Department of Natural Resources
1000 Assembly St.
Columbia, SC 29201
(803) 734-3886 (hunting & fishing)
(803) 734-3893 (Heritage Preserves)
dnr.sc.gov

South Carolina Department of Transportation
955 Park St.,
Columbia, SC 29201
(855) 467-2368
scdot.org

GIS/Mapping
955 Park St.
Columbia, SC 29201
(803) 737-1677
https://www.scdot.org/travel/travel
-mappinggis.aspx

South Carolina Forestry Commission
5500 Broad River Rd.
Columbia, SC 29212
(803) 896-8800
scfc.gov

**South Carolina Institute of
Archaeology & Anthropology**
1321 Pendleton St.
Columbia, SC 29208
(803) 777-8170

South Carolina State Library
1500 Senate St.
Columbia, SC 29201
(803) 734-8666
statelibrary.sc.gov

South Carolina State Museum
301 Gervais St.
Columbia, SC 29201
(803) 898-4921
scmuseum.org

United States Government

**US Department of Agriculture
(USDA) Forest Service**
Francis Marion & Sumter National
Forests
4931 Broad River Rd.
Columbia, SC 29212
(803) 561-4000
fs.usda.gov/scnfs

**Francis Marion National Forest
US Forest Service
Ranger District Office**
2967 Steed Creek Rd.
Huger, SC 29450
(843) 336-2200
fs.usda.gov/scnfs

*Sewee Visitor & Environmental
Education Center*
5821 US 17 North
Awendaw, SC 29429
(843) 928-3368

**Sumter National Forest
US Forest Service**
fs.usda.gov/scnfs

Andrew Pickens Ranger District Office
112 Andrew Pickens Circle
Mountain Rest, SC 29664
(864) 638-9568

Enoree Ranger District Office
20 Work Center Rd.
Whitmire, SC 29178
(803) 276-4810

Tyger Ranger District Office
3557 Whitmire Hwy.
Union, SC 29379
(864) 427-9858

Long Cane Ranger District Office
810 Buncombe St.
Edgefield, SC 29824
(803) 637-5396

National Wildlife Refuges

**Cape Romain National Wildlife
Refuge**
5801 US 17 North
Awendaw, SC 29429
(843) 928-3264
fws.gov/refuge/cape-romain

Carolina Sandhills National Wildlife Refuge
23734 US 1
McBee, SC 29101
(843) 335-8350
fws.gov/carolinasandhills

Ernest F. Hollings ACE Basin National Wildlife Refuge
Grovetown Plantation Manor
8675 Willtown Rd.
Hollywood, SC 29449
(843) 889-3084
fws.gov/refuge/ernest-f-hollings-ace-basin

Pinckney Island National Wildlife Refuge
Savannah Coastal Refuges Complex
694 Beech Hill Lane
Hardeeville, SC 29927
(843) 784-2468
fws.gov/pinckneyisland

Santee National Wildlife Refuge
2125 Fort Watson Rd.
Summerton, SC 29148
(803) 478-221
fws.gov/santee

Savannah National Wildlife Refuge
694 Beech Hill Lane
Hardeeville, SC 29927
(843) 784-2468
fws.gov/savannah

Waccamaw National Wildlife Refuge
21424 N. Fraser St.
Georgetown, SC 29440
(843) 527-8069
fws.gov/waccamaw

National Park Service Sites

Charles Pinckney National Historic Site
1254 Long Point Rd.
Mount Pleasant, SC 29464
(843) 577-0242
www.nps.gov/chpi

Congaree National Park
100 National Park Rd.
Hopkins, SC 29061
(803) 776-4396
nps.gov/cong/index.htm

Gullah/Geechee Cultural Heritage Corridor National Historic Area
PO Box 787
Beaufort, SC 29901
(843) 818-4587
gullahgeecheecorridor.org

Cowpens National Battlefield
4001 Chesnee Hwy.
Gaffney, SC 29341
(864) 461-2828
nps.gov/cowp

Fort Sumter and Fort Moultrie National Historic Park
1214 Middle St.
Sullivan's Island, SC 29482
(843) 577-0242
nps.gov/fosu

Kings Mountain National Military Park
2625 Park Rd.
Blacksburg, SC 29702
(864) 936-7921 x 3
nps.gov/kimo

Ninety Six National Historic Site
1106 Hwy. 248
Ninety Six, SC 29666
(864) 543-4068
nps.gov/nisi

Overmountain Victory National Historic Trail
338 New Pleasant Rd.
Gaffney, SC 29341
(864) 461-2828
nps.gov/ovvi

Reconstruction Era National Historic Park
706 Craven St.
Beaufort, SC 29902
(843) 962-0039
nps.gov/reer

Private Sources of Information

Foothills Trail Conservancy
PO Box 3041
Greenville, SC 29602
(864) 467-9537
foothillstrail.org

International African American Museum
14 Wharfside St.
Charleston, SC 29401
PO Box 22761
Charleston, SC 29413
Iaamuseum.org

Palmetto Conservation Foundation & Palmetto Trails
722 King St.
Columbia, SC 29205
(803) 771-0870
palmettoconservation.org

Palmetto Cycling Coalition
808-D Lady St.
Columbia, SC 29201
(803) 445-1099
pccsc.net

South Carolina Nature-Based Tourism Association
scnatureadventures.com

Tourism Regions

Capital City & Lake Murray Country
Richland, Lexington, Saluda, & Newberry Counties
2184 N. Lake Dr.
Columbia, SC 29212
(803) 781-5940
(866) SC-JEWEL
lakemurraycountry.com

Historic Charleston & Resort Islands
Charleston & Dorchester Counties
Charleston Area Convention & Visitors Bureau
375 Meeting St.
Charleston, SC 29403
(843) 774-0006
charlestoncvb.com

Lake Hartwell Country
Anderson, Oconee, & Pickens Counties
Pendleton District Commission
120 History Lane
Pendleton, SC 29670
(864) 646-3782
lakehartwellcountry.com

Lowcountry & Resort Islands
Beaufort, Colleton, Hampton, & Jasper
Counties
1 Lowcountry Lane, PO Box 615
Yemassee, SC 29945
(843) 717-3090
(800) 528-6870
southcarolinalowcountry.com

Myrtle Beach Area & Grand Strand
Horry & Georgetown Counties
Myrtle Beach Area Chamber of
Commerce
1200 N. Oak St.
Myrtle Beach, SC 29577
(843) 626-7444
(800) 356-3016
visitmyrtlebeach.com

Old 96 District
Abbeville, Edgefield, Greenwood,
Laurens, & McCormick Counties
Old 96 Tourism Commission
204 E. Public Sq.
Laurens, SC 29360
(864) 984-2233
visitold96sc.com

Olde English District
Chester, Chesterfield, Fairfield,
Kershaw, Lancaster, Union, and York
Counties
3200 Commerce Dr.
Richburg, SC 29729
(803) 385-6800
oldenglishdistrict.com

Pee Dee Country
Darlington, Dillon, Florence, Lee,
Marion, Marlboro, & Williamsburg
Counties
Pee Dee Tourism Commission
Hamer, SC 29547
(843) 669-0950
peedeetourism.com

Santee Cooper Country
Berkeley, Calhoun, Clarendon,
Orangeburg, & Sumter Counties
9302 Old #6 Hwy. E.
Santee, SC 29142
(803) 854-2131
santeecoopercountry.org

Thoroughbred Country
Aiken, Allendale, Bamburg, & Barnwell
Counties
2748 Wagener Rd.
Aiken, SC 29801
(803) 649-7981
tbredcountry.org

The Upcountry
Anderson, Cherokee, Greenville,
Pickens, Oconee, & Spartanburg
Counties
Discover Upcountry Carolina
Association
500 East North St.
Greenville, SC 29601
(864) 233-2690
upcountrysc.com

Bibliography and Further Reading

South Carolina: A History, by Walter Edgar, and *The South Carolina Encyclopedia,* edited by Edgar, are the authoritative works on the state's historical setting. This appendix provides information on some of the many other excellent published sources for learning more about South Carolina's natural resources and other attractions.

We must note, however, that many of our best sources for writing this book, in addition to our personal experiences and observations from driving each and many alternative routes, were locally produced brochures and pamphlets, websites, historical markers, and conversations with a variety of helpful folks across the state, especially including those staffing visitor centers and museums, along with public servants working for the state and federal agencies that manage and protect our natural wonders. Also helpful was the fact that both authors are native South Carolinians and have lived the large of majority (but not all) of our lives in our home state.

Google Maps, Mapquest, and GPS systems have replaced our earlier reliance on road atlases for finding our way around the back roads of South Carolina. Nevertheless, we still found *South Carolina State Road Atlas,* published by RLM Enterprises, to be helpful.

Helpful Sources and Selected Reading

Able, Gene, and Jack Horan. *Paddling South Carolina: A Guide to Palmetto State River Trails.* Rev, edition. Orangeburg, SC: Sandlapper Publishing, 2001.

Alderfer, Jonathan K. *National Geographic Field Guide to Birds: The Carolinas.* Washington, DC: National Geographic Society, 2005.

Barbour, R. L. *South Carolina's Revolutionary War Battlefields: A Tour Guide.* Gretna, LA: Pelican Publishing Company, 2002.

Baldwin, Agnes L., N. Jane Isely, and William P. Baldwin Jr. *Plantations of the Low Country: South Carolina 1697–1865, Rev. edition.* Greensboro, NC: Legacy Publications, 1987.

Barefoot, Daniel W. *Touring South Carolina's Revolutionary War Sites.* Winston-Salem: John F. Blair, 1998.

Barry, John M. *Natural Vegetation of South Carolina.* Columbia: University of South Carolina Press, 1980.

Blagden, Tom. *South Carolina's Wetland Wilderness: The ACE Basin.* Englewood, CO: Westcliffe Publishers, 1992.

Blagden, Tom, and Barry Beasley. *The Rivers of South Carolina.* Englewood, CO: Westcliff Publications, 1999.

Blagden, Tom, Jane Lareau, and Richard Porcher. *Lowcountry: The Natural Landscape.* Greensboro, NC: Legacy Publications, 1988.

Blouin, Nicole. *Mountain Biking South Carolina.* Helena, MT: Falcon Publishing Company, 1998.

Brooks, Benjamin, and Tom Cook. *The Waterfalls of South Carolina,* 3rd edition. Columbia: Palmetto Conservation Foundation, 2007.

Bull, John. *National Audubon Society Field Guide to North American Birds, Eastern Region,* Rev. edition. New York: Alfred A. Knopf, 1993.

Carter, Robin M. *Finding Birds in South Carolina.* Columbia: University of South Carolina Press, 1993.

Clark, John F., and John Dantzler. *Hiking South Carolina.* Helena, MT: Falcon Publishing Company, 1998.

Clark, Robert C., and Tom Poland. *Reflections of South Carolina.* Columbia: University of South Carolina Press, 1999.

Edgar, Walter. *South Carolina: A History.* Columbia: University of South Carolina Press, 1998.

Edgar, Walter, editor. *The South Carolina Encyclopedia.* Columbia: University of South Carolina Press, 2006.

Epps, Edwin C. *Literary South Carolina.* Spartanburg: Hub City Writers Project, 2004.

Everett, Roger S. *Birds of Coastal South Carolina.* Atglen, PA: Schiffer Books, 2007.

Foothills Trail Conservancy. *Foothill Trails Guidebook,* Rev. edition. Greenville, SC: Foothills Trails Conservancy, 2022.

Jackson, Sherry. *Five Star Trails: South Carolina Upstate.* Birmingham, AL: Menasha Ridge Press, 2013.

Jones, Lewis P. *South Carolina: A Synoptic History for Laymen,* Rev. edition. Orangeburg, SC: Sandlapper Press, 1971.

King, Thomas E. *Waterfall Hikes of Upstate South Carolina,* 2nd edition. Athens, GA: University of Georgia Press, 2008.

Lambert, Yon, and Oliver Buckles. *The Palmetto Trail Lowcountry Guide,* 2nd edition. Columbia: Palmetto Conservation Foundation, 2008.

Little, Elbert L. *National Audubon Society Field Guide to North American Trees, Eastern Region,* Rev. edition. New York: Alfred A. Knopf, 2001.

National Audubon Society Field Guide to North American Wildflowers, Eastern Region. New York: Alfred A. Knopf, 2001.

Naturaland Trust. *Mountain Bridge Trails.* Greenville, SC: Naturaland Trust, 1994.

Neuffer, Claude and Irene. *Correct Mispronunciations of Some South Carolina Names.* Columbia: University of South Carolina Press, 1983.

Poland, Tom. *South Carolina Country Roads.* Charleston: The History Press, 2018.

Porcher, Richard. *A Guide to the Wildflowers of South Carolina.* Columbia: University of South Carolina Press, 2001.

South Carolina Wildlife. A bimonthly magazine published by the South Carolina Department of Natural Resources.

Tekiela, Stan. *Birds of the Carolinas Field Guide.* Cambridge, MN: Adventure Publications, 2020.

Todd, Caroline W., and Sidney Wait. *South Carolina: A Day at a Time,* Rev. edition. Orangeburg, SC: Sandlapper Publishing, 2008.

Whitaker, John O. *National Audubon Society Field Guide to North American Mammals.* New York: Alfred A. Knopf, 1996.

Williams, Jai. *Plantations and Historic Homes of South Carolina.* Guilford, CT: Globe Pequot Press, 2019.

Wyche, Tom. *South Carolina's Mountain Wilderness: The Blue Ridge Escarpment.* Englewood, CO: Westcliffe Publishers, 1994

Index